# DAILY WISDOM FOR TEEN GIRLS

# DAILY WISDOM FOR TEEN GIRLS

BARBOUR
PUBLISHING

Compiled by Barbour Staff.

Print ISBN 979-8-89151-268-9

Text compiled from *Daily Wisdom for Teen Girls* © 2020 published by Barbour Publishing, Inc.



Published by Barbour Publishing, Inc., 1810 Barbour Drive, Uhrichsville, Ohio 44683, www.barbourbooks.com

*Our mission is to inspire the world with the life-changing message of the Bible.*

ecpa Member of the Evangelical Christian Publishers Association

Printed in China.

# WISDOM FOR EVERY DAY OF THE YEAR STARTS RIGHT HERE!

Beginning a new year is like planning a party. You wake up with fresh expectations for all the good that will occur, envision the joy and companionship of loved ones, and eagerly imagine all the delicious food and sweets that will be shared. There is anticipation and excitement for the new memories you will create, the adventures you will experience, and the friendships you will strengthen.

But like a carefully planned party, the year ahead may have unforeseen challenges: bumps in the road, strangers at your door, and moments when everything goes wrong. There may be times when illness strikes a family member or you find yourself in deep trouble. There may even be moments when you have found yourself feeling totally alone.

*Daily Wisdom for Teen Girls: Morning & Evening* reminds you to begin every day and end each night with the foundation of God. It encourages you to love Him and trust in His presence. Let this book remind you that in moments of celebration and joy, as well as in times of fear and worry, God is always with you—guiding you, loving you, and holding you in His arms.

Who wouldn't want to celebrate that?

## DAY 1

# YOU ARE A NEW CREATION

*Therefore, if anyone is in Christ, the new creation has come: The old has gone, the new is here!*
2 CORINTHIANS 5:17 NIV

### MORNING

New Year's often turns into an excuse for excess. There are too many relatives around the house, too much food on the table, too many football games to watch. But the day rarely lives up to its promise. It turns a little flat around midafternoon, and by evening we're relieved that it's nearly over.

The thing we like about New Year's Day, though, is that it marks a new beginning. Maybe last year was a bummer, but now we celebrate hope for the year to come. Tomorrow we'll probably break all our resolutions, but today we allow ourselves to dream a little.

### EVENING

We don't have to settle for the hope of our dreams. As today's verse says, if you've given your life to the Lord, everything really is new. Your old sins are forgiven, and you're as clean as the falling snow. Anything *is* possible with God's help. And that is really something worth celebrating!

*Father, on this day of celebration and resolutions, remind me that I have good reason to hope. You will be by my side this year, helping me make my dreams come true every day. Amen.*

# DAY 2

## USE YOUR ABILITIES

*And Jesus grew in wisdom and stature, and in favor with God and man.*
Luke 2:52 NIV

### MORNING

If there had been a "gifted" class when Jesus was a child, He would have been in it. We're really not sure how it all played out in His 100-percent divine/100-percent human nature, but He was definitely different from the other kids in the neighborhood. Yet He was enough like them that the town elders erroneously thought of Him as "the carpenter's son" when He came back as an adult and performed miracles! We don't know the details about Jesus' childhood, whether He experienced development and maturity in the same manner as we do. Yet we do know that He never sinned; He never rebelled against what was right.

### EVENING

Scripture tells us that Jesus "learned"—increased in wisdom—so we can assume He was "taught" in some manner. In so many ways, He was way ahead of the other kids around Him. Talk about gifted! He was God in the flesh; He could heal diseases, correct deformities, multiply meals, and resurrect the dead. He always used His divine abilities to bless others. He did not seek to gain earthly glory, to get even with His enemies, or to curry favor with the ruling powers. He brought honor to His Father and help to others.

*Lord, I want to be like You. I want to use the abilities You've given me to bless those You bring into my life. Give me the wisdom and grace to manage my gifts so that others may be helped. In Jesus' name, amen.*

# DAY 3

## TAKE TIME TO THINK

*Desire without knowledge is not good—*
*how much more will hasty feet miss the way!*
PROVERBS 19:2 NIV

### MORNING

You've got dreams and goals and energy to spare. Like a cat locked out of a bedroom, you want to throw yourself against all obstacles. Well, the cat never gets on the bed that way. It doesn't know how to turn the doorknob, after all.

But one night the cat tries another approach. He cries—pitifully, loudly, for minutes on end—and because you love him, you open the door and let him hog the bed. The cat has achieved his goal, hasn't he? He may never learn how to turn a doorknob, but he figured out a way around that problem.

### EVENING

Sometimes, like the cat mentioned in this morning's reading, you must step back and think a problem through. Hitting your head against a door may not do the trick.

*Father, I know what I want out of life, and I'm determined to achieve my goals with Your help. Give me the sense to figure out how to do this with the least possible amount of pain, and if my goals are not pleasing to You, put me on the right track. Amen.*

# DAY 4

# IN HIS PRESENCE

*So let us come boldly to the throne of our gracious God. There we will receive his mercy, and we will find grace to help us when we need it most.*
HEBREWS 4:16 NLT

## MORNING

Abigail was only three, but she knew that when she was at Grandpop's house, he made the best playmate ever. Sometimes she only had to ask twice to get him to play tea party with her and several of Grandmom's stuffed animals or special dolls. He was usually pretty quick to turn on the sprinklers so Abigail could run through the grassy yard in her bare feet. More than anything, she enjoyed crawling up on his lap with her favorite book and presenting it to him to read. If he ever got tired of the same old story, he never let on. Instead, he read it each time with surprise and sincerity—as if he'd never seen the words before. What a joy to know that just like Abigail with her grandfather, we can come into the presence of God and make our requests known to Him!

## EVENING

Just like grandparents love to see joy in their grandchild's eyes, God loves to give us gifts and see us delight in time spent with Him. Whatever we have need of, we can come in and sit down with our heavenly Father and tell Him everything.

*Heavenly Father, thank You for always welcoming me into Your presence. I have assurance that You know what I need and that I can always rest in Your mercy and grace. Amen.*

# DAY 5

## ARE YOU KEEPING YOUR PROMISES?

*The Lord is not slow in keeping his promise, as some understand slowness. Instead he is patient with you, not wanting anyone to perish, but everyone to come to repentance.*

2 PETER 3:9 NIV

### MORNING

A week has passed since you made your New Year's resolutions. How many of them are you still keeping? Well, we're all human. Promises come easily to us and are just as easily forgotten.

Of all the promises we make and break, perhaps the most tragic are those we make to God. "Get me out of this and I promise. . ." Every time we say something like that, in the back of our minds we can hear God say, "Oh, sure!" Yet we keep promising, for who else can we turn to in times of real crisis?

### EVENING

Isn't it wonderful to know that "[God] is patient with you, not wanting anyone to perish"? As often as we make and break our little promises, God never breaks even one. Once His word is given, it's forever.

*Father, help me be more faithful at keeping my word. My track record is pretty bad, but I look to You and Your promises as examples to follow. Amen.*

# DAY 6

## PROMISES OF GOD

*"For the Lord your God is living among you. He is a mighty savior. He will take delight in you with gladness. With his love, he will calm all your fears. He will rejoice over you with joyful songs."*
ZEPHANIAH 3:17 NLT

### MORNING

Look at all the promises packed into this one verse of scripture! God is with you. He is your mighty Savior. He delights in you with gladness. He calms your fears with His love. He rejoices over you with joyful songs. Wow! What a bundle of hope is found here for the believer. Like a father attuned to his newborn baby's cries, so is your heavenly Father's heart for you. He delights in being your Father. He knows when the storms of life are raging all around you. He senses your need to be held close and for your fears to be calmed. It is in those times that He is for you a prince of peace, a comforter. He rejoices over you with joyful songs.

### EVENING

Can you imagine that God loves you so much that you cause Him to sing? God sings over you, and the songs He sings are joyful. He loves you with an unconditional, everlasting love. Face this day knowing that your God is with you. He calms you and He sings over you. You are blessed to be a child of the King.

*Father, thank You for loving me the way You do. You are all I need. Amen.*

# DAY 7

## THE HEART OF GOD

*"If you forgive those who sin against you, your heavenly Father will forgive you. But if you refuse to forgive others, your Father will not forgive your sins."*
MATTHEW 6:14–15 NLT

### MORNING

Forgiveness is closely related to trust. God knows it's your greatest need, so He provided a Savior for you. In return, you choose to respond to Him in faith, trusting Him to save you. Then you are to extend forgiveness to others—both the news of God's forgiveness in Christ and to those who have wronged you personally.

Saying "I'm sorry" is a start, but it can only express your regrets. To ask someone to forgive you is to put the power in their hands—to say, "In order to make this right, I need you to let go of the wrong I've done to you." It's a gift to forgive and be forgiven.

### EVENING

God loves to turn your mistakes into blessings, but forgiveness is key to that. When you put your trust in God (Psalm 7:1), He will help you deal with the consequences of all the things that need to be forgiven.

*God, I trust You to turn mistakes into blessings. Help me to forgive and to seek forgiveness from others. Amen.*

# DAY 8

## LOVE ONE ANOTHER

*I am not writing you a new command but one we have had from the beginning. I ask that we love one another. And this is love: that we walk in obedience to his commands.*

2 JOHN 5–6 NIV

### MORNING

Sometimes being a Christian gets confusing. Pressures bear down and your love grows cold. Spiritual winter sets in. So you start looking for something you've missed, some new trick to alter your life.

The truth is, you probably don't need a trick. You just need to get a handle on the old truth that's stared you in the face for a long time. Then you need to obey what you know.

When your love for God grows cold, take a fresh look at what He's already said. Draw close to the fire of His Word, and your life will brightly burn.

### EVENING

When the cold, dull days of winter make you feel dull, renew your love for God. Warm yourself in God's Word just as you'd seek the heat of a fireplace.

*Jesus, I already know so much about You, but sometimes I don't use that knowledge in my life. Help me bridge the gap between my head and heart. Amen.*

# DAY 9

## BEING A GOOD EXAMPLE

*Don't let anyone think less of you because you are young. Be an example to all believers in what you say, in the way you live, in your love, your faith, and your purity.*
1 TIMOTHY 4:12 NLT

### MORNING

When someone is referred to as a "good example," that person is most likely middle-aged or older. We tend to look to those who are older than we are for inspiration, figuring they have more experience and wisdom. That is not necessarily true; there are plenty of old fools around.

Don't rule yourself out of the good-example population because you're young. Being a good example has nothing to do with age and everything to do with how you live your life.

### EVENING

You don't have to be a Goody Two-shoes, but you should try to live your life with courage and fairness and faith. If you can do that long enough, you're on your way toward becoming a good example. A good reputation opens doors that might otherwise stay closed to you.

*Lord, I'm not sure I'm ready to be someone's role model. Maybe for now I'll just concentrate on doing the right thing day by day and see how it works out. Teach me how I should act. Amen.*

## DAY 10

# WHEN WORDS FAIL ME

*Before a word is on my tongue you, Lord, know it completely.*
Psalm 139:4 NIV

### MORNING

Pastor John's message on Sunday morning had been about prayer. After the service, Melissa, a teenager in the congregation, asked the pastor if they could speak privately.

"Pastor," she said, "I can't pray. Your prayers sound so beautiful. But when I pray, I sometimes have no words, and when I do, they sound. . .well. . .stupid."

Her pastor smiled reassuringly. "Melissa, God doesn't care how fancy your words are. He cares about what's in your heart. Without you telling Him, God already knows your thoughts and desires. When you pray, speak to Him as if you're talking with your loving Father."

### EVENING

Sometimes Christians feel so overwhelmed by their needs or by the greatness of God that they simply can't pray. When the words won't come, God helps to create them. Paul says in Romans 8:26 (NLT), "And the Holy Spirit helps us in our weakness. For example, we don't know what God wants us to pray for. But the Holy Spirit prays for us with groanings that cannot be expressed in words."

God hears your prayers even before you pray them. When you don't know what to say and the words won't come, you can simply ask God to help you by praying on your behalf.

*Dear God, I'm grateful today that in my silence You still hear me. Amen.*

# DAY 11

## AGAINST OUR NATURE

*"You have heard that it has been said, 'You must love your neighbor and hate those who hate you.' But I tell you, love those who hate you. (*Respect and give thanks for those who say bad things to you. Do good to those who hate you.) Pray for those who do bad things to you and who make it hard for you. Then you may be the sons of your Father Who is in heaven. His sun shines on bad people and on good people. He sends rain on those who are right with God and on those who are not right with God."*

MATTHEW 5:43–45 NLV

### MORNING

Jesus sure didn't believe in doing things the easy way, did He? Loving the people who wish us harm, the people who curse us and shame us and make our lives miserable. . .that goes against every natural instinct we have.

Yet that's the point, isn't it? We are sinful by nature. When we live for Christ, He calls us to die to our natural instincts and develop a new nature. If He called us to do what comes naturally, everyone would follow Christ. However, everyone would also be self-centered and greedy, because that's who we are.

### EVENING

Christ calls us to turn against what *feels* right and do what *is* right. He tells us that if we want to be great, we must be servants; and if we want to be rich, we must give up all our stuff. Perhaps the hardest thing He requires of us is the mandate He lays out in this verse: Love those who hate us. Pray good things for those who persecute us. Then we will develop the family resemblance He longs for us to have, and everyone will know that we are children of God.

*Dear Father, help me to truly love those who don't love me. Amen.*

# DAY 12

## GET ABOVE IT ALL

*Keep your minds thinking about things in heaven.*
*Do not think about things on the earth.*
COLOSSIANS 3:2 NLV

### MORNING

If you've ever taken a trip by airplane, you know with one glimpse from the window at thirty thousand feet how the world seems small. With your feet on the ground, you may feel small in a big world; and it's easy for the challenges of life and the circumstances from day to day to press in on you. But from above the clouds, things can become clear.

Sometimes the most difficult challenges you face play out in your head—where a struggle to control the outcome and work out the details of life can consume you. Once removed—far away from the details—you can see things from a higher perspective.

### EVENING

Close your eyes and push out the thoughts that try to grab you and keep you tied to the things of the world. Reach out to God and let your spirit soar. Give your concerns to Him and let Him work out the details. Rest in Him and He'll carry you above it all, every step of the way.

*God, You are far above any detail of life that concerns me. Help me to trust You today for answers to those things that seem to bring me down. I purposefully set my heart and mind on You today. Amen.*

# DAY 13

## WHY ARE YOU AFRAID?

*When Jesus woke up, he rebuked the wind and said to the waves, "Silence! Be still!" Suddenly the wind stopped, and there was a great calm. Then he asked them, "Why are you afraid? Do you still have no faith?"*

MARK 4:39–40 NLT

### MORNING

One day Jesus and His disciples were on a boat heading to the other side of the lake. Then a storm came up. Jesus was so secure, He'd fallen asleep. The disciples weren't feeling very secure, however. They tried to be brave, but things were getting out of hand—even for those among Jesus' disciples who had made their living on boats. Finally, they woke Jesus and He calmed the storm.

### EVENING

Jesus was speaking to His disciples, but He was also speaking to you when He asked, "Why are you afraid? Do you still have no faith?" Trust is a main part of faith, but too often fear rather than faith is a first response. Burdens become personal, not shared. Outcomes include best efforts, not God's help.

When the storm was the worst for the disciples, Jesus was with them. And when He spoke, things immediately became calm.

*Lord, You want me to replace fear with faith and anxiety with trust. You give examples of what that looks like, and I'm left to remember that even mighty men and women of the Bible struggled with trust. Help me learn what they learned and to trust You in doing so. Amen.*

# DAY 14

## ANSWER ME!

*Answer me when I call to you, my righteous God. Give me relief from my distress; have mercy on me and hear my prayer.*

PSALM 4:1 NIV

### MORNING

Have you ever felt as if God wasn't listening? We've all felt that from time to time. David felt it when he slept in a cold, hard cave night after night while being pursued by Saul's men. He felt it when his son Absalom turned against him. Time and again in his life, David felt abandoned by God. And yet David was called a man after God's own heart.

No matter how old we are, there will be times when we feel abandoned by God. There will be times when our faith grows weak. That's okay. It's normal.

But David didn't give up. He kept crying out to God, kept falling to his knees in worship, and kept storming God's presence with his pleas.

### EVENING

David knew that God wouldn't hide His face for long, for he knew what we might sometimes forget: God is love. He loves us without condition and without limit, and He is never far from those He loves. No matter how distant God may seem, we need to keep talking to Him, to keep praying, and to keep pouring out our hearts to Him. We can know, as David knew, that God will answer in His time.

*Dear Father, thank You for always hearing my prayers. Help me to trust You even when You seem distant. Amen.*

# DAY 15

## DO YOU SEE GOD AS A LOVING PARENT?

*He has removed our sins as far from us as the east is from the west. The Lord is like a father to his children, tender and compassionate to those who fear him.*
Psalm 103:12–13 NLT

### MORNING

When the author of Psalm 103 looked for a way to describe God, he settled on the image of a father caring for his children and treating them with compassion regardless of their failures. There's no mistaking that God desires obedience and trust from His children, but He's not about to cast away His beloved children if they sin. In fact, God makes a point of separating His children from their sin. Their sins play no part in what He thinks of them.

### EVENING

Can you imagine that God looks at you without any thought of your past failures and mistakes? Whatever story from your past makes you cringe or causes you to feel unworthy before God, He has made into a distant memory.

This is not an excuse to sin. God desires to be close to you and wants what's best for you. That includes your obedience. However, God has taken your worst parts and thrust them from you as far as possible.

*Thank You, Lord, for making me Your beloved child and removing my sins from what You think of me. Amen.*

# DAY 16

## THROWING STONES

*"Let any one of you who is without sin be the first to throw a stone at her."*
JOHN 8:7 NIV

### MORNING

Nobody likes to be judged. Especially when those people judging us don't know the whole story or the road we've walked. That's why God is so clear in His Word. He states it time and again: We're not supposed to judge each other. That's *His* job.

It's easier, and a whole lot more fun, to focus on someone else's shortcomings instead of our own. It's been said that we're supposed to hate the sin and love the sinner. . .and that's true. Yet we'd be better off to hate our own sin before we focus on the sins of others. We all have plenty in our own lives that doesn't measure up to God's standards.

### EVENING

Since we each have our own sins to deal with, God wants us to concentrate on doing the one thing He's put us here to do: love.

Hate our own sins. Love each other. Hmmm. . .that is an interesting concept.

Next time we catch ourselves making a judgment call about another person's choices, let's take a close look at our own weaknesses. Before we point out their flaws, let's figure out a way to show them love.

*Dear Father, thank You for not focusing on my sin and shortcomings. The minute I admit those sins, You forgive me. Thank You for investing so much into showing me love. Help me pour my energy into loving others, not finding their faults. Amen.*

# DAY 17

## YOUR PARENTS' LESSONS

*Listen, my son, to your father's instruction and*
*do not forsake your mother's teaching.*
PROVERBS 1:8 NIV

### MORNING

You learned a lot from your parents, mostly through example. You learned that Sunday feels empty without church. You learned that sharing often gets you twice as much as hogging. You learned that hitting causes more problems than talking. . .and that disrespect is often worse than hitting. You absorbed all these lessons and more through your day-to-day life at home.

At the same time, you were learning at school and on the playground. Some of these lessons were harsh, but they were also useful. You had to know what the world was really like.

### EVENING

You often laughed when your parents told you, "We don't do things like that in this family," but the next time it came up in the world, you didn't do it. It didn't feel right.

The older you get, the more you will remember your parents' lessons, and the more thankful you will be. Soon enough, you might be telling your own children, "We don't do that in *this* family!"

*Father, I hope I'll be able to teach my children as well as my parents taught me. Their lessons always came out of their love for me. I'll do my best to pass them on. Amen.*

# DAY 18

## BLESSABLE

*Love the* L*ORD* *your God and. . .serve him with all your heart and with all your soul—then I will send rain on your land in its season.*
DEUTERONOMY 11:13–14 NIV

### MORNING

We all want God's blessings. We want it to rain on our flowers, we want the sun to shine on our picnics, and we want a gentle breeze to relieve us from summer's scorch. We want good grades and lots of friends.

Although God allows some blessings to grace every person, there are some keys to receiving more of God's goodness. If we want God's blessings, we must be blessable.

So how do we become blessable? We must love God, and we must serve Him with all our hearts. Loving God is the easy part. But the evidence of that love comes through our service to Him, and that's a little harder.

### EVENING

When we love God, we serve Him by loving others. We serve Him by taking the time to mow the elderly neighbor's lawn or help a friend with their homework or provide a coat for someone who's cold. We serve Him by offering a hand of friendship to the friendless or by saying something positive about a victim of gossip.

When we love God and our actions show evidence of that love, we become blessable. That's when God will pour out His goodness on us in ways we could never imagine.

*Dear Father, I love You. Show me ways I can serve You today. Amen.*

## DAY 19

# THE TRUTH ABOUT GOD

*They traded the truth about God for a lie. So they worshiped and served the things God created instead of the Creator himself, who is worthy of eternal praise! Amen.*

ROMANS 1:25 NLT

### MORNING

The world's obsession with pick-and-choose reality would be hilarious if it weren't so tragic. People who hate God will think, feel, believe, and say *anything* to avoid facing the truth about Him. Those who love God, however, will think, feel, believe, and say the truth about Him.

### EVENING

- God is almighty. He is everywhere. He knows everything. Nothing is outside His infinite sovereignty.
- God is the Creator and sustainer of all that exists, temporal and eternal. He knows and controls every subatomic particle in the universe.
- God is love, and all people benefit from His goodness.
- God is absolutely just, pure, and holy. He's perfect in every way. Everything He says is true. Everything He does is best.
- God is a triune being: God the Father, God the Son, and God the Holy Spirit. God desires that none perish but that all repent, turn to Him, trust Him, and receive all that faith in Jesus offers.
- God is mystery. God has infinite knowledge, insight, and understanding. His ways are light-years higher than man's ways.

*Lord, I love the truth about who You are. I will worship and serve You, my Creator. You alone are worthy of eternal praise. Amen.*

# DAY 20

## THE NAME OF JESUS

*The Lord will be king over the whole earth. On that day there will be one Lord, and his name the only name.*
ZECHARIAH 14:9 NIV

### MORNING

"The name of Jesus used to grate against my nerves. Saying it was like squealing chalk against a blackboard," Alicia remembered. "I think, even before I knew Him, I couldn't get away from His authority."

There is something about the name of Jesus. In many settings, you'll hear it uttered often—but not prayerfully. Yet who misuses the name of Allah, Buddha, or any other religious figure when things aren't going right? It's as if even people who don't believe in Jesus can't get away from His authority. Maybe they blame Him for anything that goes wrong, but they unknowingly recognize Him.

### EVENING

One day Jesus will return to rule the entire earth. Then, at His name, "every knee should bow" (Philippians 2:10 NIV). Christians will kneel willingly, glorifying the risen one, but nonbelievers will be forced to acknowledge their judge.

Today, recognize Jesus for who He is. There's a lot of power, glory, and love in that name.

*Lord, Your name is wonderful. I want the world to know it today. Amen.*

# DAY 21

## HANGING ON

*"He spreads out the northern skies over empty space; he suspends the earth over nothing."*
Job 26:7 NIV

### MORNING

An old, dry petunia bloom had fallen from its hanging pot and was caught in a mere two-threaded spiderweb. Suspended in midair, it was seemingly held by nothing at all and flittered wildly in the softest of breezes. God and the curious cat are likely the only ones who knew how long it had been there.

Do you ever feel this way—barely hanging on, struggling like crazy, and no one seems to notice? When the struggle *is* recognized by others, they can't see why it's so hard; and then, on top of your hardship, you may be judged too. Sometimes the only person who notices knocks you around, like the cat leaping and batting at the hovering debris. . .

### EVENING

Does God notice your struggles? Is He going to help you through them?

Remember that God absolutely notices and cares immensely. He holds up the universe, and He holds you up even when you feel alone, mocked, and discouraged. He will not forget your plight.

*Lord God, thank You for knowing exactly where we are all the time and for holding us up even when we don't understand the hows and the whys. Amen.*

# DAY 22

## ALL ABOUT ME

*You know me inside and out, you know every bone in my body;*
*you know exactly how I was made, bit by bit, how I was sculpted from nothing into something. . . . All the stages of my life were spread out before you, the days of my life all prepared before I'd even lived one day.*

PSALM 139:15–16 MSG

### MORNING

Have you ever considered how matchless you are in this world? No one is created in exactly the same way. We each have our own personalities, gifts, ideas, and dreams. C. S. Lewis wrote, "Why else were individuals created, but that God, loving all infinitely, should love each differently?"

Accepting our individuality is a lifetime lesson since there will be many times we will want to compare ourselves to others. But God has shown His love through the unique manner in which He creates and guides our lives.

### EVENING

We are distinct from each other. God's presence in our lives keeps us on a path He created just for us. It's hard to fathom that kind of love.

With that knowledge, we can learn to love ourselves and others with Christlike love and enrich our relationship with Him. Ever growing and ever learning, we can trust the heavenly Father to mature us into what He created us to be: "Just ME."

*Thank You, Father, for loving me each day.*
*Keep me on the path You created. Amen.*

# DAY 23

## CHRIST HAS OVERCOME

*"These things I have spoken to you so that in Me you may have peace. In the world you have tribulation, but take courage; I have overcome the world."*
JOHN 16:33 NASB

### MORNING

In today's verse Jesus says that you can count on struggles and hardships in this world. It is just the way this fallen world operates. Thankfully, He doesn't leave us there. In fact, this verse is one of the most comforting verses to go to when you are in the midst of the world's tribulations. Jesus says that in Him you have peace. Everything around you might be chaotic and unstable, but while resting in Him, there is perfect calm and peace. How is it that He can promise you His peace even when He guarantees that you will have struggles in this world? *He has overcome the world.* Could any words be more uplifting?

### EVENING

God has overcome this world's fear, heartache, regret, violence, sorrow, and death. Run to the one who has conquered and ask Him to give you this peace that He promises. The troubles and struggles of this world may touch you for a time, but they are no match for the eternal peace of Christ that is promised to you who believe.

*Lord, thank You that You have already conquered all the world's struggles that are surrounding me right now. Let me rest in Your peace and focus on that time when all my tears will be wiped away. Amen.*

# DAY 24

## BEYOND PEAK EXPERIENCES

*You are my God, and I will praise you!*
*You are my God, and I will exalt you!*
PSALM 118:28 NLT

### MORNING

What are your favorite college and professional sports teams? Can you remember scenes from some of their most famous victories? Have any of your favorite teams ever won a national championship? If so, how did you feel? Elated? Electrified? Ecstatic? Enthusiastic beyond words?

Who are your favorite musicians and music groups? Can you remember specific songs from some of their concerts? Have they ever had a number one hit? If so, how did you feel when you heard it for the first time?

The funny thing about peak experiences is that they never last. That's true not only in sports and music but in every other sphere of life. Sadly, some peak experiences end up leaving a bitter taste in your mouth. That team isn't so special anymore. That number one hit song now just gets on your nerves. . .

### EVENING

How good it is that you can thank the Lord every day for who He is and what He means to you!

As you continue to read God's Word, be sure to look for "peak" reasons to keep praising God.

*Lord, You are my God, and I want to honor and praise You every day of my life. Help me notice and remember scores of reasons why. You are worthy beyond measure! Amen.*

# DAY 25

## MUCH, MUCH MORE

*Now all glory to God, who is able, through his mighty power at work within us, to accomplish infinitely more than we might ask or think. Glory to him in the church and in Christ Jesus through all generations forever and ever! Amen.*

EPHESIANS 3:20–21 NLT

### MORNING

Think back to a time when something happened in your life that you never saw coming—something that happened out of the blue and absolutely amazed you. When God's power is at work within you, the possibilities are beyond your imagination.

The New International Version of the Bible says that He can do "immeasurably more" than what you could imagine. Whatever problem you are facing right now—big or small—God cares. As you pray about it and seek God's will, don't put Him in a box thinking that there's no way out or that there is only one right answer. His response just might be beyond your understanding and your wildest imagination.

### EVENING

Remember that things aren't always what they seem. When you feel disappointed in God's answers to your prayers, look outside the box. God is always, always working everything out for your good. God sees all. What may feel like the best answer may be totally destructive to you or someone you love. Trust that God can do much more than anything you could ever ask or imagine!

*Heavenly Father, help me trust You with my whole heart. When I'm disappointed, help me to see outside of myself and what I think are the best answers for my life. Thank You for working everything out according to Your great plan. Amen.*

# DAY 26

# HIS MASTERPIECE

*For we are God's masterpiece. He has created us anew in Christ Jesus, so we can do the good things he planned for us long ago.*

EPHESIANS 2:10 NLT

## MORNING

When artists envision a creation, they spend time plotting, planning, and preparing. Did you know that God, as the divine artist, conceived of you—with your special blend of talents, personality, and intelligence—this way? He has a present and future in mind for you that far exceeds your wildest expectations. Not just in heaven, either. He wants to give you unspeakable joy, unquenchable hope, and unfathomable grace—right here, right now.

It's up to you, though, whether to receive His grace and live out His masterful plans for you. With His help, the Holy Spirit's comfort, and Jesus' compassion, you can be a world changer! In the corner of the universe where God has placed you, you can spread Jesus' love, tell others about Him, and help them find their way to the God who loves them as much as He loves you.

## EVENING

Will you take God's word that you are divinely inspired and uniquely equipped for the calling He has on you? Will you believe Him for the strength, endurance, and power that only He can give? Our world needs young people who will dig deep into His Word and impart the life-changing truths of the gospel message with fearless abandon.

Say yes to His design this very moment. You won't regret it.

*Divine Creator, thank You for the way You fashioned me. Help me live the calling You envisioned for me with grace and humility. Amen.*

# DAY 27

## DESTINED FOR GREATNESS

*For we are God's handiwork, created in Christ Jesus to do good works, which God prepared in advance for us to do.*
EPHESIANS 2:10 NIV

### MORNING

Many of us want to do great things. We feel it in our bones—we're destined for greatness. While this is true, our definition of greatness may differ slightly from God's definition.

We're not great because of who we are, but because of who created us. Just as any work signed by Michelangelo has great value simply because of the signature, so we have great value because of God's imprint on our lives. He created us so we could glorify Him, not ourselves.

### EVENING

The way we honor God is by doing good works. Sometimes those works are amazing. More often, they're simple and go without notice. He created us to share His love by speaking to the outcast, by helping the helpless when no one else sees, by helping with the laundry, by clearing the dinner table, and by feeding the dog—all with a pleasant attitude.

Just think: God prepared those little opportunities in advance just so we'd have ways to share His love and point people to Him. Some of those actions are easy, and others are hard. Still, they are all worth it for they help us live out our purpose and fulfill the destiny God designed. When we do good things and share His love, we become truly great in His eyes.

*Dear Father, I want to do all the good things You've planned for me, no matter how big or small they may seem. Help me to stay true to Your purpose for my life. Amen.*

# DAY 28

## ORGANIZE YOUR LIFE

*For God is not a God of disorder but of peace.*
1 CORINTHIANS 14:33 NIV

### MORNING

The Bible is talking about worship in today's verse, suggesting that a certain amount of order should be maintained during services, but it's easy enough to see how the same idea can have wider application. After all, if a worship service can be turned into disorder, imagine what we can do the rest of the week.

Some of us are more comfortable with disorder than others. A few thrive on it, feeling that it keeps them on their toes. Others can't stand disorder and feel frustrated or insecure when faced with it.

Can we agree that we're a pretty disorderly bunch?

### EVENING

We don't have the discipline of ants or bees, and who would want that? We tend to throw our dirty socks on the floor and neglect to take out the garbage. We like a little disorder now and then.

But when it comes to school or jobs, we need order and routine. Reports need to be written on time, tools need to be cleaned and put away, and work must be prioritized—or nothing will get done. Leave your fondness for disorder at home, and be as organized as possible everywhere else.

*Father, I'm not the most orderly person in my private life,*
*but teach me how to be organized at school and work. Amen.*

# DAY 29

## HIS MERCIES NEVER CEASE

*The faithful love of the* Lord *never ends! His mercies never cease. Great is his faithfulness; his mercies begin afresh each morning.*
Lamentations 3:22–23 NLT

### MORNING

Troubles seemed to overflow Craig. He spent more and more time on his "part-time" job as his boss loaded him with work. His mom went into the hospital for tests. His girlfriend disappeared from his life. The pastor of his church resigned, and Craig wondered if anything in life was stable. Troubles seemed to eat Craig up inside.

Life's challenges can hit us hard—and suddenly. One moment you're dealing with one problem, and the next moment you have three or four. *Has God forgotten me? Will He leave me stranded?* you may wonder.

Never. Compassion is God's "middle name."

### EVENING

Every day, even the lousy ones, God remains faithful. You may not see the way He's working, but He's out ahead, protecting you.

No trouble can eat you up when you belong to God. It may nibble at your edges, but you won't be consumed.

*Lord, faith isn't just emotions. When I get that empty, stranded feeling, I know it's nothing You put in my heart. I don't want to be eaten up with worry—just consumed with Your Word. Amen.*

# DAY 30

## THE THIEF HAS NO POWER

*"The thief comes only to steal and kill and destroy; I have come that they may have life, and have it to the full."*
JOHN 10:10 NIV

### MORNING

Satan's tactics are discouraging. He often seems one step ahead of us, anticipating our every move, hiding behind rocks, just waiting to trip us up. While it feels overwhelming at times, in reality, Satan has only a few tricks up his sleeve. Quite simply, he aims to steal, kill, and destroy. He's not that creative and certainly doesn't have any power to harm a child of God. Ephesians 1:13 tells us that we are sealed with the Holy Spirit and are therefore protected from Satan's schemes.

### EVENING

In stark contrast to Satan, Jesus boldly states that He came so that we no longer have to fear Satan's (limited) power. Jesus brings us a full and abundant life. What are some things that Satan tries to steal, kill, and destroy in you? What does it mean to live abundantly for Jesus? Turn your back on Satan, the liar. Turn to Jesus, the truth. Seek Him and receive a life beyond your wildest dreams.

*Jesus, I am so grateful for Your coming and the promise of an abundant, full life! What a joy it is to know that Satan no longer has the power to steal from me, kill what I love, and destroy what I hold dear. You are Life. Help me to live my life abundantly for You. Amen.*

# DAY 31

## CREATIVE IMAGE-BEARER

*So God created mankind in his own image, in the image of God he created them; male and female he created them.*
Genesis 1:27 NIV

### MORNING

As children we learned we are different from animals because we reason, but much more than that sets humans apart. We are made in God's image. We can reason because God reasons. But what else do we do that bears His likeness?

Is bearing God's image limited to demonstrating character qualities such as love, forgiveness, hope, and honesty? Is it doing good deeds and acts of kindness? Does it mean every conversation should be peppered with spiritual language? Or is there a larger sense in which we bear God's image?

In the context of Genesis 1, when we imagine, create, and bring order to our world, we are bearing God's image.

### EVENING

To bake a beautiful cake or design a quilt is to reflect God's creativity. To put a budget together in a systematic fashion, write a report, or bring organization to a pile of dirty laundry is to show God's ability to make order and beauty out of chaos.

As we work on projects and do our jobs, we reveal the Creator God to a world that doesn't recognize Him. When we get stuck, when no idea will come to mind, we can ask the one whose imprint we bear. The Creator who made us and loves us puts every good, true, and lovely thought in our minds.

*Father, may we bear Your likeness better today than yesterday. Cause us to remember that You are the source of creativity, imagination, and organization. Help us do Your will. Amen.*

# DAY 32

## THE TEMPTATION TO GOSSIP

*At the same time they also learn to be idle, as they go around from house to house; and not merely idle, but also gossips and busybodies, talking about things not proper to mention.*

1 TIMOTHY 5:13 NASB

### MORNING

Gossip usually starts innocently enough. We hear some juicy bit of news and share it with just one close friend, starting with the disclaimer "I really shouldn't tell you this, but. . ." and concluding with "Now be sure not to tell anyone else." How often does the gossip truly stop there?

When we choose to gossip, we are not being good stewards of our time. The Bible warns us not to give in to idleness. This doesn't mean that we should never rest; it means we should find constructive uses for the time God has given us.

### EVENING

Instead of talking about others to others, consider taking those concerns to God. Be the one in your circle of friends to stop gossip in its tracks by speaking words of encouragement, gently reminding those who talk about other people that you'd rather discuss something else. Soon you'll find that gossip is no longer your go-to topic of conversation.

*Father, may our conversation be pleasing to You. May we honor You with each word, spoken and unspoken. Amen.*

# DAY 33

## WISDOM

*Do not deceive yourselves. If any of you think you are wise by the standards of this age, you should become "fools" so that you may become wise.*

1 CORINTHIANS 3:18 NIV

### MORNING

*Why don't you guys just leave me alone!* Punxsutawney Phil probably thinks as those strange humans drag him out of his nice, cozy hole every year. *You fools! Ask a weatherman about spring. I just want more sleep.*

From all the groundhog hoopla, you'd think a lot of silly humans take seriously a rodent's "prediction" about how long winter will last!

Spiritually, people can be pretty ridiculous too—such as the nonbelievers who see Christians as fools for believing they can really know God. These people ignore God, but *you're* the fool. *Right?*

### EVENING

What does the world really know about wisdom? Can your boss understand a worker's deep-hearted needs? Can your non-Christian friends explain how the universe got here?

God can.

Why accept what a fool says is wise? Go instead with wisdom's Creator!

*Lord, I feel uncomfortable calling people fools. But that's what You call those who reject Your love. Help me reach out to them today. Amen.*

# DAY 34

## FEELING PRESSED?

*By his divine power, God has given us*
*everything we need for living a godly life.*
2 PETER 1:3 NLT

### MORNING

People need you—your family and your friends need you. Adding their needs to your commitments at school or work can sometimes be too much. Maybe your boss demands extra hours or your sister needs you to help her with a family birthday party.

People pulling you here and there can have you going in circles. Somehow you keep pushing forward, not always sure where the strength comes from, but thankful in the end that you made it through the day.

In those situations, you're not just stretching your physical body to the limit, but your mind and emotions as well. Stress can make you feel like a grape being stepped on. But there is good news. God has given you everything you need, but you must choose to use the wisdom He has provided.

### EVENING

Don't be afraid to say no when you feel you just can't add one more thing to your to-do list. Don't become involved in too many activities, don't agree to a part-time job unless you know it won't interfere with your studies, and do your homework before spending time watching television.

Lessen the pressure where you can, and then know that God's power will make up for the rest.

*Lord, help me to do what I can do, and I'll trust You to*
*do for me those things that I can't do. Amen.*

## DAY 35

# PERFECTION STEMS FROM GOD

*"God is my strong fortress, and he makes my way perfect."*
2 SAMUEL 22:33 NLT

### MORNING

Trapped! You're on a plane, and you can't help but overhear that whining, complaining voice. *Could I climb out on the wing for a little quiet?* you wonder. You soon know all about the whiner, who tells more with that whine than with words.

As a Christian, you're as public as that whiner. Everyone hears and sees all you do. But instead of griping, you exude kindness, gentleness, and sweetness. You make your fair share of mistakes, yet hecklers call you "Goody Two-shoes" or "Ms. Perfection" just to get a less-than-perfect reaction from you.

Any perfection doesn't stem from you but from God.

### EVENING

God is making you strong in Him. People see His righteousness, and it challenges them. Some react negatively. But don't worry. If they don't like you, it's not *you* they're really seeing anyway—it's Jesus.

*Jesus, even if they don't like it, I want others to see You in my life. Your perfection is better than anything I could offer. Amen.*

# DAY 36

## JESUS IS THE LIGHT

*In the beginning was the Word, and the Word was with God, and the Word was God. He was with God in the beginning. Through him all things were made; without him nothing was made that has been made. In him was life, and that life was the light of all mankind. The light shines in the darkness, and the darkness has not overcome it.*

JOHN 1:1–5 NIV

### MORNING

Before Jesus enters our lives, we may believe we are living well, but in the end, we are stumbling along a path in the darkness if we aren't following Him. Jesus, the Light of the World, taught us to love Him by loving us first. His love is the light by which we can see all things more clearly.

### EVENING

Even now, we need Jesus' light. Ask your Savior to cast light on the sins you haven't been able to see in yourself. Ask Him to illuminate your community's needs and hurts so you can pray and serve the best you can. Don't be afraid, but don't rush out into darkness headlong; follow the Light, for He leads us to the work He has for us (Ephesians 2:10). Be saturated in His brightness and glory; if we live like Jesus, wholeheartedly desiring to know and love our heavenly Father, then we will be like stars shining in the darkness (Philippians 2:14–16).

*Jesus, shed Your glorious light on all parts of my life. Help me to move forward in faith, following where You lead, my path lit by Your wisdom. Don't let me run ahead of where You would have me. Amen.*

# DAY 37

## WHY NOT ME?

*God gave Paul the power to perform unusual miracles.*
*When handkerchiefs or aprons that had merely touched his*
*skin were placed on sick people, they were healed.*
ACTS 19:11–12 NLT

### MORNING

It's probably safe to say that none of your clothing has ever resulted in an amazing healing. Maybe we have witnessed some unexplainable cures. We prayed, and God healed a friend of cancer. Perhaps God spared a loved one in an accident that claimed the lives of others. Most of the time, however, these kinds of miracles don't happen. . .

### EVENING

When his fellow missionary, Trophimus, fell sick, Paul was given no miracle to help him. When Timothy complained of frequent stomach problems, Paul had no miracle-working handkerchief for Timothy's misery. Paul himself suffered from an incurable ailment (2 Corinthians 12:7), yet he was willing to leave it with God. We may be clueless as to why God miraculously heals others but not us or our best friend.

Like Paul, we must trust God when there's no miracle. Can we be as resilient as Job, who said, "Though he slay me, yet will I hope in him" (Job 13:15 NIV)? We can—waiting for the day when health problems and bad accidents and death cease forever (Revelation 21:4).

*When healing doesn't come, Lord Jesus,*
*give us grace to trust You more. Amen.*

# DAY 38

# EXPERIENCE GOD'S LOVE ANEW

*Those who trust God's action in them find that God's Spirit is in them—living and breathing God! Obsession with self in these matters is a dead end; attention to God leads us out into the open, into a spacious, free life.*

ROMANS 8:5–6 MSG

## MORNING

Slow down and take a minute to carefully reread today's scripture verses. Isn't that the kind of life *you* want to experience?

Sadly, many people think God doesn't look on them with love, favor, or delight—let alone desire to fill every fiber of their being. In their heart of hearts, they feel that God is angry at them. . .or, at best, distant and uncaring. They certainly don't trust what He does in their lives. This is the great disconnect that the Father wants to deal with in your heart today.

## EVENING

When you trust and embrace God's deep love for you, you become better able to love others in return. Loving what God loves is the key—and yes, He absolutely loves you. Both Jesus and the apostles affirm this truth repeatedly.

One pastor told his congregation that he knew God loved him but that the past week, for the very first time, he had experienced a profound revelation of "Jesus loves me, this I know" deep within his heart. He was completely transformed by this experience.

*Lord, I want to experience Your love anew. Transform me, I pray. Amen.*

# DAY 39

## ASK IN FAITH

*But when you ask him, be sure that your faith is in God alone. Do not waver, for a person with divided loyalty is as unsettled as a wave of the sea that is blown and tossed by the wind.*

JAMES 1:6 NLT

### MORNING

What does it mean to ask God for something *in faith*? Does it mean we believe that He *can* grant our requests? That He *will* grant our requests? Exactly what is required to prove our faith?

These are difficult questions. Many who have prayed for healed bodies and healed relationships have received exactly that on this side of heaven. Others who have prayed for the same things, believing that only God could bring healing, haven't received the answers they wanted.

There is no easy fix that makes all our longings come true. The secret ingredient, if there is one, is faith that God is who He says He is. It's faith that God is good and will use our circumstances to bring about His purpose and high calling in our lives and in the world.

### EVENING

When we don't get the answers we want from God, it's okay to feel disappointed. He understands. But we must never doubt His goodness or His motives. We must stand firm in our belief that God's love for us will never change.

*Dear Father, I know that You are good and that You love me. I know Your love for me will never change, even when my circumstances are hard. Help me cling to Your love even when You don't give the answers I want. Amen.*

## DAY 40

# STAND FIRM!

*Cast your cares on the Lord and he will sustain you;*
*he will never let the righteous be shaken.*
Psalm 55:22 NIV

### MORNING

The storm tore through the neighborhood, upending patio furniture and blowing trash cans down the street. After the tempest passed, the neighbors ventured outside to inspect the damage. Roof shingles were found in some yards. Several large tree branches had narrowly missed damaging vehicles, and some trees were completely uprooted. It was a horrendous and frightening sight, one that was very unsettling to many.

We believers often have horrible storms in our own lives: parents' unemployment, the death of a loved one, a serious illness, a brother or sister in trouble. . .

### EVENING

She who stands with Christ stands firmly, as if anchored to the ground. Although it seems as if we will be destroyed in these life storms, God will not allow it.

*Dear Lord, I will trust in You, despite what life throws at me. You have promised to never let the righteous be shaken, and I am holding on to that promise by holding on to You. Thank You that You can be trusted to keep Your promises to protect and sustain me. In Jesus' name. Amen.*

# DAY 41

# NEVER ABANDONED

*We are hard pressed on every side, but not crushed; perplexed, but not in despair; persecuted, but not abandoned; struck down, but not destroyed. We always carry around in our body the death of Jesus, so that the life of Jesus may also be revealed in our body.*

2 Corinthians 4:8–10 niv

## MORNING

Have you felt abandoned or ignored by God? We often transfer our anger and feelings of betrayal (about a person who wounded us) onto the God who hurts with us. Rest assured that God has not left you alone. He may be silent, and you may not feel His presence, but He is with you. Trust the truth of the Word, even when your emotions say something different. Emotions can't be trusted, but God can be. His promises hold whether or not we feel we can hold on.

Satan wants you to give up. He doesn't want you to be victorious, because he knows how much you can do for God—and how much God can do in you—if your wounds are healed.

## EVENING

God, who loved you so much that He gave His only Son to die on the cross, is *for* you. He wants your heart's restoration more than you do. Do you believe that? Whatever you've done, whatever you've been through, He is still the same: perfectly forgiving, perfectly faithful, and perfectly compassionate.

Lean into that. Let the truth soak into the driest parts of your soul. . .and be encouraged.

*Reveal Your life-giving truths to me, Holy One. Though I am hard pressed and perplexed, I trust that You are for me and not against me. Amen.*

# DAY 42

## RECONCILED TO GOD

*Ezra wept, prostrate in front of The Temple of God.*
*As he prayed and confessed, a huge number of the men,*
*women, and children of Israel gathered around him. All the*
*people were now weeping as if their hearts would break.*

EZRA 10:1 MSG

### MORNING

Sin is not a politically correct topic these days. Yet God talks about sin all throughout His Word. The Bible says God hates sin and that He sent His Son to die on the cross to save us from the results of sin—our eternal separation from God.

Sins can be "big" (murder, adultery) or "little" (gossip, envy)—but in God's eyes, they're the same. That's why we need His sacrifice, His righteousness. Only through Jesus' death on the cross can we be reconciled to God.

### EVENING

Satan loves to remind us of our sins to make us feel guilty. He adores it when we wallow in them. But God never intended for us to do that. Instead, God wants us to confess our sins—daily, or hourly if need be! He wants us to receive His forgiveness and move on to live with renewed fervor.

What sins have separated us from God today? Let's draw near to the throne of grace so we can receive His pardon. He longs for us to come near to Him, and He will cover us with Jesus' robe of righteousness so that we don't have to feel guilt or shame anymore.

*Lord, forgive me for the sins I've committed today. Make me ever aware of Your grace and forgiveness so that I may share Your love with others. Amen.*

# DAY 43

## A CLEAR FOCUS

*Hope deferred makes the heart sick,*
*but a longing fulfilled is a tree of life.*
PROVERBS 13:12 NIV

### MORNING

We all have dreams and a desire to pursue them. But then life gets busy, and we become distracted with the choices we must make daily. Do you go right or left, choose this way or that? Too much too fast is overwhelming, and looking for balance can leave us lost, not knowing which way to turn. The best way to gain your balance is to stop moving and refocus.

Jesus is your hope! He stands a short distance away, bidding you to take a walk on water—a step of faith toward Him. Disregarding the distractions can be hard, but the rough waters can become silent as you turn your eyes, your thoughts, and your emotions on Him.

### EVENING

You can tackle the tough things as you maintain your focus on Jesus. Let Him direct you over the rough waters of life, overcoming each obstacle one at a time. Don't look at the big picture during the storm; instead, focus on the one thing you can do at that moment to help your immediate situation—one step at a time.

*Lord, help me to not concentrate on the distractions but to keep my focus on which step to take next in order to reach You. Amen.*

# DAY 44

## DEFINITION OF HOPE

*Praise be to the God and Father of our Lord Jesus Christ!*
*In his great mercy he has given us new birth into a living*
*hope through the resurrection of Jesus Christ from the dead,*
*and into an inheritance that can never perish, spoil or fade.*

1 PETER 1:3–4 NIV

### MORNING

It's interesting to watch how language shifts over time. Words change. Their definitions change. Sometimes a subtle change in meaning can result in big misunderstandings.

One word that has an altered definition is the word *hope*. Today, hope often refers to a weak, unreasonable optimism. It means "It probably won't happen, but we'll try to stay positive." Yet when Peter wrote about hope, his definition meant absolute belief in a certain, positive outcome.

In Christ, we have hope—not just for heaven, but for this life we're currently living. No matter where we are on our journey, He has good things in store for us.

### EVENING

We can look forward to heaven. We can also look forward to today because He has great things in store. We have hope for tomorrow and next week and next year because God loves us, and Christ made the way for us to have a close relationship with our adoring Father.

Next time we find ourselves thinking, *I hope today is a good day*, we can adjust the definition of the word *hope*. Then we'll know that today, and every day, will be filled with amazing reminders of God's unfailing love.

*Dear Father, thank You for giving me hope for today and for eternity. Amen.*

# DAY 45

## IS ANYONE LISTENING?

*"I have labored in vain; I have spent my strength for nothing at all. Yet what is due me is in the LORD's hand, and my reward is with my God."*
ISAIAH 49:4 NIV

### MORNING

Some days you just can't win. The shirt you just got has a stain on it. Your cat turned over the goldfish bowl and ate the body. You said something at school, and the silence that followed made you want to creep under a desk. Nothing went right all day.

Doesn't anyone care that you had a rotten day and need a little encouragement? Well, you could call home and get some sympathy, but Mom might remind you that you still need to clean your room. . .

### EVENING

Why not just talk out your worries and troubles with God? He listens without comment. He knows exactly what kind of day you had, and He weeps for you. He's there, and He cares.

*Even if no one seems to appreciate me, I know that You do, Lord. In just a second, my day can become holy when I reach out to You. Amen.*

# DAY 46

## PUT ON LOVE

*And over all these virtues put on love,*
*which binds them all together in perfect unity.*
COLOSSIANS 3:14 NIV

### MORNING

How many mornings have we stood in front of our closet, looking hopelessly at its overstuffed contents and thinking we have nothing to wear? What we're really thinking is that we have nothing to wear that makes us feel cute or pretty or sporty—or whatever look we're going for that day. We want to look good. We want others to be drawn to us. And sometimes, no matter how many shirts we have to choose from, nothing feels right.

But there is one accessory we all have available to us that always fits. It always looks right, is always appropriate, and always makes us more attractive to others. When we wear it, we look great, no matter how faded or dated our wardrobes may be. When we wear it, we become more popular, more sought after, and more admired.

What is that accessory, you ask, and where can you buy it?

It's love, and you can't buy it anywhere. It's free!

### EVENING

Love is always available through the Holy Spirit. When we call on Him to help us love others, He cloaks us in a beautiful covering that draws people to us and makes us perfectly lovely in every way.

*Dear Father, as I get dressed each day, help me to remember that the most important accessory I can wear is Your love. Amen.*

## DAY 47

# PUT FAITH FIRST

*"But seek first his kingdom and his righteousness,*
*and all these things will be given to you as well."*
MATTHEW 6:33 NIV

### MORNING

Following Jesus means trusting Him to keep this promise. You understand that He will do so because of who He is and all He has done for you. When it comes down to reality, though, part of you wonders, *I know He can, but will He?*

Even Abram found this difficult. He had God's promise of blessing—of guidance, presence, descendants, and land—yet he ran away from the Promised Land and lied about his wife out of fear and uncertainty.

Small faith fails to put God and His priorities first, but a little faith gets you back on track.

### EVENING

How big is God? Let David remind you: "GOD, brilliant Lord, yours is a household name. . . . I look up at your macro-skies, dark and enormous, your handmade sky-jewelry, moon and stars mounted in their settings. Then I look at my micro-self and wonder, Why do you bother with us?" (Psalm 8:1, 3–4 MSG). He's the mighty Creator, but He's also your loving Father.

*Lord, You put humanity at the pinnacle of creation. Help me to embrace the provision You've given me in Christ and trust You for every need. Amen.*

## DAY 48

# FOLLOW THE LEADER

*Lead me, LORD, in your righteousness because of my enemies—make your way straight before me.*
PSALM 5:8 NIV

### MORNING

Today's world is full of enemies of righteousness. We seek instant gratification instead of practicing patience. Rudeness is seen as strength, while gentleness is devalued as weakness. Indulgence is promoted, but self-control is not. Greed and deceit are excused as part of competition. Image seems more important than honesty. Rationalization has become an accepted form of making excuses for bad behavior.

Yet the psalmist offers us hope for learning to live as a Christian in an environment that does little to help us. He reminds us to ask the Lord to lead us in righteousness.

### EVENING

Too often we believe in the Lord for our eternal salvation but go about trying to live our daily lives as if being righteous is something we must figure out on our own. Christ is the righteousness of God embodied for us. In Him, we have been accepted by the Father and given the Spirit, who enables us to live in right relationship to God and others. Daily and hourly, we can pray for Christ's leading, asking Him to keep us focused on Him and mindful that we are following Him. He has a path that He desires to walk with each of us, guiding us each step of the way.

*Lord, help me remember to ask for Your leading. Show me the path You have designed for my life and give me clear direction. Amen.*

# DAY 49

## CALLED TO BE DIFFERENT

*[Jesus said,] "In this world you will have trouble. But take heart! I have overcome the world."*
John 16:33 NIV

### MORNING

Would you intentionally accept a job that is difficult and dangerous and requires intense commitment? If you hesitated in answering, you should know that people make this decision every day. Some examples of those who face this choice include firemen, policemen, military personnel, and parents.

We have the example of those who willingly accept a role in life that they know will bring its own share of inconvenience. There's another application to this idea when following Jesus. We're enriched beyond anything we can think by following Jesus, but our verse reminds us that trouble will be part of our lives. . .

### EVENING

We've been called to be different. This difference is seen in the way we talk, the places we go, and a myriad of choices we make. When noticed by those who don't like Jesus, there may be tension and trouble. We should always keep in mind that no matter how difficult things may be, the time we live on earth will be the worst of our eternity. When we die, we will spend the rest of eternity with God. Stand strong. Whatever difficulties you face won't last forever.

*You overcame the world, and You're willing to lead. Let me rest in knowing that any trouble I face is temporary at best. Where You lead is somewhere I can never get to on my own. Each day brings me closer to seeing You face-to-face. Lead on, O King eternal. Amen.*

# DAY 50

## STRENGTH IN GOD

*I am in the midst of lions; I am forced to dwell among ravenous beasts—men whose teeth are spears and arrows, whose tongues are sharp swords.*

Psalm 57:4 NIV

### MORNING

Does today's scripture sound like a description of your school or neighborhood? Does your apartment have bars over the windows, and does your door have at least three locks? Do you come home and stay inside from dusk to dawn? In many places, this is the only safe way to live—and you must deal with it.

You also must rise above it, to refuse to be a prisoner in your own home. When you are old enough, you can join other neighbors and help take back the streets. You can stay in the neighborhood when you have the chance to get out. You can volunteer to be a mentor, to help with a neighborhood sports program—to invest yourself and your money where it will make a difference.

### EVENING

It's not easy, but Psalm 57:7 (NIV) says, "My heart, O God, is steadfast, my heart is steadfast; I will sing and make music." Make music wherever you live.

*Father, it's tempting to get out as soon as possible and leave all these problems behind me. Give me the strength to make music in places where there is only discord and trouble. Amen.*

# DAY 51

## LOVING FULLY

*Jesus replied: "'Love the Lord your God with all your heart and with all your soul and with all your mind.'"*
MATTHEW 22:37 NIV

### MORNING

When Jesus commanded His followers to love God with all their hearts, souls, and minds, He meant that loving God fully means putting aside everything that gets in the way of a relationship with Him. Everything. That's no small order in a world filled with distractions.

So how can today's Christians set aside everything to fully love God? The answer is to shift their desire from serving themselves to serving Him. Love requires action, and the Holy Spirit gives believers power to glorify God with everything they do. Praising Him for His provisions is one way to love Him. Doing selfless acts of service for others as if working for Him is another way. So is loving others as He loves us. Studying the Bible and being intimate with God in prayer is the ultimate act of love toward Him. When Christians center their lives on their passion for God, they learn to love Him fully.

### EVENING

Loving God with heart, soul, and mind takes practice. It means thinking of Him all day and working to glorify Him through every thought and action. It means putting aside one's own desires to serve someone greater.

Is it possible to love God more than you love anyone or anything else? You can try. That in itself is an act of love.

*Dear God, I love You. Help me to love You more through everything I do. Amen.*

## DAY 52

# THE PERFECT REFLECTION

*"Give careful thought to your ways."*
HAGGAI 1:7 NIV

### MORNING

You probably know how it feels to have a bad hair day or a huge zit on your face. On those days, we try to avoid the mirror. The last thing we want is to keep running into a reflection of ourselves when we look less than our best.

Our Christian lives often have a similar feel. Instead of facing our imperfections as followers of Christ, we work hard to avoid any mention of them. God's command to give careful thought to our ways may fill us with dread because the reflection can be so unattractive.

As we give careful thought to our ways, we should first look back to where we have come from and reflect on God's work in our lives.

### EVENING

We are on a journey. Sometimes the road is difficult; sometimes the road is easy. We must consider where we were when God found us and where we are now through His grace. Even more importantly, we must think about the ways our present actions, habits, and attitudes toward God reflect our lives as Christians. Only when we are able to honestly assess our lives in Christ can we call on His name to help perfect our reflection.

*Dear Lord, help me to look honestly at the ways I live and make changes where necessary. Amen.*

# DAY 53

## GO FORTH

*Then Jesus came to them and said, "All authority in heaven and on earth has been given to me. Therefore go and make disciples of all nations, baptizing them in the name of the Father and of the Son and of the Holy Spirit, and teaching them to obey everything I have commanded you. And surely I am with you always, to the very end of the age."*
MATTHEW 28:18–20 NIV

### MORNING

Some Christians thrive on evangelism, stopping and asking folks in the grocery store if they know Jesus. More introverted believers may shudder at the thought. However, Jesus doesn't tell His disciples that the Great Commission is limited to the fearless extroverts. His command to carry His gospel to the world is for *all* who believe in Him.

The Holy Spirit has given different spiritual gifts to believers to help them obey this command (see 1 Corinthians 12). Any spiritual gift can be used to share the gospel, whether it's teaching, showing mercy, or hospitality. Your friendships with others in your community could lead to conversations about who you serve. Inviting a new friend into your home and life gives you the opportunity to share about the one who invited you to be His friend.

### EVENING

In our work, our hope is always in Jesus. His authority and power are more than sufficient to bring His plan to completion, but we have the profound privilege of joining in His mighty work. In His power, go forth to share His goodness!

*Holy Spirit, grant me wisdom and strength to share the gospel through the gifts You've given. Help me recognize the opportunities when they come! Amen.*

# DAY 54

## WE ARE NOT PERFECT

*I am on the verge of collapse, facing constant pain. But I confess my sins; I am deeply sorry for what I have done.*
PSALM 38:17–18 NLT

### MORNING

Jesus was the only perfect person in the world. David, who wrote the verses above, was as sinful as the next man, yet God favored him over all other kings and chose his descendants to be the earthly ancestors of Jesus.

### EVENING

God knows we will sin. It's in our nature to do so. Not that we can use that as an excuse, but it is a fact of life we must live with. God meant us to live happy lives, not to be weighed down by an unnatural burden of sin. Jesus has accepted that burden for us. Give it over to Him, accept His sacrifice with joy, go on with your life, and try to sin no more.

*Father, thank You for forgiving all my sins through Your Son, Jesus Christ. Let me dwell on what You have done for me, not on the many ways I have failed You. In Jesus' name, amen.*

# DAY 55

# NOT A GAME

*"Don't bargain with God. Be direct. Ask for what you need. This isn't a cat-and-mouse, hide-and-seek game we're in."*
MATTHEW 7:7–8 MSG

## MORNING

Life tests you. God allows it to challenge you to learn and grow, but the lessons are almost always about learning to trust more in Him. God shows you who He is—His power and holiness, but also His mercy and grace. The only way to pass such tests is to take God seriously.

When God told Abraham to sacrifice his only son, Abraham didn't hesitate to obey. He reasoned that if God was going to let him take Isaac's life, God would then have to raise Isaac from the dead to keep His promises. That's why he told his servants, "The boy and I are going over there to worship; then we'll come back to you" (Genesis 22:5 MSG). Only faith prepares you for such a test, and only faith will help you pass it.

## EVENING

It's dangerous to play at following God. To act the Christian on Sunday and spend the rest of the week living how you want to is not truly believing. That reveals a person living in fear of other people instead of reverent fear of God. Worship isn't part of your Sunday face; it's your life each day.

*Father, I choose to recognize and honor You with all I have and all I do, today and every day. Amen.*

# DAY 56

## NO LIARS ALLOWED

*"God is not a man, so he does not lie. He is not human, so he does not change his mind. Has he ever spoken and failed to act? Has he ever promised and not carried it through?"*

NUMBERS 23:19 NLT

### MORNING

Have you ever let someone else down? Have you experienced disappointment when others didn't follow through with what they said they'd do? As imperfect humans, we've all been on the giving and receiving ends of such circumstances.

But God is different. It's not just that He's upstanding and reliable; instead, God, by His very nature, is incapable of lying, indecision, manipulation, or going back on His word.

What does this mean for His children? It means that we never have to wonder if God is planning to follow through with His promises. It means we can count on Him to do what He says, never wavering or being wishy-washy. God's truth will remain true now and forever.

### EVENING

No matter what frustrations or disappointments are happening in your life, take comfort in the fact that God remains constant. Praise Him for His very nature of stability and support, and thank Him for His everlasting goodness.

*I am amazed by You, dear Lord. When I am surrounded by the sins of the world, still Your awesome perfection shines through. You are my rock, my Redeemer, and my ever-faithful friend. Amen.*

# DAY 57

## OFFER GOD YOUR TALENTS

*One generation commends your works to another; they tell of your mighty acts. They speak of the glorious splendor of your majesty—and I will meditate on your wonderful works.*

PSALM 145:4–5 NIV

### MORNING

There was no internet in the days of David, no instant communication. Most people couldn't read or write. Traditions were taught to a young generation by the older generation, often through stories, songs, and dances, which were memorable and enjoyable ways to learn. The psalms and hymns of the church not only lift people's spirits but serve as teaching tools.

Perhaps you were not cut out to be a witness. The thought of speaking to another person about your beliefs may scare you into silence. But there are other ways to communicate. . .

### EVENING

Can you tell stories? Can you sing? Can you dance? Can you draw? Faith, and the joy it brings you, can be communicated through many means. Offer God the talents you do have, and He will find a way to use them.

*Father, show me how I can tell others about Your mighty works and pass on the faith I treasure. You know what I am capable of, and I do want to help. Amen.*

# DAY 58

## FAMILY RESPONSIBILITY

*When Jesus saw his mother standing there beside the disciple he loved, he said to her, "Dear woman, here is your son." And he said to this disciple, "Here is your mother." And from then on this disciple took her into his home.*

JOHN 19:26–27 NLT

### MORNING

Little is known about the home life of Jesus when He lived on earth. Before He began His public ministry, the record is sparse, and God must have a reason for that. We can surmise that He grew up as many children did in His little town. His family wasn't well-to-do; His earthly father was a carpenter, and we know He had half brothers and sisters. He was respectful of His earthly parents and obedient to their wishes, as shown in the account of them finding Him in the temple talking to the teachers.

### EVENING

Some scholars think that Joseph had died before Jesus went to Calvary. If so, as the oldest son, Jesus had been responsible for the family since that time. This may be the reason why He speaks to John, "the disciple he loved," from the cross, committing His mother to John's care. Jesus was concerned for His mother, knowing the trauma she was experiencing and feeling the responsibility of His earthly duty to her. He was careful to assure that she would be safe and well.

Likewise, we must embrace the roles given to us as children and all the responsibilities entailed. In this way, we follow His great example.

*Heavenly Father, thank You for creating the home and the family in it. Help me to accept and embrace my place and my responsibilities. In Jesus' name, amen.*

# DAY 59

## RELEASING YOUR HOLD ON ANXIETY

*Search me, God, and know my heart; test me and know my anxious thoughts. See if there is any offensive way in me, and lead me in the way everlasting.*

PSALM 139:23–24 NIV

### MORNING

We live in an age of anxiety. Worry and stress soak our lives, and most of us accept it as a given that we will not live in a personal state of peace.

This is not how God intended it to be. He asks us to place our trust and our hope in Him. If we worry, we are not trusting. If we let the cares of this world weigh on our hearts and distract us from participating in God's work, then that worry becomes sinful.

### EVENING

What is it that weighs you down? Your family's financial issues? An unhealthy relationship? Your busy schedule? Surrender these misgivings to God, who wants to take them from you. Ask Him to search your heart for any and all anxieties, for any and all signs that you have not truly put your trust in Him. Find the trouble spots in your life to which you direct most of your thoughts and energy, and then hand these troubles over to one who can truly address them.

Realize that you are only human and that God is infinitely more capable of balancing your cares than you are.

*Lord, take from me my worries, big and small. May I remember to give these to You daily so that I will not find myself distracted by the things of this world. Amen.*

# DAY 60

## FAIR JUDGMENT

*"Just as I swore in the time of Noah that I would never again let a flood cover the earth, so now I swear that I will never again be angry and punish you."*

ISAIAH 54:9 NLT

### MORNING

The last time God really cut loose in anger, He killed off everyone in the world except Noah and his family and a representative sample of every animal that filled the world. God must have known that humans couldn't live with a threat like that hanging over their heads, and He promised that this sort of mass punishment was a thing of the past. Humanity itself was safe, even though individuals still had to deal with individual judgment. God promised to differentiate between individuals and humanity.

### EVENING

Besides taking a load of fear off our backs, God's promise also serves as an example of how we should deal with our own anger. We must differentiate too. Just because a bald man unfairly fired you doesn't mean all bald men are bad bosses. You don't kick all dogs after one bites your leg. If God in His righteous anger promises not to punish by category, can we do anything less?

*Father, thank You for judging fairly, no matter how we displease You with our actions. Teach me to do the same. Amen.*

# DAY 61

## HOLD HIS HAND

*"For I am the Lord your God who takes hold of your right hand and says to you, Do not fear; I will help you."*
Isaiah 41:13 NIV

### MORNING

Holding hands communicates love and protection. Courage and strength are imparted from one person to another. Holding hands acknowledges that a strong bond exists between two people.

Imagine facing surgery, a new school, the death of a parent, or a move to a new town. Many circumstances may cause us to become fearful. We need to feel love and protection. We yearn for courage and strength to face another day. If only we had someone's hand to hold!

God desires to help us. When we walk through life hand in hand with God, we can face anything. His love covers us. His presence is our guard. We can do all things through Christ because we are given His strength.

### EVENING

Do you feel as though you're walking through life alone? Do not fear. Are you in need of love, protection, courage, and strength? Reach out your hand. Allow Jesus to take hold of it. Receive His love and protection. Bask in His courage and strength. Take hold of His hand!

*Dear Lord, thank You that I do not have to fear.
You will help me by taking my hand. Amen.*

# DAY 62

## ABSOLUTE COMMITMENT

*"Whoever does not take up their cross and follow me is not worthy of me. Whoever finds their life will lose it, and whoever loses their life for my sake will find it."*
MATTHEW 10:38–39 NIV

### MORNING

You may have heard people say they have a "cross to bear." That usually means they are going through a rough time, such as a hard relationship, a chronic disease, or an addiction. But the cross really means only one thing: suffering and death. Jesus' call to take up your cross is about dying to self, letting go of your plans and desires, and letting God replace them with His.

This is especially difficult for those who think they're doing God a favor by receiving Christ: *Imagine God using my talents and connections for the good of the kingdom!* But if they had anything to offer God, would the cross have been necessary?

### EVENING

In Christ, you're reborn spiritually, but you'll bear the difficulties of life until either you die or Jesus comes back. However, you'll share in the suffering that Christ endured, and because you belong to Him, God can redeem all your mistakes and hardships, self-made or not. He can turn them into bridges to others' pain. It's not easy to love people the way Jesus loves you, but it's worth it.

*God, strengthen me for the journey ahead. I willingly share in Your suffering, knowing that You will be with me and that the reward is worth the pain. Amen.*

# DAY 63

# READY, WILLING, AND ABLE

*He said, "Then you see how every student well-trained in God's kingdom is like the owner of a general store who can put his hands on anything you need, old or new, exactly when you need it."*
MATTHEW 13:52 MSG

## MORNING

God does things in unexpected ways, at unexpected times, and through unexpected people. He tends to turn conventions upside down, doing things in what seems to us like the most difficult and convoluted ways. God uses the least likely people to do the least likely things, all so He gets His rightful glory even as He blesses His people.

You won't always know how God is going to work, but you know the ultimate result: "The LORD gives victory to his anointed. . . . Some trust in chariots and some in horses, but we trust in the name of the LORD our God" (Psalm 20:6–7 NIV).

## EVENING

The key to working *with* an unpredictable but always victorious God (instead of against Him) is to make yourself available. Then, as Matthew 13:52 suggests, you must stock your shelves with the right supplies, and the Bible is your chief supplier. It's so important to be filled with His Word daily so you will be topped up and available for His purposes at any given time.

*Father, teach me more about You and Your ways through Your Word so that I can know You more and be useful to You in any situation You put me in. Amen.*

# DAY 64

# LONELINESS

*God places the lonely in families.*
Psalm 68:6 NLT

## MORNING

It's kind of hard to be lonely in a family. Someone's always sitting at the kitchen table, waiting for you to get off the computer, or banging on the bathroom door. Eventually, you move out, get your own place, and rule your own roost. It's wonderful for a while. You do what you want, eat what you want, and leave your clothes where you want.

But soon the silence gets to you. You start leaving the television on just for the company. You sing along with the commercials. You call home just to hear your sisters fighting in the kitchen. You begin the frightening process of dating, at first just for the company. If you're fortunate, you find the right person and—bingo—you have your *own* family.

## EVENING

Loneliness has its purpose. It forces most of us to relate to others in meaningful ways, to build families of one sort or another. The ultimate success of loneliness is its own defeat.

*Lord, sometimes I get so lonely I can't stand it. Help me find the family I need, whether it's a group of close friends from school, a circle of people from church, or a boyfriend. Amen.*

# DAY 65

## JUNGLE OF LIFE

*God's Word is living and powerful. It is sharper than a sword that cuts both ways. It cuts straight into where the soul and spirit meet and it divides them. It cuts into the joints and bones. It tells what the heart is thinking about and what it wants to do.*

HEBREWS 4:12 NLV

### MORNING

Since the time Adam and Eve disobeyed God, the consequences of sin have often stood between us and God's best for our lives. Choosing a life of faith can feel like we are lost in a jungle, tangled in the underbrush. But God has given us a powerful tool that will cut through the debris of life in a fallen world.

When you take the Bible and live according to His plans, obeying Him, God's Word cuts like a knife through the entanglements of life. When you choose to use the sword of truth, it clears a path and can free you from the weights of the world that try to entrap and ensnare you.

### EVENING

No matter what the challenges of life are saying to you today, take God's Word and speak His plans into your life. Choose His words of encouragement and peace instead of the negative things your circumstances are telling you.

*God, I want to live in Your truth. I want to believe what You say about me in the Bible. Help me to speak Your words today instead of letting the problem speak to me. Help me believe. Amen.*

# DAY 66

## GOD'S UNSTOPPABLE PLAN

*"I know that you can do anything, and no one can stop you."*
JOB 42:2 NLT

### MORNING

Melinda's passion is music. Ever since she was a little girl, she has loved to sing and play the piano. As a teen, she won several competitions, and her college of choice offered her a scholarship to study music. Melinda spent four years immersed in her favorite subject, enjoying almost every minute of her studies.

However, as graduation neared, Melinda couldn't find a job in music. Week after week, she prayed for a way to make money from her passion. But none came. Melinda eventually took a job in sales, an area in which she was naturally gifted but that didn't excite her much. Now she sings in a community chorus and participates in music groups at her church. And she prays for a way to get paid to do what she loves. During her times with God, He assures her that He has a plan and that He will open a door for her, in His time and way.

### EVENING

Whatever you're waiting for, hold on to God's promises with faith, knowing that He who parted the Red Sea has a very good plan and purpose for your life.

*Lord, thank You for giving me unique talents. Help me to trust You to open doors for me so I can use those talents for Your glory. Amen.*

# DAY 67

## ONLY BELIEVE

*"He who puts his trust in Me and is baptized will be saved from the punishment of sin. But he who does not put his trust in Me is guilty and will be punished forever."*
MARK 16:16 NLV

### MORNING

Many people have a hard time with the concept that belief in Jesus is all it takes to be saved. Some think they must do something important or be really good; they hope their good works will outweigh the bad when Judgment Day comes.

Maybe part of the problem stems from not understanding what *believe* means when it's used in the Bible. We might say, "I believe it's going to rain" or "Can you believe that game?" Yet the word we're talking about here is much more powerful. It means to adhere to, trust in, and rely on. The object of our reliance must be Jesus. It does no good to depend on a church or our own good works or any person except Jesus Christ.

### EVENING

Jesus came as a human being because of profound love. He took our place, suffered excruciating agony, and died because He wanted you and me to have a rich, abundant life and spend eternity with Him. All He asks in return is that we trust Him. Such love demands a response. The only acceptable response is for us to believe that what Jesus did is enough.

He loves for us to pray and sing praises and study the Bible, but those things don't make us any more worthy. It's all about Jesus and what He did.

*Dear Lord, I believe You've done it all. I long to worship You forever and give myself to You totally, to glorify You in every way. Amen.*

# DAY 68

## MORE BLESSED TO GIVE

*"Give, and it will be given to you. A good measure, pressed down, shaken together and running over, will be poured into your lap. For with the measure you use, it will be measured to you."*
LUKE 6:38 NIV

### MORNING

When Cassie learned that her church's homeless ministry needed help, she volunteered, eager to give what she could. Lending a hand seemed like the right thing to do, and she expected to find lots of needy people with whom she could share her gifts. She found plenty of needy people, and she definitely lent a hand. However, what she hadn't expected was to be blessed so much. Not only did she make some new friends, but they taught her a great deal about thankfulness, contentment, and how to make the best of a hard situation.

### EVENING

In God's economy, giving means receiving. When we give to others, we receive more than the satisfaction of a job well done. Jesus promises blessings when we give to others. They can be simple blessings, such as a smile or a kind word of thanks. Blessings can also be life-changing, such as making a new friend or acquiring a new skill. Getting something shouldn't be our motivation for serving others, but it is an added bonus. What can *you* do today to be a blessing to others?

*Lord, thank You for the promise of giving and receiving. Help me to bless others as You have blessed me. Amen.*

# DAY 69

## CONTROL YOUR ANGER

*A quick-tempered person does foolish things.*
PROVERBS 14:17 NIV

### MORNING

People handle anger in various ways. Some manage to push it down and continue as if they never felt it—probably giving themselves ulcers in the process. Others kick chairs in private but soon come to terms with their anger. Still others blow up and immediately feel better. We tend to react to anger the same way our parents did, for better or for worse.

In the same way, we all have different boiling points. It takes a lot to get some people angry, while others erupt at the slightest provocation.

However you react to anger, you need to maintain control.

### EVENING

Uncontrolled anger makes us stupid. We do and say things we would never do under normal circumstances, starting fistfights or saying words we can never take back.

When anger takes over, we need to get away if we can't control ourselves. Go hide out in the restroom, if necessary. Shut a door behind you until you are back in control. A real man does not hit. A strong woman asserts control over herself, not over others.

*Father, when I want to strike out in anger, whether verbally or physically, give me the self-control I need to avoid doing anything stupid. Amen.*

# DAY 70

## FIRST-NAME BASIS

*Moses protested to God, "Who am I to appear before Pharaoh? Who am I to lead the people of Israel out of Egypt?" God answered, "I will be with you."*

EXODUS 3:11–12 NLT

### MORNING

Moses didn't jump at the chance to deliver Israel. He had spent his first forty years in Egypt and had blown his exit badly. He spent the next forty years in the wilderness, staying out of trouble but hiding from his past. So, in a sense, he was right; he had no business going back to Egypt or leading God's people. But in God's eyes, that made him the perfect candidate. At that point, Moses didn't need to see himself as he was, but he needed to see God as He is.

### EVENING

God can handle your doubts if you don't let them hide your view of Him. Don't let fear make you forget who is calling you to serve Him. You have chosen to ally yourself with God. Almighty God wanted Moses to know Him on a deeply personal level, anticipating the access you now have to Him through Jesus.

The next time you face an overwhelming situation, remember that God is with you. You know Him on a first-name basis: Jesus.

*Jesus, here I am. I make myself available for whatever You want me to do today, knowing that You are with me and for me. Amen.*

# DAY 71

# ABUNDANT LIFE

*God, my shepherd! I don't need a thing. . . . Your beauty and love chase after me every day of my life. I'm back home in the house of God for the rest of my life.*

Psalm 23:1, 6 MSG

## MORNING

Psalm 23 is a comforting passage that is often read at sickbeds or funerals. But even with its famous reference to God's presence in the valley of death's shadow, the psalm is really about life. Most of its words describe God's presence, protection, and provision as you go *through* life's mountaintops and valleys.

God wants you to walk with Him so you get the most out of life.

## EVENING

You can see God's desire for relationship with His people when He told Moses how to introduce Him to Israel: "I am the LORD. . . . I will redeem you with a powerful arm and great acts of judgment. I will claim you as my own people, and I will be your God" (Exodus 6:6–7 NLT).

God had been known as God Almighty to the patriarchs, but here He opened a whole new level of intimacy. It's even deeper today—through Jesus, you are an adopted daughter of God. Consider what that means for you. Consider the resources at your disposal to do your Father's work, to experience His blessings, and to just enjoy knowing Him.

*Father, I can't wait to come home to You, but until then, let me walk more closely with You each day. Amen.*

# DAY 72

## WHEN THE ROAD BECOMES BUMPY

*"For I know the plans I have for you," says the Lord. "They are plans for good and not for disaster, to give you a future and a hope."*

JEREMIAH 29:11 NLT

### MORNING

We all have plans for our future, even if they're a little fuzzy. We know whether we want to go to college, what places we want to travel to, and what things we hope to accomplish. Most of us are realistic about our plans, knowing that some will work out and some won't. We also know that our plans will change from year to year as we mature and see more of the world.

### EVENING

What we don't like is to have our plans blown out of the water and to have our lives take a sudden change of direction. There's nothing more frightening than losing the anchor that's been holding our life in place and being forced to start over again.

Fortunately, some of these disasters turn out to be blessings. Even when we have no idea which way to turn, the Lord knows where we're going and will keep us on the right path, even if the trip's a little bumpy.

*Father, when my life suddenly turns upside down,*
*I will trust in You to lead me in the right direction. Amen.*

# DAY 73

# PRAYERS FOR BOLDNESS

*Pray that I may declare [the gospel] fearlessly, as I should.*
EPHESIANS 6:20 NIV

## MORNING

The apostle Paul was an amazing follower of Christ. He endured countless hardships, all in order to preach the gospel to those who had never heard it. He was in prison when he wrote to the Ephesians.

One might think Paul was fearless about his faith, courageously overcoming obstacles and boldly preaching the good news. In Ephesians 6:20, however, Paul asks the Ephesians to pray for him. He realized that without the prayers of the saints and the faithfulness of God, he would not be an effective ambassador for Christ.

## EVENING

In today's world, proclaiming our faith can be difficult. Our family and friends can make us feel shy about sharing the gospel. We might feel unworthy to talk about our faith, or we may be worried that we will not use the right words. Paul's request for prayer should encourage us. Paul worried about his ability to effectively communicate the gospel to those around him. He relied on his brothers and sisters in Christ to lift him up to God. In the same way, we should rely on our brothers and sisters to pray for us so that we may declare the gospel fearlessly, as we should.

*Dear Lord, thank You for Your Word. Surround me with people who will pray for me, and place people in my life for whom I can pray. Together let us boldly proclaim Your name. Amen.*

# DAY 74

# PRUNING PRODUCES FRUIT

*"I am the vine; you are the branches. If you remain in me and I in you, you will bear much fruit; apart from me you can do nothing."*
JOHN 15:5 NIV

## MORNING

What does it mean to remain in Christ so that He can produce much fruit in us and through us? John 15 speaks about sanctification (living the Christian life), not salvation (becoming a Christian). When we remain in fellowship with Christ, the true vine, His nourishment enables us to grow in holiness and be useful to Him. His process, however, includes painful pruning. He cuts away our willfulness, apathy, distractions, and sins that prevent holiness.

## EVENING

When grapevines are pruned, they weep, as sap drips from every wound. Pruning makes us weep as well, but tears teach lessons we could not learn any other way. Weeping sends us running to Christ for comfort, endurance, and wisdom. Pruning hurts, but it helps our fellowship with Christ if we submit to the sanctification process. A branch cannot bear fruit on its own. It must stay attached to the vine for its nourishment. How do we remain in fellowship with Christ? By resisting sin, staying connected through prayer, and occupying our minds with God's Word and thoughts about Him. Because He remains in us, His life can provide the power we need to remain in fellowship with Him.

*Lord Jesus, You are my source. Forgive my self-reliance and independent spirit. When I forget You during my day's activities, I accomplish nothing for eternity. Please help me be faithful and fruitful for Your glory. Amen.*

# DAY 75

## CONSTANT REMEMBRANCE

*Examine me, God, from head to foot, order your battery of tests. Make sure I'm fit inside and out so I never lose sight of your love, but keep in step with you, never missing a beat.*

Psalm 26:2–3 msg

### MORNING

You're a few months into the new year. Take stock of what God has been doing in and around you. It's all too easy to lose sight of what it took to make you His, which is why God commanded His people to hold regular remembrances of His works, such as the Passover (Exodus 12:14). Human nature is to forget the things worth remembering.

Look past the familiarity of the story. As surely as the lamb's blood provided cover for the Jews from the plague of death, so Christ's blood saved you from eternal damnation. And when God delivered His people, He was also looking down the road to the day when you would receive Him as Lord and Savior.

That's worth celebrating!

### EVENING

Keep celebrating, girl! Return to that place of wonder, reminding yourself of your need for God, having the trust of a child relying on her dad for her needs (Matthew 18:3). Avoid saying, "I've seen too much and know too much to ever be that innocent again." The moment you surrendered to God was the truest moment of your life. Trust its lessons.

*Father, never let the awe and wonder of what You did to save me become stale to me. Thank You for giving me life and eternity with You. Amen.*

# DAY 76

## LEAD US, LORD

*I know, God, that mere mortals can't run their own lives, that men and women don't have what it takes to take charge of life. So correct us, God, as you see best.*

JEREMIAH 10:23 MSG

### MORNING

So many changes would happen in our lives if we lived Jeremiah's words, if we really believed that God was in control. We would be able to release our worries and problems in a prayer of thanksgiving and then wait. And that's the difficulty that trips us up. In our crazy world, we feel that we need immediate answers, and we rush to solve situations our own way. Sometimes that works; however, often we become enmeshed in less than desirable circumstances.

The last line of the verse above entreats God to correct us, and that's certainly not a desirous thought. Not many people hope to be straightened out. But when we yield our lives to Him and trust Him implicitly, understanding full well that our Creator God wants the best for us, then our prayers of thanksgiving and trust fall more easily from our mouths.

### EVENING

Adoration and praise should fall from our lips before our requests. A prayer of total surrender gives glory to God the Father and pleases Him. It allows Him to work in our lives in ways we often don't understand.

*Lord, I bless You and give You my heartfelt praise. Thank You for all You do to work on my behalf. Amen.*

# DAY 77

## BELIEVE BOLDLY

*A crowd gathered, jamming the entrance so no one could get in or out. [Jesus] was teaching the Word. They brought a paraplegic to him, carried by four men. When they weren't able to get in because of the crowd, they removed part of the roof and lowered the paraplegic on his stretcher. Impressed by their bold belief, Jesus said to the paraplegic, . . . "Get up. Pick up your stretcher and go home." And the man did it—got up, grabbed his stretcher, and walked out.*

MARK 2:2–5, 11–12 MSG

### MORNING

Jesus was impressed by the faith of this man and his friends. Why? They did something unusual, out of the ordinary, and unexpected. They were so solid in their foundation of faith that they didn't allow the circumstance they faced to block them from receiving Jesus. They went against the protocol of society, opened someone else's roof, and pursued what they needed from Jesus.

What a great example they are to us today!

### EVENING

When we are faced with insurmountable odds, what is our response? Do we find a way to reach Jesus? Do we get creative in the choices we make? Or do we sit back and let circumstances dictate our decisions?

These men who lowered their friend through the roof could have easily stopped when they saw the crowded house, but they didn't. Next time you are faced with difficulty, remember: Jesus responds to bold belief.

*Jesus, help me to push beyond my limits today and do something extraordinary and unexpected. I want to impress You with my bold belief. Amen.*

# DAY 78

## WHAT IS REQUIRED

*But he's already made it plain how to live, what to do, what God is looking for in men and women. It's quite simple: Do what is fair and just to your neighbor, be compassionate and loyal in your love, and don't take yourself too seriously—take God seriously.*

MICAH 6:8 MSG

### MORNING

Micah has pretty much summed up what God expects of us. We are to be fair, and we are to be caring and humble. It really isn't difficult to understand, but it is often hard to put into practice.

So often we ignore God's instructions and try to find other ways to please Him, but what He really wants is obedience. By society's standards, God's expectations don't make sense. Our idea of justice is that what works for me is fine, and what works for you is all right too as long as you don't bother me with it. . .

### EVENING

True mercy is virtually unheard of. Many people have the attitude that they are number one, and anyone who interferes with their desires is in danger. In a world where we are taught that we deserve everything, humility is not a priority. We are actually taught to be proud.

These are not God's ways. He expects us to be fair, merciful, and humble, and He will give us the strength to be so.

*Father, You've made clear what You require of me.*
*Please help me live according to Your way. Amen.*

# DAY 79

## CHRIST'S ATTITUDE

*Have this attitude in yourselves which was also in Christ Jesus, who, as He already existed in the form of God, did not consider equality with God something to be grasped, but emptied Himself by taking the form of a bond-servant and being born in the likeness of men. And being found in appearance as a man, He humbled Himself by becoming obedient to the point of death: death on a cross.*

PHILIPPIANS 2:5–8 NASB

### MORNING

You are to have the same attitude as Christ had. So what should you be emulating?

Christ did not feel that He was entitled to anything. He is God and therefore has abundantly more reason to feel entitled than anyone on earth. Still, He did not consider Himself equal with God, and He became just like us.

Christ was willing to step into the experience of another. Instead of keeping His distance from those who could give Him nothing in return, He became human in order to fully understand and ultimately redeem us.

### EVENING

Christ emptied Himself for the good of others. He was not thinking at all about Himself and what He wanted. His only thought was to fulfill the will of God by loving humanity more than we could possibly deserve.

Christ was humble. With complete absence of pride, Christ silently endured unjust accusations and treatment and willingly died a shameful death on the cross.

*Lord, help me to be like You by being humble, unselfish, and concerned for the interests of others over my own desires. Amen.*

# DAY 80

## RESPECT OTHERS' SPACE

*Seldom set foot in your neighbor's house—*
*too much of you, and they will hate you.*
PROVERBS 25:17 NIV

### MORNING

This verse isn't saying you should avoid your neighbors or refrain from having a social life with them. The Bible is full of verses that applaud neighborliness and caring for others. But there are limits. Some neighborhoods are remarkably close and friendly; others aren't. When you move into a new neighborhood, you need to learn the neighborhood rules and not be a pest when people want to be left alone.

### EVENING

When friends begin to pursue new interests and the old gang begins to break up, it's easy to blame the girlfriends or boyfriends or teammates instead of admitting that *you* are part of the problem. If you want to stay close, you'd be wise to become friends with the "new kids" and give everyone the space they need. Then they won't (using the Bible's phrase) "hate you."

*Father, give me the good sense to allow my friends the space they need and to realize that relationships change with time. Amen.*

## DAY 81

# THE BRAVE HEART OF FREEDOM

*Moses said to the people, "Always remember this day. This is the day when you came out of Egypt from a house of slavery. GOD brought you out of here with a powerful hand."*
EXODUS 13:3 MSG

### MORNING

It should have been a day of rejoicing. God had released Israel from captivity. No longer would they need to make bricks all day long. No longer would they need to cower before brutal slave drivers. God had delivered them, but the people had trust issues.

So many choices had been made for the Israelites that they struggled to embrace freedom. The people actually suggested that things had been better when freedom was a dream and hope was drowned out by harsh Egyptian commands.

When *normal* is abuse, addiction, and anger, freedom can seem like a very radical idea. Many former captives return to familiar chains because they don't value the day freedom visited them and invited them to leave bondage behind. . .

### EVENING

You can trust in the God who breaks chains, repairs hearts, and restores futures. He can. He has. He will. His power is great enough to deliver a new normal. He can destroy the heavy chains that have kept you from the good He has planned for you.

*Lord, help me remember the day freedom came to visit. May I refuse to be chained to a past that You have freed me from. Thanks for removing my life from the slavery of sin. Amen.*

# DAY 82

# SNIPER ON THE FIFTY-YARD LINE

*Nothing in all creation is hidden from God's sight.*
HEBREWS 4:13 NIV

## MORNING

Tiffany's boyfriend, Brett, asked her to come out to the fifty-yard line with him after his victorious college football game. Brett assured Tiffany this was a brief meeting with a sportswriter. "It will just be a few minutes," he said.

Once on the fifty-yard line, Brett knelt down on one knee and took Tiffany's hand. This wasn't a meeting with a sportswriter. Brett asked Tiffany to become his wife.

Tiffany didn't see their families—still in the stands—witnessing Brett's carefully planned surprise. And there was one other person hidden from the new fiancée too. Brett gently turned Tiffany around. There, crawling across the field like a sniper, was Tiffany's future sister-in-law, snapping picture after picture. . .

## EVENING

We can hide all kinds of things from each other. We cannot, however, ever surprise God or hide anything from Him. He knows us inside and out—all the good and all the not-so-good. He needs no camera. He knows us intimately and individually. That knowledge can be our incentive for right living and our comfort when we're wronged. There's both warning and assurance that "everything is uncovered and laid bare before the eyes of him to whom we must give account" (Hebrews 4:13 NIV).

*Lord, teach me to live and rest in the knowledge*
*that I can't hide anything from You. Amen.*

# DAY 83

## OVERFLOWING HOPE

*May the God of hope fill you with all joy and peace as you trust in him, so that you may overflow with hope by the power of the Holy Spirit.*

ROMANS 15:13 NIV

### MORNING

How do we find hope when life overwhelms us? Each day, the news is filled with reports of terrorist attacks, plane crashes, school shootings, and more. All the chaos swirling around the planet can make us want to crawl back into bed, pull the covers over our heads, and never come out.

Instead of burrowing our heads in our beds, let's hit our knees right after our feet hit the ground in the morning. There, we can ask God for His perspective. He knows the future because He is already there. We don't have to worry about what will happen; we just need to trust that He will be with us, no matter what.

### EVENING

On our knees, we can listen to God's voice and determine to obey what He calls us to do. Perhaps He wants to use us to minister to those who have been hurt by the sinful choices of broken people. Perhaps we've made sinful choices and we need to ask forgiveness, or we need to forgive someone who hurt us.

If we live with ears tuned to the Spirit's voice and eyes open to see His workings in the world, our lives become a living, dynamic portrait of God's presence, promises, and power.

*Lord, You hold me close when the world seems out of control. You have the power to heal our broken world. Use me, Lord, to bring light to the darkness. Amen.*

# DAY 84

# LIKE THE CHILD JESUS WELCOMED

*Jesus said, "Let the children come to me. Don't stop them! For the Kingdom of Heaven belongs to those who are like these children."*
MATTHEW 19:14 NLT

## MORNING

In first-century Israel, it was not unusual for parents to disown children. Parents could treat their children like property. Husbands could sell their wives. So, when you read that Jesus said, "Let the children come to me," know that His words were beyond revolutionary.

Jesus didn't view children as a substandard group. He even went so far as to say that children can be examples of what trust looks like. To Jesus, children weren't a nuisance. They were pictures of the way everyone should come to Him.

## EVENING

You might come to Jesus as a doubter thinking He needs to prove Himself. But Jesus is building a kingdom on a foundation of love, enhanced by grace, and growing when people like you trust God like the child Jesus welcomed.

Jesus removed barriers for the forgotten, lost, and marginalized to come to Him. He warned those who thought differently to stay out of the way. If you think there are barriers keeping you from Jesus, please remember that those obstacles are not put in place by the one who came to rescue you.

*Dear God, help me look past the barriers I have erected and see Your invitation to forgiveness. May I come to You trusting that Your answers are greater than my questions. Amen.*

# DAY 85

## THE ULTIMATE ACT OF LOVE

*Bring joy to your servant, Lord, for I put my trust in you. You, Lord, are forgiving and good, abounding in love to all who call to you.*
PSALM 86:4–5 NIV

### MORNING

The modern theologian Lewis Smedes once said, "You will know that forgiveness has begun when you recall those who hurt you and feel the power to wish them well." It seems that the most unnatural thing in the world for us is to forgive someone who has hurt us deeply, let alone to hope good things will happen for them. However, that is really the only loving thing to do.

### EVENING

Forgiveness doesn't require that the person who did the hurting apologize or acknowledge what they've done. It's not about making the score even. It doesn't even require forgetting about the incident. But it is about admitting that the one who hurt us is human, just like we are. We surrender our right for revenge and, like God, let go and give the wrongdoer mercy, therefore blessing them.

*Gracious and loving Father, thank You that You love me and have forgiven me of my sins. May I be more like You in forgiving others. Although I may not be able to forgive as easily as You do, please encourage me to take those small steps. In forgiving others, Father, I am that much closer to being like You. Amen.*

# DAY 86

## WHEN YOU GIVE YOUR LIFE AWAY

*"Is there anyone here who, planning to build a new house, doesn't first sit down and figure the cost so you'll know if you can complete it?"*
LUKE 14:28 MSG

### MORNING

Henry David Thoreau, an American writer and philosopher, once said, "The price of anything is the amount of life you exchange for it." Busy lives often dictate that there is no time for the important things. People say, "Oh, I don't have time for this or that," or "I wish I had the time." The truth is that you make the time for what you value most.

Every person has the same amount of life each day. What matters is how you spend it.

### EVENING

It's easy to waste your day doing insignificant things—what many people call time wasters—leaving little time for God. The most important things in life are eternal endeavors, such as spending time in prayer to God for others, giving your life to building a relationship with God by reading His Word and growing in faith, and sharing Christ with others and giving them the opportunity to know Him. These are things that will last.

What are you spending your life on? What are you getting out of what you give yourself to each day?

*Heavenly Father, my life is full. I ask that You give me wisdom and instruction to give my life to the things that matter most. The time I have is precious and valuable. Help me to invest it wisely in eternal things. Amen.*

## DAY 87

# SPEAK YOUR PIECE

*Listen, for I have trustworthy things to say;*
*I open my lips to speak what is right.*
PROVERBS 8:6 NIV

### MORNING

You can't always keep your mouth shut. Sometimes others really need your help. You may have already gone through a problem they're facing now and have some good advice on how to get through it.

On a larger scale, you may want your opinion heard on a local, national, or international issue. You may feel compelled to join a group working for a cause you believe in. Don't be afraid to wade in and speak your piece.

### EVENING

You may be young, but you're not stupid. If you feel you have something to contribute, have faith in yourself and do it. You must pay your dues, actually and figuratively, but once people see you pulling your weight, they will begin to listen when you have a good idea you just can't keep to yourself.

*Lord, I do have things I want to say. Give me the courage to say them, and help me earn the respect of others so my voice will be heard. In Jesus' name, amen.*

# DAY 88

## DAILY CONFIDENCE

*For I can do everything through Christ,*
*who gives me strength.*
PHILIPPIANS 4:13 NLT

### MORNING

Philippians 4:13 isn't talking about being able to do anything you set your mind to do. It's not about having superpowers or amazing abilities to serve your own purposes. Philippians 4:13 is about being able to complete the tasks God has given you through His strength and power.

Do you feel a gentle nudging from the Spirit to do something about which you are unsure and insecure?

### EVENING

Maybe the Spirit is urging you to talk to the new girl at school and invite her to a movie. Or maybe the Lord is prompting you to solve a family relationship, help with a new youth ministry, or even stand up for your beliefs in class.

You won't be able to accomplish any of those things without the strength that comes only from Christ living and working in you. If the Lord asks you to do something, you can count on Him to give you the strength and the resources to accomplish His will.

*Dear Lord, please give me the confidence that I need to do Your will each day. I pray that You will work in my heart so that I can know what it is that You want me to do and that You will give me the strength to do it. Amen.*

# DAY 89

## A FOREVER LOVE

*But I trust in your unfailing love;*
*my heart rejoices in your salvation.*
PSALM 13:5 NIV

### MORNING

The Bible tells us that God's love for us is unfailing. The dictionary defines *unfailing* as "completely dependable, inexhaustible, endless." Our hearts can truly rejoice knowing that we can never exhaust God's love. It won't run out. We can completely depend on God and His love for us at all times and in all situations.

### EVENING

Many people—even Christians—go through life believing that God is just a grumpy old man at the edge of heaven looking down on us with disappointment and disgust. That couldn't be further from the truth! Through Jesus Christ and His power at work within us, God sees us as "holy and dearly loved" (Colossians 3:12 NIV) children. His love is unfailing, and that can never change! The next time you start to think that God is upset with you, remember His unfailing and unchanging love.

*Father in heaven, Your unfailing love surrounds me as I trust in You. Thank You for Your amazing promise! Amen.*

# DAY 90

## PEACE IS A GUARD

*Do not be anxious about anything, but in every situation, by prayer and petition, with thanksgiving, present your requests to God. And the peace of God, which transcends all understanding, will guard your hearts and your minds in Christ Jesus.*

PHILIPPIANS 4:6–7 NIV

### MORNING

A guard stands at the gate of the White House. His job is to protect and defend the nation's president.

Most of us do not need a bodyguard. What we do need is a guard over our hearts and minds. Anxious thoughts and worry will try to attack us on a regular basis. Fear can so easily creep into our thinking and rob us of joy, the very treasure we hold because we know Jesus.

Thankfully, we have been given the key to protecting our minds and hearts—prayer.

### EVENING

In coming to God with our petitions and in giving thanks to Him for all He has already done for us, we receive His peace. Beyond our ability to understand or explain, a heaven-sent peace will abide with us.

What a beautiful picture: the soldier of peace standing at the door of our hearts and minds, guarding the treasure of fellowship with Christ. It is ours for the asking when we go to our Father with all our requests.

*Father, cause me to remember that Your peace is available to guard me night and day. Help me to bring everything to You in prayer, trusting in Your faithful provision. Amen.*

# DAY 91

## BOLD ENOUGH TO ASK

*Two blind men were sitting by the roadside, and when they heard that Jesus was going by, they shouted, "Lord, Son of David, have mercy on us!"*

MATTHEW 20:30 NIV

### MORNING

When life is good and problems are few, you might think there's less need for God. You might think you're relieving God of the burden of taking care of you. If you can meet your own needs, you might think God is simply an option for when things get tough.

Interestingly, the greater your need, the more likely you are to be bold enough to make requests when praying. There are times in everyone's journey of faith when they discover it's impossible to manage life alone.

### EVENING

Two blind men encountered Jesus. They had heard stories of His healing, restoration, and forgiveness. These men made their audacious request to Jesus and trusted enough to ask for mercy. Their bold faith was rewarded. They started by hearing His voice, and they ended up seeing His face.

You must believe before you see God's plan. This was true for two blind men. It's equally true in your personal journey with Jesus.

*Dear God, You want me to see life from Your perspective. I always see more clearly when I trust in the truth that You've always been for me. May I remember that You help those who ask for help. Amen.*

# DAY 92

## EXPECT GOD

*Be brave. Be strong. Don't give up. Expect God to get here soon.*
Psalm 31:24 MSG

### MORNING

God is never late. He isn't slow. He doesn't tease you by dangling a spiritual carrot of hope with no intention of actually providing help. God asks for patience and perseverance, however. He wants you to be courageous. God will show up. You'll discover that your trust in Him is never misplaced.

God doesn't hide from those who stumble and make mistakes. His love was ensured when Jesus arrived with a rescue plan for all who wanted rescue. His actions are designed to bring you closer to Him.

### EVENING

Why would God ever push you away? His connection with you is lasting. Jesus died to create an uninhibited connection between His Father and mankind. Virtually everything He does is an introduction, invitation, and enhancement of that friendship.

When you're weary, weak, or wandering, remember that the God of rescue never leaves you. If you've been waiting for His arrival, don't worry. He will get here soon. The truth is, He's already here.

*Dear God, there's nothing I can offer to make You love me, but You do. There's nothing I can do to make You fulfill my wish list, but You give me life. There's nothing I can do to change my past, but You can change my future. Help me be courageous while waiting for You. I'm grateful You keep Your promises. Amen.*

# DAY 93

## "GOOD SHEPHERD" SALVATION

*[Jesus said,] "I am the good shepherd. The good shepherd lays down his life for the sheep."*
JOHN 10:11 NIV

### MORNING

Sheep are not smart animals. They require the care of a compassionate shepherd who leads, refreshes, guides, prepares, anoints, and loves (see Psalm 23). It would be strange if we naturally thought that being compared to sheep makes us look good. We are called sheep because we need protection, guidance, and love.

We are described as sheep because we need a picture of the vulnerability we experience due to our greatest adversary, the devil, who is described as a thief who comes to steal, kill, and destroy (see John 10:10).

### EVENING

Jesus paints a picture of a place of protection for His sheep. He describes Himself as the gate through which we enter. He came to give us abundant life. This life is available through the protection He offers, and He demonstrated that love all the way to the cross.

Sheep recognize the voice of their shepherd, they express trust in his goodness, and they know that he loves them without condition. The good shepherd would die before He'd ever allow the adversary to take His sheep, but *this* shepherd can—and did—take up His life again (John 10:18).

Sheep need a shepherd. Humanity needs a Savior. Jesus *is* the good-shepherd Savior.

*I need Jesus. While I may not be thrilled with the idea of being compared to sheep, I also know that I look to You for protection, guidance, and love. Keep me in Your care, and keep my feet from stumbling. Amen.*

# DAY 94

## KINDNESS

*"Here is my servant, whom I uphold, my chosen one in whom I delight."*
ISAIAH 42:1 NIV

### MORNING

Jackie and her sisters celebrated Advent in a unique way. They decided that every day they would perform little acts of kindness. They wrote their ideas down, and with much excitement they planned to surprise friends, family, and strangers with unexpected blessings. They paid parking meters that were about to expire, sang carols at nursing homes, gave hot chocolate to the mail carrier, babysat for free, and did many other things anonymously or expecting nothing in return. The result? They were blessed with smiles, thank-yous, and even a few happy tears; and they hoped that their acts of kindness would prompt others to do the same.

First Peter 5:2 (NIV) says, "Be shepherds of God's flock that is under your care, watching over them—not because you must, but because you are willing, as God wants you to be; not pursuing dishonest gain, but eager to serve."

### EVENING

God calls His people to serve, and service comes in many forms. Some work actively in the church as lectors and Sunday school helpers. Others volunteer in their communities through homeless shelters, fundraising projects, food banks, and other causes. And every day, Christians like Jackie and her sisters work silently in the background performing little acts of kindness.

Can you encourage someone today through a little act of kindness?

*Dear God, how can I serve You today?*
*What can I do to show kindness to others? Amen.*

# DAY 95

## LOSE TO GAIN

*"If you cling to your life, you will lose it;*
*but if you give up your life for me, you will find it."*
MATTHEW 10:39 NLT

### MORNING

Life is precious. It has been said that life is but a dash, as represented by the dash between one's birth and death dates on a tombstone. Certainly, our physical lives are a mere dash compared to eternity. How will we choose to spend this gift of life that our Creator has given us?

### EVENING

Some people selfishly cling to possessions and spend their entire lives trying to get more. They use people to gain possessions. They use time to pursue worldly passions. They use God to advance their cause. They are blind to truth. Someday, when their physical life closes in death, they will lose everything.

Others believe that physical life is just the beginning. Jesus came to give spiritual life as well. These people use their possessions to reach people with the love of Jesus. They willingly sacrifice time and talent by allowing God to use them to advance His kingdom. When they draw their last breath on earth, they will be ushered into eternal life. Having given their life on earth for God's purposes, they will live forever.

Are we clinging tightly to what God has given us? Or are we willing to give it back to Him and gain so much more? Let's lose to gain.

*Dear Lord, use my life on this earth for Your glory.*
*Help me unselfishly give myself to be used by You. Amen.*

# DAY 96

## BE GENTLE

*Let your gentleness be evident to all.*
PHILIPPIANS 4:5 NIV

### MORNING

Gentleness doesn't seem to have much going for it today. It's macho time, every man for himself, and heaven help the weak. At least, that's what the movies and television tell us, and a lot of people seem to be buying into it.

But movies and television aren't into reporting the truth. They're into entertaining, and gentleness can look boring, even in 3D. For every graphic murder scene in the news, there are at least one thousand acts of kindness that go unreported. For every man who strikes out in anger, there are one thousand who reach out in peace. For every maniac oppressor, there are one thousand Peace Corps volunteers.

### EVENING

Occasionally, you'll see a movie, hear a report, or read a story about a really good person—usually around Christmas. Who are your role models today? For the good of the world, "let your gentleness be evident to all."

*Father, teach me how to be that rare and endangered species—a gentle person, one who gives of themselves for the benefit of others. Amen.*

# DAY 97

# MY STRENGTH

*I love you, Lord, my strength.*
Psalm 18:1 NIV

## MORNING

Ever feel like you want to crawl into a hole and pull the earth in around you? Most of us have felt that way at some point. Sometimes life overwhelms us, and we feel like we will drown at any moment.

At times like that, we often don't have the strength to even pray. We don't know what to say to God, and we don't have the energy to form the correct words or thoughts. That's when we need to keep it simple. "I love You, Lord" is all we need to say.

When we utter those four little words to God, we bend His ear to us. We bend His heart to us.

## EVENING

When we whisper our love for God, although we don't have strength to say another word, He shows up and becomes our strength. He wraps His mighty arms around us, pulls us into His lap of love and comfort, and pours His life and love into our spirits.

Truly, it is in those moments of weakness, when we have nothing else to offer God, that He is made strong in us. He longs for our love above all else. When we give it, as weak as we may feel, He becomes strength for us.

*Dear Father, sometimes I feel weak, like I can't go on. But Lord, I love You even then. I know in my weak moments that You are my strength. Amen.*

# DAY 98

## A HEART THAT SINGS

*I will sing of your strength, in the morning I will sing of your love; for you are my fortress, my refuge in times of trouble. . . . I sing praise to you.*
PSALM 59:16–17 NIV

### MORNING

Talk about trouble—David had a lion's share of it! Day in and day out, year after year, fueled by a king's jealousy, David was a wanted man—homeless, on the run, and accompanied by a bunch of lowlifes. Yet amazingly, in the book of Psalms we see that David's crying out to God turns into joyful music or praise. What an example he sets for us!

### EVENING

You can be that real with God by telling Him your heart's burdens. Vent your hurts, disappointments, and struggles to Him. He can handle it. David didn't try to sound spiritual. He was genuine before the Lord. Once he cleared the air, his heart turned to thanksgiving and praise. He'd bring out the instruments, write a song or two, and regain his strength.

Playing God-focused music and joining in a song of praise can become a spirit booster. Humming along can help refocus a grumbling heart and brighten a dull day. Keep songs of praise and worship handy to maintain a cheerful heart.

*Mighty Father, thank You for the wonder of music. Help me to sing Your praises, to sing of Your strength and love daily, for You are my refuge. Amen.*

# DAY 99

## ONE COUPLE, ONE FAMILY, ONE GOD

*Jesus was indignant. He reached out his hand and touched the man. "I am willing," he said. "Be clean!" Immediately the leprosy left him and he was cleansed.*

MARK 1:41–42 NIV

### MORNING

The people in Jesus' time feared leprosy. They saw it as a terrifying contagious disease. Aside from it being incurable at the time, it was a deal-breaker in families, marriages, and communities.

Scaly sores that identified leprosy in Jesus' time were only the beginning. Lepers became shunned outcasts. No longer allowed to worship in the synagogue or to mingle with family, friends, and community members, they lost the ability to work and live in their own homes. Many lost fingers, toes, and noses. Their eyes became deformed. The victims' only destiny was a leper colony—and death.

Yet God celebrates the whole person. After Jesus healed the leper, He sent the man to a priest, who would pronounce the victim clean. Then the former leper could return to his family, work, community, and place of worship.

### EVENING

Jesus gave the leper more than the gift of health. He gave him back his life. The head of household and his wife again became one couple, one family, worshipping one God. There is no better endorsement of God's love of the family.

*Thank You, Jesus, for valuing family and giving the strength of healing to all in difficult family roles and responsibilities. Amen.*

# DAY 100

## LOVE AND FAITHFULNESS

*So the Word became human and made his home among us. He was full of unfailing love and faithfulness. And we have seen his glory, the glory of the Father's one and only Son.*

JOHN 1:14 NLT

### MORNING

God came in human flesh—fully knowing what would be done to Him—to allow complete access to God. Jesus said that the only way to God is through Him (John 14:6). Before Jesus came, one could know about God. Through Jesus, we all can have an intimate relationship with God.

Christ came full of unfailing love and faithfulness. No other relationship can fill you with the love that comes through Jesus. No other relationship can meet all your needs. No other relationship can be depended on in the way that you can trust God's faithfulness.

### EVENING

Earthly relationships will leave you lacking if you come to count on them for your happiness. People will let you down. It's a guarantee. Even your most trusted loved ones cannot be faithful all the time. But Jesus' love is unfailing. He promises to never leave or forsake you (Hebrews 13:5). Put your faith and trust in the only one who is worthy.

*Heavenly Father, I'm eternally grateful that Your love and faithfulness will never leave me. Help me depend fully on Your faithfulness alone, and give me a healthy perspective and balance in my earthly relationships. Amen.*

# DAY 101

## UNSHAKABLE LOVE

*"For even if the mountains walk away and the hills fall to pieces, my love won't walk away from you, my covenant commitment of peace won't fall apart." The God who has compassion on you says so.*

Isaiah 54:10 MSG

### MORNING

We live in a scary world. The daily news warns of global warming, terrorist attacks, earthquakes, and hurricanes. Anxiety is a very real part of our human journey, and fear can easily cloud our view of God and distort our perspective. If we're not careful, we can dissolve into frightened, anxious people who rarely take risks or initiate new adventures.

However, God doesn't want us to live isolated, dull lives. His Word encourages us to be bold, passionate, and faithful. *Yikes*, we think. *I'm scared to go anywhere by myself. How can I venture out in a dangerous world without fear?*

The answer is love.

### EVENING

All throughout the Bible, God assures us of His constant, comprehensive love for us. He promises in Isaiah that even if our world literally caves in (as it has for people who have endured natural disasters), He will never walk away. Because of His compassion for His frail children, He has a commitment to give us peace. And if we take Him at His word, we will be filled with confidence and inner peace. That kind of peace comes from knowing that we are deeply, eternally cared for—no matter what happens.

*Lord, thank You for Your love and Your covenant commitment to peace for me. Help me to take You at Your word. Amen.*

# DAY 102

## WHAT DO YOU BELIEVE?

*For since we believe that Jesus died and was raised to life again, we also believe that when Jesus returns, God will bring back with him the believers who have died.*

1 THESSALONIANS 4:14 NLT

### MORNING

Since we live in a sinful world, we have the opportunity, when we are young, to develop negative belief systems about ourselves and others. For example, a young child who is abandoned by a parent may feel that everyone will abandon him. A child whose physical needs were neglected may come to believe that he is not worthy of receiving care. In psychology, these are called *schema*, and they have a profound effect on our ability to function well. We typically are not consciously aware of schema, but our behavior is greatly impacted.

We can develop spiritual schema as well.

### EVENING

We may develop faulty beliefs, such as *God loves others, but He doesn't love me* or *I'm not worthy of forgiveness*. Take a moment to examine your beliefs about Jesus. Do they match what the Bible says? If you believe that Jesus died and was raised to life again, you will live in a way that shows that you are expectant and eager for His return.

*Jesus, thank You for Your death on the cross. Examine my heart and see if there are any faulty beliefs in me. Use scripture to correct my faulty thinking, and allow my behavior to reflect what I know to be true about You. Amen.*

# DAY 103

## THE ONLY QUESTION THAT COUNTS

*Examine yourselves to see if your faith is genuine.*
*Test yourselves. Surely you know that Jesus Christ is among*
*you; if not, you have failed the test of genuine faith.*
2 CORINTHIANS 13:5 NLT

### MORNING

*Oh, no! Not another test! And it's not even going to be multiple choice!*

Still, a little introspection is always a good idea. At least you'll know how far off the mark you've wandered. So, what are the criteria here? Who gets an A and who fails?

First of all, this is an open-book test. Take your Bible and read all of Matthew. Read every word Jesus spoke and every command He ever gave. Give yourself a grade on every command. How did you do?

### EVENING

The open-book test could be pretty dismal until you hit Matthew 22:37–39 (NIV): "'Love the Lord your God with all your heart and with all your soul and with all your mind.' This is the first and greatest commandment. And the second is like it: 'Love your neighbor as yourself.'"

This is the only question that counts! (By the way, the person doing the grading is you, and you can grade on a curve. That wasn't so hard, was it?)

*Father, in a real test, I'm sure I'd fail, but You forgive me*
*and only require my love. I can do that. Amen.*

# DAY 104

# PERFECT PEACE

*You will keep in perfect peace those whose minds are steadfast, because they trust in you.*
Isaiah 26:3 niv

## MORNING

Peace: that inner sense that all is well, the calm assurance that all is under control. The canvas of peace depicts a glassy sea and clear, blue skies.

Peace is something we all desire, yet few obtain. Why? We mistakenly think a different life scenario will quiet our hearts. But perfect peace is not contingent on perfect circumstances. In fact, many times just the opposite is true. Perfect peace can be experienced in the most terrifying storms of life. How is that possible?

## EVENING

Perfect peace can be found only in the Prince of Peace, Jesus. He imparts peace to our souls. Regardless of the circumstances, when we completely surrender ourselves to the Lord, we experience His peace. It is unexplainable. It passes all understanding. The Lord has all things under control even when we lack spiritual eyes to see that truth. Faith enables us to believe that all is well even when our emotions scream the opposite.

Is your spirit at peace or is it stirred up? Jesus calmed the storm while in a boat with His terrified disciples. The Prince of Peace can calm the raging waters in your soul. Trustfully turn to Him. Receive His peace. He will bring you safely through.

*Dear Lord, help me trust You regardless of my circumstances. Impart Your peace to my heart and give me the assurance that all is well. Amen.*

# DAY 105

## SING HIS PRAISES

*Give praise to the Lord, proclaim his name; make known among the nations what he has done. Sing to him, sing praise to him; tell of all his wonderful acts.*

1 Chronicles 16:8–9 niv

### MORNING

We often think of giving thanks as a private event, something strictly between us and God. At most, we join with our family or church in thanksgiving. Public thanksgiving makes us uneasy. We don't want to seem like we're boasting.

Yet the Bible urges us to sing His praises loudly for others to hear. But how do you do it?

### EVENING

Start small with your out-loud praises. The next time you feel you have been blessed, tell another believer. She'll tell someone else, and the story will get around, as all stories do. Once you feel comfortable talking about such things to believers, tell a close friend who isn't a churchgoer, speaking humbly but surely, and then move on to another topic. In time, you will find your comfort level. Good news is meant to be shared.

*Father, give me the courage I need to sing Your praises and the discernment to know who needs to hear Your message. Amen.*

# DAY 106

## WORLD CHANGERS

*"A new command I give you: Love one another.*
*As I have loved you, so you must love one another."*
JOHN 13:34 NIV

### MORNING

Christ had one rule: Love. Love God first. Love others like you love yourself. Though it sounds simple, it's easier said than done.

Oh, it's no problem to love those who love us. It's a piece of cake to love the lovable, the kind, the compassionate, the witty, and the beautiful. However, what about those people who curse us and spit in our faces? What about those people who make it their goal to wreak havoc and create misery in our lives? We're supposed to love them too?

Yes, we are. Jesus said to love one another the way He has loved us. It's a self-sacrificing kind of love.

### EVENING

One thing to remember is that Jesus was no pushover. He stood for what was right and even got angry when it was appropriate. After all, how often do we equate turning over some tables in a fit of rage with love?

Yet that was love. It was Christ putting God first. Notice that He didn't hurt anyone when He did it. Though He called them a "brood of vipers," He did so out of tough love to get their attention and show them a better way.

Overall, Jesus' life was a display of gentleness, compassion, and a servant's heart. When we model our lives after Him, we'll change the dynamics of our world.

*Dear Father, teach me to love like Jesus loved. Amen.*

# DAY 107

## CONVEY THE MESSAGE CLEARLY

*My goal is that they may be encouraged in heart and united in love, so that they may have the full riches of complete understanding, in order that they may know the mystery of God, namely, Christ.*

COLOSSIANS 2:2 NIV

### MORNING

When it came to writing papers, Jessi struggled. Nothing seemed to work. No matter how she tried, she always got more criticism than encouragement. Finally, she asked Rachel, another Christian, to help her.

After reading her latest paper, Rachel pointed out that Jessi was so busy using large words that her writing wasn't clear. "Say what you want to get across, not what you think will impress someone," she advised. Then Rachel turned to Colossians. "Paul didn't focus on himself when he wrote. He wrote things his readers could understand and learn from. You can make your message clear if you use this method too."

### EVENING

The next time you write—a paper, a personal note, or a letter, for example—think first about the other person. What words will express what you want her to understand? How can you help him know your need? Then boot up your computer or pick up your pen.

*Lord, when I communicate, I want to do it in a way that glorifies You, not me. Help me write clearly and lovingly. Amen.*

# DAY 108

## FIRST THINGS FIRST

*Jesus [said,] "First things first. Your business is life, not death. Follow me. Pursue life."*
MATTHEW 8:22 MSG

### MORNING

Part of being a responsible person is making plans and following through on commitments. Take a moment and think of all the things you've done in the past week and all the things on tap for this week. When your head stops spinning, think of how often you deliberately brought God into those plans. You've probably brought Him into a lot of what's going on—maybe all of it—and that's good.

But is it God's best for you? Why should we ask that? Well, trusting God includes trusting His timing.

### EVENING

Life is just plain busy, and with school and family appointments and church activities, it's easy to reach a level of not only spiritual exhaustion but unrealistic expectation—that just because you're doing the best you can, God's schedule is going to fit into yours. Stay focused on God, not the tyranny of the urgent.

Are you willing to let God interrupt your plans? Part of being His child means letting Him do just that. Be willing to slow down, ask Him for perspective, and trust that His interruptions are for your ultimate benefit.

*Father, Your business is my business. Help me to make sure what I'm doing is what You want me to be doing. If it's not, help me to shift the focus to You and Your priorities. Amen.*

# DAY 109

## HURT HAPPENS—LOVE ANYWAY

*"I have loved you even as the Father has loved me. Remain in my love."*
JOHN 15:9 NLT

### MORNING

Do you ever feel like Jesus overcame life's challenges more easily than you because He was God? It's important to realize that Jesus lived His life as a man—empowered just as you are today as a believer. He relied on His relationship with God and the Holy Spirit working in Him to do all that He did. He too was human. He suffered pain, hurt, and disappointment just as you do.

Imagine His feelings when brothers, sisters, aunts, uncles, and cousins refused to believe He was the Messiah or discounted His words of truth because He was family. How painful it must have been to have those closest to Him reject Him! Jesus knew that Judas would betray Him and Peter would deny Him. Jesus must have felt that hurt deeply—yet He loved them anyway. In the face of the cross, He asked God to forgive those who put Him there.

### EVENING

When faced with pain or disappointment, it's easy to become angry, defend yourself, or even sever the relationship. The same Spirit who empowered Jesus to live His faith can empower you. When hurt happens, choose to love anyway!

*Lord, You have shown me how to respond in love. Give me strength by Your Holy Spirit to love others in the face of pain, disappointment, and hurt. Comfort me and provide ways for me to show love to others. Amen.*

# DAY 110

## HEAVENLY TREASURE

*"But store up for yourselves treasures in heaven, where moths and vermin do not destroy, and where thieves do not break in and steal."*
MATTHEW 6:20 NIV

### MORNING

You have ten minutes to leave your home before it is destroyed by fire. What will you take with you? Once you knew that your loved ones were safe, you would likely grab the things that remind you of them—photos or a precious family Bible.

Questions like these have a way of whittling our priorities down to the bare essentials. Most of what we own is easily destroyed and just as easily replaced. There are, however, a few things really worth having, and Jesus reminds us that these are things on which we can't put a price tag.

### EVENING

Relationships. Eternal life. The assurance that our loved ones will live eternally with Him.

What will *you* take with you? This isn't a rhetorical question. The practicality of Jesus' words reminds us that the way we live our lives each and every day should be guided by this principle. Invest yourself in the things that matter.

*Lord, You know it is easy to get distracted by earthly things—things that will ultimately be worth nothing. Help me to shift my focus to matters that have eternal significance, and help me to invest my life in those things that will bring eternal dividends. Amen.*

# DAY 111

## GOD'S CHILDREN

*He gave the right and the power to become children of God to those who received Him. He gave this to those who put their trust in His name.*
JOHN 1:12 NLV

### MORNING

What an awesome privilege! When we welcome Jesus into our lives, we become God's kids. We're adopted into His holy family. Don't rush past this verse; let it sink into your spirit. Picture what it means.

None of us has a perfect family here on earth. Our family members may be fun and full of love, but there are imperfections because humans are flawed. All of us have defects, not just that troublesome uncle or that weird cousin who always says the wrong thing. Some family relationships feel scratchy and uncomfortable.

Only God is perfect, yet He gives us the right to be His children, to live and thrive in His family.

### EVENING

Most parents experience amazing love for their children—especially when babies are brand new and the parents marvel at the miracle of life. Now multiply that feeling many times, wrap it in love beyond our comprehension, and know how much God loves each of us. When we repent and are born into God's family, all heaven rejoices (Luke 15:7). The angels have a celebration.

*Thank You, dear Father, for allowing me to be part of Your family. I am humbled and overjoyed to be called Your child. Amen.*

# DAY 112

## ALL IN

*I've already run for dear life straight to the arms of God. So why would I run away now when you say, "Run to the mountains. . . . The bottom's dropped out of the country; good people don't have a chance"?*

Psalm 11:1–3 MSG

### MORNING

Much more than the ongoing misadventures of a slick trickster, Jacob's life is the story of the faithful God who stuck with him even when he messed up. And when he feared the consequences of his past the most, God didn't chew him out. Instead, He told him, "I am with you, and I will protect you wherever you go. . . . I will not leave you until I have finished giving you everything I have promised you" (Genesis 28:15 NLT).

Jacob realized that God was there *with* him and—even more amazingly—*for* him! He then committed wholeheartedly to God for the first time in his life—all his provision, resources, and plans—and left the rest up to God.

### EVENING

All your mistakes, all the things that haunt your memories—God knows all of it and still gave Himself for you. Let that sink in. When it does, you'll see that the only reasonable response is gratitude followed by commitment. There's nothing you can do to earn God's grace, but you can respond to it by giving all of yourself to Him.

*God, there's no turning back. I trust that You are here with me now and always. I'm all in. Amen.*

# DAY 113

## A RETURN TO CLARITY

*He built an altar there, and gave the place the name El-bethel. Because God had shown Himself to him there, when Jacob ran away from his brother.*
GENESIS 35:7 NLV

### MORNING

After a disastrous episode in his life when God seemed far away and he didn't seek Him (Genesis 34), Jacob was in dire need of clarity. He returned to Bethel, the place where God had revealed He was with him, where Jacob had come alive spiritually and God reminded him of His protection and provision (Genesis 35:7–14).

To be fully available to God, you must get to a place where you truly recognize your need and His presence in your life. To have a Bethel moment, clear away the cobwebs of cluttered thinking (and schedules). Remind yourself of what you know to be true about God. Make time to worship, thanking and honoring Him with your words and actions.

### EVENING

David wrote a primer on drawing close to God: "Walk straight, act right, tell the truth. Don't hurt your friend, don't blame your neighbor; despise the despicable. Keep your word even when it costs you, make an honest living, never take a bribe. You'll never get blacklisted if you live like this" (Psalm 15:2–5 MSG).

*I want to get back to basics, God, focusing on godly behavior as a response to You and Your faithfulness, goodness, and mercies. Help me to see You on the path ahead of me. Amen.*

# DAY 114

## WHEN YOU WANT TO GIVE UP

*I know how to live on almost nothing or with everything. I have learned the secret of living in every situation, whether it is with a full stomach or empty, with plenty or little. For I can do everything through Christ, who gives me strength.*

PHILIPPIANS 4:12–13 NLT

### MORNING

Being satisfied with what God provides is the best way to hang on when things get tough.

Paul said he lived through times when he had everything he needed, but he also lived through challenges that left him with little. He "learned the secret of living in every situation." That secret was satisfaction in the God who provides.

### EVENING

We may want to give up, throw up our hands, and admit defeat. But God didn't send us a note indicating He's no longer able to take care of things.

As long as God is in control, there's no need to panic or surrender to despair. Because Jesus gives us strength, we can watch that strength overcome our weakness. This is where we find the encouragement to resist giving up.

*Dear God, You've always been in control, and You'll be in control forever. It can be easy to think everything is falling apart. When I'm satisfied that You love me enough to take care of me, then I discover that when You're with me there is nothing that cannot be done if You want it to be done. Help me trust You more and worry less. Amen.*

# DAY 115

## ABIDE IN CHRIST

*"If you remain in Me, and My words remain in you, ask whatever you wish, and it will be done for you."*
JOHN 15:7 NASB

### MORNING

At first glance, this verse could be misunderstood to mean that Jesus is your "genie." You ask whatever you wish, and He'll do it. Sounds pretty good, right? That's not quite the point.

Do you really abide in Christ? Surrender your false sense of independence so that you can fully understand your reliance on Christ for every aspect of your life—then you can rest in His grace, love, and plan for you.

Do His words abide in you? Read, memorize, and meditate on His Word on a regular basis so that your thoughts and words are more like His.

### EVENING

Imagine how different your wishes would be if you truly abided in Christ and His words abided in you. Gone would be the wishes that everything would go your way and that God would remove those things or people that make life difficult for you. Instead, you would wish for God to make you and those around you more like Him every day. You would desire justice, lasting peace, and the spread of the gospel. You would ask that God be glorified, no matter the circumstances.

*Lord, help me to abide in You every day. Make Your words alive in my thoughts and words today. Conform my wishes to Your perfect will. Amen.*

# DAY 116

## BATTLING PERFECTIONISM

*And Jesus grew in wisdom and stature, and in favor with God and man.*
LUKE 2:52 NIV

### MORNING

This verse gives us reason to believe that Jesus, though God in the flesh, was not born with all the knowledge that He'd had before coming to earth. Like all human babies, Jesus had a lot to learn upon arrival. The fiery, compassionate Jesus we know from scripture toddled through His first steps just like we did, His mother scooping Him up to comfort Him when He fell. Though the Gospels don't record Joseph instructing Jesus in carpentry, certainly Jesus learned from observing His earthly father's skilled hands and then practiced honing those techniques Himself.

For those of us who struggle with perfectionism in our lives, we need to turn our eyes to Jesus.

### EVENING

It should comfort us that our Savior learned in His earthly life, and He learned without committing a single sin. We may view our mistakes as "wrong," but mistakes aren't necessarily sinful. Like a misplaced nail or uneven sanding, they are part of practicing and growing in a skill.

Jesus does not call us to live in shame, fearing criticism or failure, but to live trusting in Him for the grace and peace to work faithfully (*not* perfectly). When we do fail, He isn't disappointed in us but instead keeps lavishing grace and strength on us. Do you accept yourself and your shortcomings the way that Christ accepts you?

*Lord Jesus, thank You that You understand what it's like to be human and to learn new things. Please help me to practice my gifts courageously for You. Amen.*

# DAY 117

## A LESSON FROM THE BUSH

*I am glad to boast about my weaknesses, so that the power of Christ can work through me. . . . For when I am weak, then I am strong.*

2 CORINTHIANS 12:9–10 NLT

### MORNING

A cool breeze refreshed Anna's spirits, but when she took one look at her favorite hydrangea bush, her mood changed. How had the bush become so choked with vines? Dead flower heads hung limply among large, glorious blooms. Disappointed with herself for letting busyness and procrastination take over life, she began pruning. With the dead parts falling away, the bush began to take on a different shape. The remaining blooms, having stretched high for sunshine through the strangling vines, stood sturdy and tall.

After cutting a dozen blooms, she couldn't help but smile. This gangly plant had produced incredible flowers—long, strong stems for glorious arrangements of the richest shades! What she had deemed dreadful turned out to be a delight. Her shortcomings actually provided an opportunity for God's goodness and grace to be revealed.

### EVENING

Anna thought about important areas of her life. Her attempts to be financially sound seemed to repeatedly meet with failure. But God always provided—even with a car after hers died. Her weaknesses allowed His power to shine all the more. The less she had, the more she depended on Him.

*Gracious Lord, help me to remember that when I am weak, then I am strong. May Your power be revealed through me. Amen.*

# DAY 118

## SEEKING REST

*It is useless for you to work so hard from early morning until late at night, anxiously working for food to eat; for God gives rest to his loved ones.*

PSALM 127:2 NLT

### MORNING

Dirty dishes. Unexpected texts. Projects and assignments. Thing after thing, chore after chore demands your attention day after day after very long day.

So you set your alarm clock for an hour earlier. You study through lunch and hurry through dinner. You stay up an hour later than you had intended. Saturday and Sunday serve as catch-up days, and then the week begins again.

Are you tiring yourself out? Do you find yourself exhausted at each day's end? To work without rest is not only physically unhealthy; it is also spiritually unhealthy.

### EVENING

God intends for us to find a balance between work and rest. He commanded that we keep the Sabbath for just this purpose. This day should be set aside for praise and worship, certainly, but we are also to *rest*—to take quiet personal time for ourselves and to reflect on our busy lives.

Take time for solitude, for reflection, for being still. The time spent away from your work will serve to rejuvenate you—physically, mentally, and spiritually—so that you may approach life directly and positively, as you should.

*Lord, give me rest. Take my worries over the small things of life and give to me instead Your peace so that I may act kindly toward others. Amen.*

# DAY 119

## KEEPING YOUR BROTHERS

*God's way is perfect. All the LORD's promises prove true.*
*He is a shield for all who look to him for protection.*
PSALM 18:30 NLT

### MORNING

Judah had previously failed to be his brother's keeper, and the guilt and shame had plagued him for years. He took the chance to make it right at great risk to himself (Genesis 44:32–33). When a Christian fails to step up for others—as an advocate for justice or a helping hand or a true partner in accountability—they miss a golden opportunity to love like Jesus loves.

Bearing responsibility for your actions also provides an invaluable witness to God's justice and mercy. Whether you're making your wrong right or helping when someone else has been hurt, God's grace and forgiveness are the keys to looking out for others.

### EVENING

In helping the helpless and in healing hurts, God has given you a powerful calling and the power to obey it. The Bible makes it clear that the best way to show others the difference Jesus makes in your life is to step out of your comfort zone and love them.

*God, this age of grace is an amazing time to be serving You. Open my eyes, ears, and heart to Your will as I interact with others today so I can seek their highest good for Your greatest glory. Amen.*

# DAY 120

## WORKING HARD

*Whatever you do, work at it with all your heart,*
*as working for the Lord, not for human masters.*
COLOSSIANS 3:23 NIV

### MORNING

Paul encouraged his readers to work hard with all their hearts. Many of the new converts were enslaved to non-Christian masters. The tension between Christians and non-Christians increased when the non-Christian had the authority to lord it over the Christian.

But the wisdom in today's verse applies to us today. We should always work hard and always give our best, even if we don't like our teachers. Ultimately, the quality of work we do reflects on our Father. If we're lazy or if our work is below standard, it has a negative impact on the body of Christ. But when we meet our deadlines and our work exceeds expectations, we give others a positive impression of what it means to be a Christian.

### EVENING

If we want to get ahead in school and we want to help build the kingdom of God, we must have spotless reputations. One way to build a positive reputation is to be a hard worker. When we do our absolute best at any task, people notice. When we consistently deliver quality assignments, people notice. We honor God and we honor ourselves when we work hard at the tasks we've been given.

*Dear Father, I want to honor You with the work I do.*
*Help me to work hard with all my heart. Amen.*

# DAY 121

## WELCOMING OTHERS

*You are faithful in what you are doing for the brothers and sisters, even though they are strangers to you.*
3 John 5 NIV

### MORNING

We don't mind having friends over to visit. As teens, they're usually only around for a few hours, maybe overnight at the most.

But when a missionary or evangelist—or worse than that, our least favorite relative—needs a place to stay, are we "too busy"?

Gaius, an elder in a young Asian church, had plenty of demands on his time. But that didn't stop him from warmly welcoming the missionaries who crossed his path. Because he did such a great job, someone told the apostle John about it.

### EVENING

Gaius probably shared the doubts we have about entertaining guests. Would they make a mess of the house? Would they eat him out of house and home? Would they be so irritating that after one day he'd want to toss them out on the street? But he invited them in anyway.

Even if your cousin Poindexter messes up your bathroom, you can clean it again once he's gone. But you can't clean up your own heart if you sin by ignoring God's commands for hospitality.

*Giving up some of my space is hard, Lord. But I want to use my home to show Your love. Open my heart to help. Amen.*

## DAY 122

# PROVERBS WISDOM FOR LIFE

*My son, if you accept my words and store up my commands within you, . . .then you will understand the fear of the* Lord *and find the knowledge of God.*

Proverbs 2:1, 5 NIV

### EVENING

In an age of electronic communication, isn't it fun to receive a letter in the mail? Letters are especially great when they come from someone who loves us. In the Bible, King Solomon wrote a wonderful letter to his sons. We call it the book of Proverbs, but at its core, this little gem is a heartfelt love letter from a father to his sons—not only from Solomon to his sons but from God to us.

### EVENING

Proverbs contains an abundance of short and sweet sayings that are just as relevant to us now as they were to Solomon's sons centuries ago. The wisdom of Proverbs can apply to every area of our lives. It addresses everything from relationships to our money and our work habits.

They aren't guarantees; they are timeless truths, guidelines for living, ways to increase your chances of success in life—biblical success: righteousness, integrity, honesty, and wisdom that are yours for a lifetime.

*Father, thank You for the wisdom found in the book of Proverbs. Amen.*

# DAY 123

## ONE WITH THE MARGINALIZED

*When a Samaritan woman came to draw water,*
*Jesus said to her, "Will you give me a drink?"*
JOHN 4:7 NIV

### MORNING

One of the most beautiful things about Jesus is His willingness to go where others won't go. After teaching in Judea, Jesus knew that He had to go back to Galilee. John 4:4 (NIV) says, "Now he had to go through Samaria."

Jews who lived in other regions at that time took roundabout roads to avoid passing through Samaria, where local Jews had mixed with neighboring nations and developed their own religion. However, Jesus had to meet someone special. The Samaritan woman was of little value in the eyes of others, but Jesus, a Jewish man, spoke to her. He made Himself vulnerable by asking for water in order to give her a sense of worth. He then used His question to spark a soul-searching conversation that pointed back to Him as the giver of living water that leads to eternal life.

### EVENING

Jesus knew the woman's sins, but He also knew her heart. She was part of creation that needed redemption. When He revealed His Messiah identity to the woman, she proclaimed this throughout the city, and many believed because of her testimony. Even more people believed after hearing Jesus' words. "We no longer believe just because of what you said; now we have heard for ourselves, and we know that this man really is the Savior of the world" (John 4:42 NIV).

Where is the Samaria in your life, and with which marginalized people is Jesus calling you to share His life-giving water?

*God of my salvation, open my eyes to see and my mouth to speak Your love to the unloved. Let me be blessed through blessing the least and the lowly. Amen.*

# DAY 124

## STANDING FIRM

*I. . .didn't dodge their insults, faced them as they spit in my face. And the Master, God, stays right there and helps me, so I'm not disgraced. Therefore I set my face like flint, confident that I'll never regret this. My champion is right here. Let's take our stand together!*

Isaiah 50:6–8 msg

### MORNING

Sarah had faced resistance every step of the way. Regardless of her sacrifice and dedication for many months on the project, she repeatedly met opposition from others. From the beginning, she faced their cutting remarks and hostility. She had understood the challenge of going against the grain and had braced herself, knowing she needed to stand for what was right. But she was worn thin—frayed and tattered. A soul can take only so much on its own.

Isaiah reminds us that we are not alone in our battles—even when everyone is against us and we feel outnumbered and outmaneuvered.

### EVENING

Remember that your champion, God, is right here saying, "I am not leaving you! We are sticking this out together. You can put your chin up confidently, knowing that I, the Sustainer, am on your side. Let's take our stand together!"

*Lord, boldly stand beside me. May the strength of Your arms strengthen me as I take a stand for You. Lift my chin today; give me confidence to face opposition, knowing You are right there with me. Amen.*

# DAY 125

## ENSLAVED NO MORE

*Think of your sufferings as a weaning from that old sinful habit of always expecting to get your own way. Then you'll be able to live out your days free to pursue what God wants instead of being tyrannized by what you want.*

1 PETER 4:2 MSG

### MORNING

Linda eats even when she's not hungry; it's just habit. She knows she needs to change but can't seem to for more than one day—and her yo-yo dieting produces poor health, fatigue, self-hatred, embarrassment, and guilt, sending her back to food for comfort and perpetuating this dangerous cycle. She feels resigned to being stuck in this sinful pattern of overindulging her appetite.

Isn't that what Satan wants? One more Christian bullied, paralyzed, and unintentionally making a mockery of Christ's power over sin and death?

Spiritual warfare rages every day within believers, but God's Word says we are no longer enslaved to our old habits. They may not die easily; however, we are sustained in our battle by knowing that Christ died to conquer sin.

### EVENING

Ultimately, Satan is the big loser here, not us. We must daily wag our finger in the master liar's face, claiming Jesus' name and power over all that holds us back from God's perfect will for our lives. We are no longer chained. We have soaring freedom in Christ!

*Jesus, thank You for Your sacrifice on the cross for my sin and for the victory we have every day in You. I am free to be all You created me to be because my sinful habits no longer have a grip on me. Amen.*

# DAY 126

## BLESSINGS IN GIVING

*"Will a mere mortal rob God? Yet you rob me. But you ask, 'How are we robbing you?' In tithes and offerings. You are under a curse—your whole nation—because you are robbing me."*
MALACHI 3:8–9 NIV

### MORNING

Billions of dollars are spent in America every year on movies, music, the internet, and dozens of other forms of entertainment. Meanwhile, the view in other areas of America is hardly "entertaining." Churches can barely stay above water financially because so few people tithe, and some needy families get help only when their story reaches the six o'clock news.

Is it any surprise our nation is in trouble?

If we gave as generously to God as we do to our entertainment, imagine the people who could be helped.

### EVENING

With our consistent tithes, churches could expand ministries to the inner city and support ministries all over the world. There'd be enough money to help struggling families get back on their feet.

God promises a curse to the nation that cheats Him, but the blessings that come with generous giving can hardly be imagined.

Let's start the blessing today.

*Lord, entertainment isn't anything compared to You. Help me give to You first, not last. Amen.*

# DAY 127

## A LIFE OF LOVE

*Follow God's example, therefore, as dearly loved children and walk in the way of love, just as Christ loved us and gave himself up for us as a fragrant offering and sacrifice to God.*

EPHESIANS 5:1–2 NIV

### MORNING

Are you living a life of love? Ephesians 5:1–2 tells us that Christ loved us and gave Himself up for us. John 15:13 tells us there is no greater love than when you are willing to lay down your life for someone else.

How can you apply this to your daily life? By putting others first! Think of others' needs before you worry about yourself. Be others-minded instead of selfish. Wholeheartedly loving another person is one of the most selfless things you will ever do.

### EVENING

Do you love people enough to lay down your life for them? Putting others first can be difficult to do, but when we follow God's example, He fills us with His Spirit and His power, and through Him we can do all things.

*Dear God, show me how to love people selflessly and wholeheartedly. Help me to be willing to lay my life down for someone else if necessary. Amen.*

# DAY 128

# PERSPECTIVE

*We do this by keeping our eyes on Jesus,*
*the champion who initiates and perfects our faith.*
HEBREWS 12:2 NLT

## MORNING

Disappointed. Betrayed. Overwrought. Dismayed. Denied. Jesus, in His humanness, would have experienced the depth of these feelings and beyond. It is impossible to imagine how Jesus could have maintained His composure throughout the long hours leading up to His death. No one would have blamed Him if He had heaped vile words of hatred and anger on His enemies.

As He was perfectly one with the Holy Spirit, Christ saw far beyond the darkness and into the incomparable light of eternity. He gazed into the eyes of His Father and held that gaze (even when God momentarily turned His face) with the hope of a brilliant future. This hope, this unbreakable connection to His Father, allowed Him not only to stay silent in the face of torture but to go the distance and forgive them completely.

## EVENING

How is it that we can forgive others as Christ forgives us? It is a supernatural feat, no doubt, but forgiveness is as essential to the Christian life as breathing. When we fix our eyes on the Lord—not on what is currently happening to us but, as Jesus did, on the joy set before us—we have a perspective that far surpasses this moment in time. Thanks to Christ's work on the cross, we have the power to forgive as He did, and with that power lies the path to a brilliant future with Him.

*Father, when I fix my eyes on the here and now, I am bitterly disappointed. Yet when I fix my eyes on You, I am free—free to forgive and to live, eternally, with You. Amen.*

# DAY 129

## GOOD FOR THE SOUL

*How can I know all the sins lurking in my heart? Cleanse me from these hidden faults. Keep your servant from deliberate sins! Don't let them control me. Then I will be free of guilt and innocent of great sin.*

PSALM 19:12–13 NLT

### MORNING

Confession is typically something you save for moments when you've really messed up, because even though you know you're a sinner who needs a Savior, who wants to be reminded of her mistakes all the time?

But that's why the gospel is such good news—God doesn't want to recall your sins any more than you do. Jesus told Peter, "Once you've had a bath, your body is clean; you only need to wash your feet as you go from place to place." That suggests that confession goes beyond the moment of salvation; it's part of your sanctification—a daily habit not so different from taking a shower each morning before you go to school.

### EVENING

Sometimes confession is difficult. But as hard as it is, it's the only way to bring healing to yourself and others. Trust that God has good things ahead, and when you keep a clean slate, you prepare your heart to receive and appreciate them.

*Lord, I echo David's prayer: Show me the things I need to confess, especially the things I'm not even conscious of. I want to start my day on solid ground with You. Amen.*

# DAY 130

## I FORGIVE YOU

*Smart people know how to hold their tongue;*
*their grandeur is to forgive and forget.*
PROVERBS 19:11 MSG

### MORNING

Great power comes in these three little words: *I forgive you.* Often, they are hard to say, but they are powerful in their ability to heal our own hearts. Jesus taught His disciples to pray, "Forgive us our trespasses as we forgive those who trespass against us." He knew we needed to forgive others to be whole. When we are angry or hold a grudge against someone, our spirits are bound. The release that comes with extending forgiveness enables our spirits to commune with God more closely, and love swells within us.

### EVENING

How do you forgive? Begin with prayer. Recognize the humanity of the person who wronged you, and make a choice to forgive. Ask the Lord to help you forgive the person. Be honest, for the Lord sees your heart. Trust the Holy Spirit to guide you and cleanse you. Then step out and follow His leading in obedience.

By forgiving, we can move forward, knowing that God has good things in store for us. The heaviness of spirit is lifted, and relief washes over us after we've forgiven. A new sense of hope and expectancy rises. *I forgive you.* Do you need to say those words today?

*Father, search my heart and show me areas where I might need to forgive another. Help me let go and begin to heal. Amen.*

# DAY 131

## DRAW ME CLOSE

*Don't let anyone capture you with empty philosophies and high-sounding nonsense that come from human thinking and from the spiritual powers of this world, rather than from Christ.*
COLOSSIANS 2:8 NLT

### MORNING

We expect the world to disagree with us. After all, those who don't know Jesus aren't going to believe everything we do. But what happens when people in our church face us with ideas that aren't biblical or philosophies that owe less to Christianity than something else?

It's nothing new. God hasn't forgotten His church. The Colossians had the same problem. People in this New Testament church fought off heresy from within. No longer were the apostles' teachings and the Hebrew scriptures enough. Among other things, the heretics taught the need for secret knowledge and angel worship. They said you needed something more than Jesus. . .

### EVENING

If someone comes along teaching something "new" or different about Jesus, don't listen. God hasn't hidden anything you need to know about Jesus—it's all in His Book. Anything else has no authority at all.

*Jesus, I don't need anything "new" about You. I just need to know You better and better. Draw me close to You through Your Word. Amen.*

# DAY 132

## CHOOSE FRIENDS WISELY

*The righteous choose their friends carefully.*
PROVERBS 12:26 NIV

### MORNING

We need friends at all stages of our lives, but especially when we're young and still trying to figure life out. Friends give us other viewpoints to consider. When we share experiences, we can save ourselves a great deal of time by avoiding some of our friends' mistakes. We trust friends, often more than we trust our parents, because we have more in common with them.

That is exactly why we need to be cautious in choosing our friends. Sometimes they betray us. Sometimes we discover they're not going in the direction we want to go, and it's hard to break up a friendship when we make this discovery. . .

### EVENING

Friendships change as they mature, and sometimes these changes will hurt. Friends grow apart and then reconnect as time goes by, in a sort of cyclical flow—acquaintance, friend, acquaintance, friend again. A good friendship can tolerate these changes and grow stronger with each fluctuation. Choose your friends cautiously, and when you find good ones, hang on to them throughout your life.

*Father, help me to choose my friends with care and to treasure those who stick by me through all of life's ups and downs. Amen.*

# DAY 133

## A COMPASSIONATE TOUCH

*Jesus saw the huge crowd as he stepped from the boat, and he had compassion on them and healed their sick.*
MATTHEW 14:14 NLT

### MORNING

Can you imagine the crowds? They were a dirty, dusty, hungry, sick, hopeless bunch. Oppressed by politics and poverty, they were like sheep without a shepherd. Wandering in search of something—anything—to provide relief. Perhaps they knew nothing else about this man who could heal their diseases, but they were compelled to follow Him just for the hope of sweet relief.

Jesus was overwhelmed with compassion for these people. His compassion moved Him to offer a loving touch to the sick and forgotten, to offer the precious gift of sight to the blind, to reach out a hand and invite the lame to walk.

### EVENING

When we are in a crowd, it is easy for us to become discouraged and despairing at the need. We keep our gaze straight ahead, avoiding any eye contact so we are not moved by another's suffering. After all, if we feel compassion, we may be compelled to act, and if we act. . .well, that would be risky. Ask the Lord to enlarge your heart of compassion. Dare to look into the eyes of the faces in the crowd. Wait expectantly to see what God can do through you.

*Jesus, Your heart of compassion moves me. Thank You for caring so deeply about our earthly suffering and for the gift of healing offered by You. Help me to look at others through Your eyes. Give me eyes to see the suffering hearts in need of Your gracious touch. Amen.*

# DAY 134

## USING TIME WISELY

*So then, be careful how you walk, not as unwise people but as wise, making the most of your time, because the days are evil.*
EPHESIANS 5:15–16 NASB

### MORNING

Is your testimony something you review on a regular basis? It should be. This world is full of darkness, and God needs dedicated Christians who truly love Him to shed His light on lost souls.

Our primary desire should be to bring people to Jesus. This doesn't mean that all we ever do is talk about God, but when He gives us opportunities, we should take them. No matter what we are doing or saying, it should always honor God.

### EVENING

Our time on earth is limited, and we must use every minute wisely. We will give an account of all our time, whether we waste it or use it for God's glory. That is why it is so important to look often at how we measure up to God's expectations for our lives.

Jesus is our ideal. It really doesn't matter if we are better or worse than someone else. If we don't measure up to Christ, there is work to be done. We must let God work in and through us that we might wisely use the time He gives us to make a difference for Him.

*O God, give me a desire to make every moment I have count for You. Help me be wise in how I conduct my life. Amen.*

# DAY 135

# CHECKLIST RELIGION

*"Teacher, what good thing must I do to get eternal life?"*
Matthew 19:16 niv

## MORNING

A rich man met Jesus. He consulted his mental checklist and compared his past actions with what Jesus said he needed to do.

Don't murder? *Check*. Don't commit adultery? *Check*. Don't steal? *Check*. Don't lie? *Check*. Honor your parents? *Check*. Love your neighbor? *Check*. The rich man had to have felt pretty good about his spiritual résumé. He quickly said, "All these I have kept. . . . What do I still lack?" Jesus said, "Go, sell your possessions and give to the poor, and you will have treasure in heaven. Then come, follow me" (Matthew 19:20–21 niv). In this final to-do list, Jesus offered trust and friendship. The trust was wrapped up in believing that God was worthy of greater faith than money. The friendship invited the man to stay close and follow.

## EVENING

Matthew 19 shows a beautiful picture of why Jesus ushered in a new covenant that moved from a checklist religion to a trusting friendship with God. Don't sacrifice a relationship with God for a wall filled with spiritual merit badges. Maybe you want to impress God, but it ultimately leads you to trust your own efforts while resisting God's help.

*Lord, I want to celebrate the things You've done for me, not the few things I've done right. I believe obedience transforms my heart, but Your love extends an invitation to trust and follow. I want to do both. Amen.*

# DAY 136

## PRECIOUS GIFT OF GOD

*The LORD is a jealous and avenging God; the LORD takes vengeance and is filled with wrath. The LORD takes vengeance on his foes and vents his wrath against his enemies.*

NAHUM 1:2 NIV

### MORNING

Plenty of folks are perfectly willing to accept a wimpy kind of god—a perfectly inoffensive, powerless being who never interferes with their lives, never does anything *they* don't agree with, and *never* gets angry. This isn't God. Instead they've packed their own thinking in a little plastic doll, an idol created in their own image.

Imagine the anger any father would feel at having his son slighted! Well, God isn't just any father. He gave a unique Son. The perfect Man died to save sinners.

### EVENING

To cost your Son such pain and then receive the message "Don't interfere with my life" from sinners deserves an angry response. Justice wouldn't be done if God acted otherwise.

No idol shows anger, but God is no wimp. If people won't accept the most precious gift God had to give, they can pay for it themselves—with their own lives.

What will your life cost?

*Father God, though I deserved wrath, You sent Your Son for me. I don't want to ignore His sacrifice. In Jesus' name, amen.*

## DAY 137

# OF MEEKNESS AND STRENGTH

*"Take my yoke upon you and learn from me, for I am gentle and humble in heart, and you will find rest for your souls."*
MATTHEW 11:29 NIV

### MORNING

Today, if you call someone "meek," it will probably not be seen as a compliment. That's because they don't understand that meekness is the protective layer around real strength.

Think about Jesus. See Him driving the thieves from the temple, facing the palace guards in Gethsemane, and lying on the cross while spikes were driven into His flesh. Was He weak, timid, and shrinking? Hardly. Yet He called Himself meek and gentle in heart.

To be meek (gentle) one must keep their strength in check—balanced. Only the person who understands the right use of power can be truly gentle or meek.

### EVENING

Jesus had more power than any other person who ever walked on earth. He was God in the flesh. When Peter tried to defend Him with a sword, Jesus reminded him that He had an army of angels at His command. He chose not to call them. He chose to give, to serve, to be led as a lamb to the slaughter. That is real strength.

We are often tempted to display our personal power, whatever that may be, in our families and our everyday pursuits. Christ calls us to follow Him, to choose to use our strength in meek ways, and to reflect His life in our interactions with others.

*Lord, help me to be meek like You.*
*Let Your strength keep mine in check. Amen.*

## DAY 138

# PUT ON THE ARMOR

*Finally, be strong in the Lord and in his mighty power.*
*Put on the full armor of God, so that you can take*
*your stand against the devil's schemes.*
EPHESIANS 6:10–11 NIV

### MORNING

As your relationship with the Lord grows closer, Satan will attempt to knock you off course. Has your soul ever felt oppressed for no particular reason? Satan is powerful and persistent, devising schemes that undermine the Lord's work in our lives. His attacks are more forcefully felt when we are on the front battle lines fighting for the cause of Christ. He will go to great lengths to prevent the advancement of God's kingdom on earth.

Don't get discouraged. God has already won the battle! Christ claimed the victory by overcoming death, defeating Satan once and for all. He gives that victory to us.

### EVENING

Put on the spiritual armor Christ provides. We can't fend off Satan's attacks without it. We will triumph over him as we put on the belt of truth, the breastplate of righteousness, the helmet of salvation, the shield of faith, and the sword of the Spirit. Don't face your adversary ill prepared. Put on the full armor of God and stand!

*Dear Lord, remind me to wear the full armor You*
*have given me to ensure spiritual victory. Amen.*

# DAY 139

## SPEND YOUR TIME CLOSE TO HIM

*Therefore we have been buried with Him through baptism into death, so that, just as Christ was raised from the dead through the glory of the Father, so we too might walk in newness of life.*
ROMANS 6:4 NASB

### MORNING

You've been a Christian for a while, and that brand-new, clean feeling that came with a new faith has slowly evaporated. You don't feel new anymore.

*Maybe,* you ponder, *new is only for baby Christians. I know I've made "progress,"* you think as you try to encourage yourself. *I'm not the same person I was before I knew Jesus.* But something's missing.

God didn't make Jesus new for a day, week, or month and then let Him get "old" again. He eternally raised Him from the dead, so through baptism we can share His new life forever.

### EVENING

If vibrant faith has left you, some "old" things probably tarnish your new life. Legalistic or critical attitudes, disobedience, and doubt take the shine off a once-new faith until you barely know you've been washed in the Lamb's blood.

But repentance during a let's-clear-the-air time with God returns the "new" to eternal life. Spend time with Him in prayer.

*Empty me of old things that keep me apart from You, Lord. I want to spend every new day close by Your side. Amen.*

# DAY 140

## WHEN YOU CAN'T PRAY

*And the Holy Spirit helps us in our weakness. For example, we don't know what God wants us to pray for. But the Holy Spirit prays for us with groanings that cannot be expressed in words. And the Father who knows all hearts knows what the Spirit is saying, for the Spirit pleads for us believers in harmony with God's own will.*

ROMANS 8:26–27 NLT

### MORNING

Sometimes we literally cannot pray. The Holy Spirit takes over on such occasions. Go before God; enter His presence in a quiet spot where there will not be interruptions, and just be still before the Lord. When your heart is broken, the Holy Spirit will intercede for you. When you have lost someone or something precious, the Holy Spirit will go before the Father on your behalf. When you are weak, the comforter will ask the Father to strengthen you. When you are confused and anxious about a decision that looms before you, the counselor will seek God's best for you. You are not alone.

### EVENING

You are a precious daughter of the living God. When Christ ascended back into heaven, He did not leave you on this earth to forge through the wilderness on your own. He sent a comforter, a counselor—the Holy Ghost, the Spirit of truth. When you don't know what to pray, the Bible promises that the Spirit has you covered.

*Father, please hear the groaning of the Holy Spirit, who intercedes on my behalf before Your throne. Amen.*

# DAY 141

## COMFORT IN SADNESS

*You've kept track of my every toss and turn through the sleepless nights, each tear entered in your ledger, each ache written in your book.*
Psalm 56:8 MSG

### MORNING

In heaven there will be no more sadness. Tears will be a thing of the past. For now, we live in a fallen world. There are heartaches and disappointments. Some of us are more prone to crying than others, but all of us have cause to weep at times.

Call out to God when you find yourself tossing and turning at night or when tears drench your pillow. He is a God who sees, a God who knows. He is your "Abba" Father, your Daddy.

It hurts the Father's heart when you cry, but He sees the big picture. God knows that gut-wrenching trials create perseverance in His beloved child and that perseverance results in strong character.

### EVENING

Do you ever wonder if God has forgotten you and left you to fend for yourself? Rest assured that He has not left you even for one moment. He is your good shepherd, and you are His lamb. When you go astray, He spends every day and every night calling after you. If you are a believer, then you know your good shepherd's voice.

Shhhh! Listen. . .He is whispering a message of comfort even now.

*Father, remind me that You are a God who sees my pain.*
*Jesus, I thank You that You gave up Your life for me.*
*Holy Spirit, comfort me in my times of deep sadness. Amen.*

# DAY 142

## DREAM IN PEACE

*"Walk with me and work with me—watch how I do it. Learn the unforced rhythms of grace. I won't lay anything heavy or ill-fitting on you. Keep company with me and you'll learn to live freely and lightly."*

MATTHEW 11:29–30 MSG

### MORNING

Has God given you a dream—a vision of the person He wants you to be or something He wants you to accomplish? If He hasn't, ask Him for one. If He has, trust Him with it.

God gave Joseph dreams, but to his brothers, they seemed like a brat's fantasies (Genesis 37:8). What if instead, you saw Joseph as the dreamer God wants *you* to be, someone attuned to His Word and His will in such a way that He gives you regular downloads that direct your steps and guide your plans?

### EVENING

Clear away thoughts and habits that create doubt. You're not doubting yourself when you doubt. You're doubting God, who gave you the dream. When Jesus spoke of living a burden-free life, He didn't refer to freedom from hardship or challenges, but liberation from your own limitations.

To live like that is to echo David's song: "I keep my eyes always on the LORD. With him at my right hand, I will not be shaken" (Psalm 16:8 NIV).

*Lord, let my dreams be Your dreams, my plans Your plans.*
*Fill my heart with Your peace as I seek to honor You*
*with all I have and am. In Jesus' name, amen.*

# DAY 143

## BUILDING FRIENDSHIPS

*A friend loves at all times, and a brother is born for a time of adversity.*
PROVERBS 17:17 NIV

### MORNING

Today's world isn't designed for friendship. It's too fast-paced, with too many demands and too much stress. Oh, we're connected to everyone, all the time, through text messaging and cell phones and Facebook. But as fun as Facebook may seem, it robs us of face-to-face time. We're so distracted with everything at once that we find it hard to focus on one thing—one person—at a time.

But friendship demands one-on-one, face-to-face time. And although most of us don't feel we have a lot of time to give, we must! We simply must make friendship and building real flesh-and-blood relationships a priority.

### EVENING

God created us for relationships. And although a well-timed email or text message may lift us up at times, there's simply no replacement for a real live hug. There's no substitute for a friend sitting beside you in the hospital holding your hand. And we won't have those things unless we're willing to put aside our high-tech gadgets and invest time in the people around us.

Let's make it a point to turn off our cell phones. Let's step away from our computers for a while and have a real conversation with someone. That person may just turn out to be a true friend.

*Dear Father, teach me to be a true friend. Help me to make friendship a priority and to invest in the people around me. Amen.*

## DAY 144

# FILLING THE HOUSE AND THE HEART WITH GOD

*"When an impure spirit comes out of a person, it goes through arid places seeking rest and does not find it. Then it says, 'I will return to the house I left.' When it arrives, it finds the house unoccupied, swept clean and put in order. Then it goes and takes with it seven other spirits more wicked than itself, and they go in and live there."*

MATTHEW 12:43–45 NIV

### MORNING

"Mom, listen! It echoes in here!" Robbie cried as the family was ready to shut the door for the last time as they moved to another home.

"Honey, it does! But we'll be able to fill up the next house with our things, your toys, fun, and laughter!"

"Will this house always echo?" Robbie wanted to know.

"Just while it's empty and for sale. Someday another family will fill up this house with their camping gear, kids, toys, and laughter!"

Jesus used similar words to clearly show that cleaning up one's life without filling it up with God leaves lots of room for Satan to enter. It's like a house that has been sitting vacant too long. Instead of being filled up with the happy sounds of a family, it may be vandalized by those with evil intentions.

### EVENING

Filling up your house and heart with God starts with devotions like the ones in this book. Fill your house, heart, mind, and soul each day with God. God's Word prevents vandalism of your heart, your home, and your family.

*Thank You, God, for filling me, my heart, and my home with Your Spirit. Amen.*

# DAY 145

# TAKE YOUR ANGER TO GOD

*Human anger does not produce the righteousness that God desires.*
James 1:20 NIV

## MORNING

"But don't I have to get all my anger in the open to get rid of it?" Tyler asked. "I've always heard it isn't good to bottle it up. Besides, my family argues all the time. I wouldn't know what else to do."

If anger resides in your home, like it does in Tyler's, you may feel baffled by this verse. You don't even know where to start.

Tyler learned he had a choice: He could go to God with the problems that caused those emotions and deal with them before he opened his mouth, or he could batter others with the feelings that kept growing inside him.

Consistently bringing your hurts to Jesus first defuses the situation.

## EVENING

The heavenly Father can show you what's wrong and give insight on how to fix it. He can soothe painful emotions by bringing understanding to both sides of a situation.

Or you can let that anger burn, ever growing and destroying your life and those around you.

Get your anger out in the open—to God.

*When I'm tempted to respond with anger,*
*Lord, turn me instead to You. Amen.*

# DAY 146

## DON'T EXPECT PERFECTION

*I do not understand what I do. For what I want to do I do not do, but what I hate I do.*
ROMANS 7:15 NIV

### MORNING

The apostle Paul was as human as the rest of us and was not afraid to admit it. "I don't know why I act the way I do," he said. "I don't do the things I want to do. Instead, I do what I don't want to do."

We don't know what Paul's sins were, but they really bugged him. It seems he never conquered them, although he obviously worked on them a lot. His standards for himself were probably pretty high.

You set yourself up to fail if you think you should be perfect. Are you better than Paul was? Have a little mercy on yourself.

### EVENING

You should never use Paul's failure as an excuse to run wild or to not even try to control yourself. Paul conquered a good portion of his weaknesses, and you can do the same. Pick out one of your least favorite behaviors and concentrate on it for a while. You may be surprised—but don't expect perfection.

*Lord, my sins are numerous and my strengths are few. Help me be the best I can be and trust Your forgiveness for the rest. Amen.*

# DAY 147

## GOD KNOWS YOUR NAME

*But now, this is what the* Lord *says—he who created you, Jacob, he who formed you, Israel: "Do not fear, for I have redeemed you; I have summoned you by name; you are mine."*

Isaiah 43:1 niv

### MORNING

Do you remember the first day of school? The teacher called the roll, and you waited for your name to be announced. When it was, you knew that you were a part of that class—you belonged there.

We wait for our names to be called a lot in life: when captains pick teams, while we're sitting in a doctor's waiting room, or when school awards are being announced. There is comfort in hearing our own names, in being recognized.

God knows your name. He created you and redeemed you from sin through His Son, Jesus, if you have accepted Him as your personal Savior. He knows you. He put together your personality and topped off His masterpiece by giving you all sorts of likes and dislikes, dreams and desires, passions and preferences.

### EVENING

You are God's unique design, His child, His beloved one.

It does not matter if you feel as if you don't belong, for *you belong to God*. He takes great joy in you. You are His treasure. He sent Jesus to die on the cross to give you an abundant life. He wants to spend eternity with you! He calls you by name, and your name is music to your Father's ears.

*Lord, I thank You for knowing my name and loving me unconditionally. Amen.*

# DAY 148

## FEELING OTHERS' PAIN

*Jesus saw her crying. The Jews who came with her were crying also. His heart was very sad and He was troubled. He said, "Where did you lay Lazarus?" They said, "Lord, come and see." Then Jesus cried.*

JOHN 11:33–35 NLV

### MORNING

Do you want to be like Jesus? Then enter into the pain of others.

Jesus did not stay away from those who were suffering. He came alongside them; He carried it with them.

As the Son of God, Jesus knew all things. He knew the reasons why people were blind, deaf, and disabled. He understood the reasons for their poverty, dysfunction, depression, and fears. He knew that He would touch many of them, healing their diseases and calming their anxieties. Yet He had compassion. He took the time to enter their pain.

We see this demonstrated here in the narrative of Lazarus' death and resurrection by Jesus. Although He knew that in a few moments Lazarus was going to walk out of the tomb, Jesus wept as He stood in front of his grave. No doubt He wept for the sisters and the crushing pain they had endured. He didn't rush to the miracle; first, He shared the grief.

### EVENING

In our times of disappointment and loss, we can know that Jesus stands beside us, feeling our hurt and bearing our pain. Like Him, we can come alongside others who suffer, crying with them, praying with them, and lifting them up to His care.

*Jesus, thank You for being the friend who shares my deepest hurts. Help me to bear the pain of others in Your name. Amen.*

# DAY 149

## THE WAY OUT

*You have never been tempted to sin in any different way than other people. God is faithful. He will not allow you to be tempted more than you can take. But when you are tempted, He will make a way for you to keep from falling into sin.*

1 CORINTHIANS 10:13 NLV

### MORNING

Everyone faces temptation. Scripture says that no one escapes it, and all become its victims (Romans 3:23). But don't be discouraged. God provides a way out.

Believers learn to endure and stand up to temptation by God's grace. When they rely on the power that comes from the Holy Spirit, God provides them with strength to resist. Jesus said that this willpower comes by watchfulness and prayer. "Watch and pray so that you will not be tempted. Man's spirit is willing, but the body does not have the power to do it" (Matthew 26:41 NLV).

### EVENING

As hard as people try, temptation sometimes wins. God has a plan for that too. He sent His Son, Jesus, into the world to take the punishment for the sins of everyone who believes in Him. Not only did Jesus suffer the consequences of sin, but through His sacrifice He provided God with a way to forgive sinfulness and to promise believers eternal life.

Watch and pray today that you don't fall into temptation; but if you do, remember this: Sin might win in the moment, but God's grace and forgiveness are forever.

*Dear Lord, lead me not into temptation but deliver me from evil today and always. Amen.*

# DAY 150

## WISDOM FROM DOING

*The fear of the Lord is the beginning of wisdom. All who obey His Laws have good understanding. His praise lasts forever.*

PSALM 111:10 NLV

### MORNING

Living in the information age, we are easily tricked into thinking that knowledge is the answer to all our problems. If we educate ourselves well on a given subject, we believe we can master it. If we identify all facets of a problem, we can solve it. But the truth is, knowing doesn't necessarily lead to doing. If it did, we would all be eating healthy foods and exercising regularly. Knowledge and obedience do not mean the same thing. Somewhere between the two is our will.

### EVENING

Scripture teaches us that fearing the Lord—not gaining information—is the source of wisdom. It is in hearing and obeying, James 1:22 tells us, that we gain clear understanding. To be only a hearer of the Word is to be deceived. To be a doer of the Word removes the spiritual blind spots and keeps our vision clear. This is the difficult part, for doing the Word often involves repentance or giving up our own agendas. Fearing the Lord is living in reverent submission to Him, seeking His will and way in our lives. That is the starting point for a life of wisdom and understanding.

*Lord, help me not to be deceived by trusting in knowledge alone. Show me the areas where I have heard and not done, and help me to obey. Give me a reverent fear of You. Amen.*

# DAY 151

## MAKING ALLOWANCES

*Always be humble and gentle. Be patient with each other, making allowance for each other's faults because of your love.*
EPHESIANS 4:2 NLT

### MORNING

Today's verse contains such a simple, forgotten truth, doesn't it? God wants us to be holy. He wants us to be righteous and good and godly. But He knows we'll never get it exactly right until we're made perfect in His presence.

Until then, we all have our faults—numerous faults, if we're honest with ourselves. And God doesn't want us standing around, whispering and pointing self-righteous fingers of condemnation. God is the *only* one who can wear the judge's robe.

And He doesn't condemn us. Instead, He pours His love and acceptance into our lives with a gentle warning to "go and sin no more" (John 8:11 NLT).

### EVENING

Jesus whispers to our hearts, "It's okay. You messed up, but it's been taken care of. The price has been paid. I still love you. Just try not to do it again."

Why do we find it so hard to extend grace to others when so much grace has been shown to us? As we go through each day, let's make it a point to live out this verse. Let's be humble, gentle, and patient, making allowances for the faults of others because of God's love.

*Dear Father, help me to be gentle and loving with others. Remind me of the grace You've shown me, and help me show the same love to those around me. Amen.*

# DAY 152

## MAKING HIS WAYS YOUR ROUTINE

*Now his boss saw that the Lord was with him.*
*He saw how the Lord made all that Joseph did go well.*
GENESIS 39:3 NLV

### MORNING

Joseph, who was sold into slavery by his jealous brothers, lived a classic riches-to-rags-to-riches tale, but the most remarkable thing about him—his greatest trait—was that God was with him. That fact explains his survival and his successes—and the wise and compassionate character he consistently showed.

Is God the core of *your* daily routine? It takes discipline not to take God for granted, to seek Him when things are going well, not just when they aren't. Joseph's consistency made him a model employee—the best worker his bosses had, a conduit of God's blessings to them. It had nothing to do with Joseph's education or accomplishments but everything to do with his trust in God.

### EVENING

God is faithful even when you're not. That's not a guilt trip but a *get-out-of-jail-free* card—a gift that can't be earned, only received, and one that changes everything. And you can tell that you have received it, not because all the storms in your life suddenly cease, but because you suddenly have a remarkable sense of peace and freedom as you face them.

*Father, "I'm not trying to get my way in the world's way. I'm trying to get your way, your Word's way. I'm staying on your trail; I'm putting one foot in front of the other. I'm not giving up" (Psalm 17:4–5 MSG).*

# DAY 153

## LET LOVE DEFUSE ANGER

*And the Lord God made clothing from animal skins for Adam and his wife.*
Genesis 3:21 NLT

### MORNING

This verse comes right after God cursed Adam and Eve and right before He chased them out of Eden. Smack-dab in the middle of all the thundering and armed angels, God took some animal skins and did a little sewing. What's going on here?

Well, that's parenting for you. He is doing what fathers do—taking care of His kids.

### EVENING

How many times has your mom yelled at you and then turned around and baked cookies before she finished her lecture? How many times has your father told you to be more careful with your money and then handed you a twenty before he told you what *not* to spend it on?

The next time you're ready to blow up at someone, follow God's example. Take a break. Do a little something to show you care for the person, and let your love defuse your anger.

*Father, thank You for Your unfailing love when I goof up. Your anger would be more than I could stand. Amen.*

# DAY 154

## BE PATIENT

*See how the farmer waits for the land to yield its valuable crop, patiently waiting for the autumn and spring rains.*
JAMES 5:7 NIV

### MORNING

If there's one thing a farmer knows well, it's patience. You can't hurry a plant's growth, and you can't do a thing to bring the rain. Standing in the field and looking at the sky is often all that can be done.

It's hard to be patient in an instant world. You need to shake off that cold right now, but your nose is still going to run for five days unless you take so much medicine that you can't function. The puppy will be housebroken when it decides to be, so don't be upset when you have to clean up another puddle. Nature has a way of telling us we're not the hotshots we think we are. . .

### EVENING

We must remember that although we can control a lot of our life, there's a lot more we can't do anything about, and there's no sense in getting upset about what we can't control. The rains will come.

*Father, teach me patience when I'm faced with something I cannot control. There is enough that I can work on to keep me busy until the time is right. Amen.*

# DAY 155

## THE TRUE LOVE

*"Love one another; just as I have loved you."*
JOHN 13:34 NASB

### MORNING

In a society that has distorted the concept of love, it's reassuring to know that God loves us with a deep, limitless love. He is, in fact, love itself. He gave His Son to die for people who didn't love Him in return. God the Father even had to turn His face from His Son when He died, as He took the sin of mankind upon Himself. What incredible love that is!

### EVENING

We Christians tell Jesus we love Him, and His response is "I love you more." We cannot comprehend that kind of love, yet we are the recipients of it. And He loves us not because of anything we've done but because of His goodness.

Jesus also commands us to love others in the same way that He loves us. We all have unlovable people in our lives. But Jesus doesn't see anyone as unlovable. Look at that difficult-to-love person through new eyes today, and love them as God has loved you.

*Heavenly Father, thank You for Your love for me. Forgive me for not loving others in that same way. Give me the ability to love others as You have instructed. Amen.*

# DAY 156

## CHRIST TASTED DEATH

*But we do see Him who was made for a little while lower than the angels, namely, Jesus, because of His suffering death crowned with glory and honor, so that by the grace of God He might taste death for everyone.*

HEBREWS 2:9 NASB

### MORNING

Death is simultaneously one of the most common and one of the most mysterious concepts. It's common because everyone goes through it and no one can escape it. Yet it's mysterious because no one currently on earth has experienced it, so no one knows what to expect. Death might not seem like an incredibly uplifting devotional topic, but for you who are in Christ, it is. In death you have the greatest hope of all—the gateway into an eternity of life with your Savior.

### EVENING

Christ has experienced death. It could not hold Him. He tasted death for everyone. This diminishes the sting and fear of death both for you and for your loved ones who are in Christ. You know someone who has been through it and will be waiting on the other side to welcome you into glory. How incredible that the God you serve has experienced and conquered that most feared of eventualities. Even through death He will hold your hand and will not let you or any of His children walk through it alone. As Romans 8:38–39 says, nothing, not even death, can separate us from the love of God that is in Christ Jesus.

*Lord, I praise You for tasting death for me so that now even in death I have the comfort of knowing that You will never leave me. Amen.*

# DAY 157

## STAYING ON TRACK

*I have fought the good fight,*
*I have finished the course, I have kept the faith.*
2 TIMOTHY 4:7 NASB

### MORNING

In our hustle-bustle world, it's easy to get so busy that we forget our priorities. Hopefully, as believers, we've established our priority list with God at the top. Staying in touch with Him and walking in His will should be our number-one goal.

The apostle Paul knew this when he exhorted the churches to stick closely to the teachings of Jesus. He knew the fickle heart and how easy it would be for them to stray. In his letters to Timothy, he reminded the young man of the importance of drawing close to God, hearing His heartbeat. Despite the pain and afflictions Paul suffered in his life, he kept his eyes on Jesus, using praise to commune with God.

### EVENING

Like Paul, we can keep in constant communion with the Father. We are so blessed to have been given the Holy Spirit within to keep us in tune with His will. Through His guidance—that still, small voice—we can rest assured that our priorities will stay focused on Jesus. As the author A. W. Tozer wrote, "Lord, guide me carefully on this uncharted sea as I daily seek You in Your word. Then use me mightily as Your servant this year as I boldly proclaim Your word in leading others."

*Lord, no better words have been spoken than*
*to say, "I surrender to Your will." Amen.*

# DAY 158

## PERSEVERANCE—A BLESSING?

*Let perseverance finish its work so that you may be mature and complete, not lacking anything.*
JAMES 1:4 NIV

### MORNING

We don't often think of perseverance as a blessing or something beneficial to our growth. We persevere because the only other options are defeat or retreat. We don't go out looking for the chance to persevere; it usually involves unpleasant experiences.

Whether or not we want these experiences, they will come. The requirements of our schoolwork may be beyond our capabilities, yet we persevere and eventually learn how to handle the work. Building muscle to make the team seems to go on forever, yet we gain a little every week and eventually get there.

### EVENING

Perseverance involves tiny little steps toward a goal, not one valiant effort that solves the problem immediately. It teaches patience, planning, and working for future rewards instead of instant gratification—all things that lead to maturity and completeness.

*Father, perseverance is hard work, no matter what the goal is. Give me the patience and foresight I need to persevere and mature. Amen.*

# DAY 159

## BAD COMPANY

*Do not be misled: "Bad company corrupts good character."*
1 CORINTHIANS 15:33 NIV

### MORNING

The young cheerleader began her new activity with stars in her eyes. However, her naive bubble quickly burst during their first break. Other cheerleaders gossiped viciously about each other and then pretended to be best friends when reunited on the gym floor. She vowed to avoid the gossip she had just witnessed. But as the weeks passed, she began chiming in during similar conversations. What was happening to her?

We are like sponges, absorbing the contents of our environment. We become like the people we spend time with. Others influence us—for better or for worse. For that reason, we must choose our friends wisely.

### EVENING

Decide what kind of person you would like to become. Spend time with people who exhibit those qualities. Good character produces good character. The opposite is also true.

Bad character is contagious. It is subtle. It doesn't happen overnight. Choose to surround yourself with positive role models who foster good character.

*Dear Lord, help me choose my friends wisely so that I will be positively influenced. Amen.*

# DAY 160

## THE FACE OF JESUS

*We're proclaiming Jesus Christ, the Master. All we are is messengers. . . from Jesus for you. It started when God said, "Light up the darkness!" and our lives filled up with light as we saw and understood God in the face of Christ, all bright and beautiful. If you only look at us, you might well miss the brightness. We carry this precious Message around in the unadorned clay pots of our ordinary lives. That's to prevent anyone from confusing God's incomparable power with us.*

2 CORINTHIANS 4:6–7 MSG

### MORNING

God illuminated the hearts and minds of people and revealed His glory in the person of Jesus. Since Adam's fall, humanity has tried to fill with false treasures the hole in society and in individual hearts that can be filled only with the beauty of being with God.

In Jesus, that dark and pointless searching comes to an end. God shines His life-giving light so that we can know and understand that His glory is in the face of Jesus.

### EVENING

When we follow Jesus, we are being brought back into that first perfect friendship with God. This powerful message reveals the depth of God's grace. Broken human bodies seem a poor enclosure for such life-changing knowledge and light; this, all the more, points to the power of Jesus' redemption work. What do we do with this knowledge? Do we recognize this treasure and allow Jesus to point us away from our corruptible bodies and back to God?

*Father, when I am overwhelmed by the limitations of my earthen vessel body, let me keep my eyes fixed on Christ and then let me see Your excellent power bring victory. Amen.*

# DAY 161

## ENCOURAGE ONE ANOTHER

*Therefore encourage one another and build each other up, just as in fact you are doing.*
1 THESSALONIANS 5:11 NIV

### MORNING

"Runners, get ready. Get set. Go!"

Travis fixed his eyes on the finish line and sprinted ahead in his first-ever Special Olympics race. As he ran, family members and friends shouted words of encouragement all along the way. "Go, Travis! You're doing great! You're almost there!" Travis beamed as he crossed the finish line and fell into the arms of his coach. "Good job!" said the coach as he embraced Travis. "I knew you could do it."

Whether it is a race, a daunting project, or just getting through life, human beings need encouragement. The apostle Paul wrote in his letter to the Thessalonians, "Encourage one another and build each other up."

### EVENING

Encouragement is more than words. It is also valuing, being tolerant of, serving, and praying for one another. It is looking for what is good and strong in a person and celebrating it. Encouragement means sincerely forgiving and asking for forgiveness, recognizing someone's weaknesses and holding out a helping hand, giving humbly while building someone up, helping others to hope in the Lord, and praying that God will encourage them in ways that you cannot.

Whom will you encourage today? Get in the habit of encouraging others. It will bless them and you.

*Heavenly Father, open my eyes to those who need encouragement. Show me how I can help. Amen.*

# DAY 162

## DOING LAPS

*The Israelites ate manna forty years. . .*
*until they reached the border of Canaan.*
EXODUS 16:35 NIV

### MORNING

You might call it "doing laps." Just as a swimmer goes back and forth in the pool to build up strength, sometimes God keeps us in the same place, doing the same thing, for a long time.

The Israelites complained that they didn't have food, so God gave them manna—today and tomorrow and the next day. Boy, were they sick of that white, wafer-like stuff! Like the swimmer in the pool, they never got anything different.

In our spiritual walk, when we get stuck "doing laps," we need to look at ourselves. Maybe, like the Israelites, we've sinned, and God is trying to humble us. Or maybe we need to gain strength, so God has us exercising the same spiritual muscle over and over.

### EVENING

If you're "doing laps," and it seems like you've been in the same place, doing the same thing over and over, search your heart. Do you need to confess some sin so you can move on? If not, don't get discouraged. God is building up your strength.

That's why you're diving into the water one more time.

*Lord, when I feel waterlogged, show me why I'm diving into the water again. Amen.*

# DAY 163

## CHANGED IN THE WAITING

*So all of us who have had that veil removed can see and reflect the glory of the Lord. And the Lord—who is the Spirit—makes us more and more like him as we are changed into his glorious image.*

2 CORINTHIANS 3:18 NLT

### MORNING

While a caterpillar is turning into a butterfly, the chrysalis is not in a resting stage. Special cells that were present in the larva grow rapidly, becoming legs, wings, eyes, and other parts of the adult butterfly. Wings are fully formed. Antennae grow, and the chewing mouthparts of the caterpillar are transformed into the sucking mouthparts of the butterfly.

While we are waiting for something, there are unseen activities going on spiritually. In the book of Daniel, Daniel prayed earnestly for many days without seeing a change in his circumstances. An angel arrived and told Daniel that he (Michael) had left immediately in answer to Daniel's prayer, but he got stopped along the way by Satan's demonic forces. The angel battled the demons, which made him "late" from Daniel's viewpoint.

### EVENING

God is always up to something. If we wait with faith in the time between a desire/prayer and its fulfillment, then, like a pupa turns into a beautiful winged creature, so we will be changed into a person who looks more like Christ. Such waiting is an active waiting, full of prayer, scripture seeking, and fellowship.

*Creator, thank You for creating miracles in nature and for the greatest miracle of all—a changed life. Help me to trust You in times of waiting and to know that You are at work. Amen.*

# DAY 164

## AT ALL TIMES

*Pray in the Spirit at all times and on every occasion.*
EPHESIANS 6:18 NLT

### MORNING

When giving instructions about important things, it's good to be specific. The more specific the instructions are, the more likely the task will be done correctly. That's why when the apostle Paul spoke to the Ephesians about praying, he didn't leave any question about when to pray.

Prayer isn't a ritual to practice before bed or first thing in the morning or when the sun is at a certain place in the sky. Though it's great to have specific times of concentrated, focused prayer, our conversations with God shouldn't be limited to a certain time on our calendar. God wants us to pray *all the time.*

### EVENING

God wants to be included in our days. He wants to walk and talk with us each moment. Imagine if we traveled through the day with our family, but we only spoke to them between 6:15 and 6:45 a.m.! Of course, we'd never do that to the people we care about. God doesn't want us to do that to Him, either.

God wants to travel the journey with us. He's a wonderful companion, offering wisdom and comfort for every aspect of our lives. But He can do that only if we let Him into our schedules every minute of every day.

*Dear Father, thank You for always being there to listen.*
*Remind me to talk to You about everything, all the time. Amen.*

# DAY 165

## LOVING YOUR NEIGHBOR—JESUS STYLE

*"'Love the Lord your God with all your heart and with all your soul and with all your mind and with all your strength.' The second is this: 'Love your neighbor as yourself.' There is no commandment greater than these."*

MARK 12:30–31 NIV

### MORNING

Thousands of years before teachers knew about learning styles and teaching with stories, Jesus taught about moral conduct using parables. His teaching stories still apply to our lives today.

To challenge attitudes about helping others, Jesus told the story of a wounded man—beaten, robbed, and left to die on the road to Jericho. It was a place His listeners knew well. Jesus knew His crowd and human nature as He told about the three who saw the injured man. Two were active in the synagogue: a priest and a Levite. Afraid of becoming unclean and unfit for service and worship, each walked on the other side of the road. Isn't that like some people who are active in church today?

Who helped? Only a man who was considered a lowlife and from the wrong side of the tracks—a person seen as "less than" stopped to help. Due to intermarriage generations before, Samaritans were a mixture of Jew and Gentile.

Jesus' challenge about attitude stands today. Who is our neighbor?

### EVENING

Jesus teaches that there are no walls when facing someone with a need. They may come from any race, creed, or social background. We are to love and care for them as God does for us. How will you step up to Jesus' challenge?

*Thank You, Jesus, for Your parables that teach us how to live and how to shine with Your light. Amen.*

# DAY 166

## THE TEMPTER

*The tempter came to him and said, "If you are the Son of God, tell these stones to become bread." Jesus answered, "It is written: 'Man shall not live on bread alone, but on every word that comes from the mouth of God.'"*

MATTHEW 4:3–4 NIV

### MORNING

The tempter is no respecter of persons. He tempts princes and paupers, senators and ordinary citizens. His goal is to destroy every human. He's smart; he identifies his prey's weakness and zooms in for the kill.

Jesus was a target, just like each of us. He was weak. He hadn't eaten for forty days. So of course Satan tempted the Son of God with food. He tried to trick Jesus by taunting Him: "You're not really God's Son, are You? If You are, show me. I know You're hungry. Turn these stones to bread."

Turning those rocks into hot, steaming rolls would have been sin—not because it was wrong for Christ to eat but because He would have done it, at that moment, out of pride, to prove His identity. He'd also committed that time to God as a time of prayer. Jesus resisted temptation with God's Word.

### EVENING

Jesus didn't argue. He didn't try to be strong enough. He simply quoted God's Word, which defeats the tempter every time. The more familiar we are with God's Word, the better chance we have against the one who wants to destroy us. We may be weak, but God's Word will win every time.

*Dear Father, help me keep Your Word in my heart so I can use it as a weapon against sin. Amen.*

## DAY 167

# TAKING GOD SERIOUSLY

*When the disciples had Jesus off to themselves, they asked, "Why couldn't we throw it out?" "Because you're not yet taking God seriously," said Jesus.*

MATTHEW 17:19–20 MSG

### MORNING

People make time for the things that matter most to them. It's one thing to say something is important, but another entirely to internalize it, spend time on it, and act because of it. This happens even with Christians who understand that Jesus is most important but put getting to know Him better behind more urgent things like school, family, or hobbies.

Good intentions aren't enough to walk fruitfully with Jesus.

### EVENING

When the disciples failed to cast out a demon, Jesus told them, "The simple truth is that if you had a mere kernel of faith, a poppy seed, say, you would tell this mountain, 'Move!' and it would move. There is nothing you wouldn't be able to tackle" (Matthew 17:20 MSG).

Don't let that discourage you though. David tells us how to take God seriously: "O LORD, I give my life to you. I trust in you, my God! Do not let me be disgraced, or let my enemies rejoice in my defeat" (Psalm 25:1–2 NLT).

*Jesus, make me aware of anything that is coming between me and You. I want to put You first in everything, knowing You'll take care of my every need. Amen.*

# DAY 168

## GENTLE BUT JUST

*"A bent reed He will not break off and a dimly burning wick He will not extinguish; He will faithfully bring forth justice."*
ISAIAH 42:3 NASB

### MORNING

Today's scripture passage is a beautiful prophecy about the Messiah. His gentleness is so evident. He mends rather than breaks. He keeps alive rather than extinguishes. If you are broken or slowly losing hope, turn to your Savior, who will never leave or forsake you. His ultimate desire for you is to bring you into closer fellowship with Him. The path to that goal may be hewn with hardships, but you serve a Lord who will gently care for you along the way.

### EVENING

While Christ is portrayed as gentle and kind in today's scripture, He is also proclaimed as one who will bring forth justice. It is overwhelming to think of all the people who are hurting others in this world. Christ does not turn a blind eye to this. In fact, it breaks His heart more than it breaks yours. Even though all is not clear in this life, you can be confident that He is a faithful judge. In His life on earth, He didn't cater to the rich and powerful. Instead, He noticed the forgotten, touched the unclean, and healed the hopeless. He was, is, and always will be the advocate for those who are hurting, lonely, and without a voice.

*Lord, I ask You to mend me and give me life today. I lean on the promise that You will judge righteously. Amen.*

# DAY 169

## GOD IS MY ROCK

*Truly he is my rock and my salvation;*
*he is my fortress, I will never be shaken.*
PSALM 62:2 NIV

### MORNING

In a world that's changing faster than ever before, many people are desperate for some sort of stability. Part of the attraction of the great outdoors is that sense of dependability, a feeling of absolute, unchanging permanency.

That's a pleasant idea, one we take comfort in. But it's not necessarily true. Think about it: The Grand Canyon becomes deeper and wider every year through erosion. Hawaii's Kilauea volcano erupted in 2019, dramatically changing the landscape forever. Earthquakes can change an area's topography in just a moment.

If you're looking for something more solid than rock, look past the canyons and beyond the mountains. . .

### EVENING

God is the one truly permanent thing in our life. Mountains and valleys will come and go, but we'll always be at the center of God's attention, the recipients of His unchanging love.

*Lord, help me remember that the things of this world will pass away.*
*Free me to more fully appreciate Your unimaginable glory. Amen.*

# DAY 170

## PERFECT PEACE IN CHRIST

*You will keep in perfect peace all who trust in you,*
*all whose thoughts are fixed on you! Trust in the LORD*
*always, for the LORD GOD is the eternal Rock.*
ISAIAH 26:3–4 NLT

### MORNING

What does perfect peace look like? Is it a life without problems? Is it a smooth ride into the future without any bumps in the road? Not for the Christian. We know life on earth won't ever be easy, but God promises to keep us in perfect peace if our thoughts are fixed on Him.

Perfect peace is found only by having a moment-by-moment relationship with Jesus Christ. It is ongoing faith and trust that God really has it all figured out. It's believing that each setback, heartbreak, problem, and crisis will be made right by God.

### EVENING

You can live in peace even during the messy stuff of life. You don't have to have everything figured out on your own. Doesn't that take off some pressure?

"And the God of all grace, who called you to his eternal glory in Christ, after you have suffered a little while, will himself restore you and make you strong, firm and steadfast" (1 Peter 5:10 NIV). That's perfect peace.

*Heavenly Father, thank You for offering me peace in the midst of the stress of this life. Thank You that I'm not in charge and that You have everything already figured out. I trust You. Amen.*

# DAY 171

## CASTING CARES

*Cast all your anxiety on him because he cares for you.*
1 PETER 5:7 NIV

### MORNING

Do you have tiresome schoolwork that calls, follows, and awaits you? No matter how demanding it is, the way you handle that work can reflect God.

Do you have relationship challenges with a parent, friend, or sibling? The way you handle those challenges can be a bright spot for everyone involved.

Are you afraid about the future, either for yourself or your family? The way you handle that fear can be a blessing into eternity.

Are there health issues that you or a loved one face? What you do with those can speak to the lives of many.

### EVENING

Do your friends or a brother or sister have things they are deeply struggling with that they have asked you to talk about with them or pray about? Listening and praying can make a world of difference for them in so many ways.

Does it seem that there are too many burdens, people, problems, and things to pray for? Give them all to God. He wants to take care of every one of them.

*Lord God, thank You for being the sovereign Almighty who can handle all of the cares we have. Amen.*

# DAY 172

# PRAYING TOGETHER

*"For where two or three gather in my name, there am I with them."*
MATTHEW 18:20 NIV

## MORNING

The pastor stood before his congregation on a rainy Sunday morning. "You have made a good choice today!" he stated, along with a joke about all those who stayed at home and pulled the covers up over their heads. "Yes, you have made a good choice," he repeated. "We have an honored guest. God is here with us this morning!" He then read Matthew 18:20: "For where two or three gather in my name, there am I with them."

Of all the passages in the Bible that emphasize the importance of gathering for worship and prayer, this one stands out. It is short and sweet and to the point. Why should we gather to pray with other Christians? Because when we do, *God shows up!* The Lord is in our midst.

## EVENING

As you gather with other Christians in your church or even in your family, God is honored. He loves to listen to the hearts and voices of His children unified in prayer. He will be faithful to answer according to His perfect will.

*Father, thank You for the promise that where we gather in Your name, there You will be also. Help me to never give up the practice of praying with fellow believers. Amen.*

# DAY 173

## STOP CROWING

*When things were going great I crowed, "I've got it made.*
*I'm God's favorite. He made me king of the mountain."*
*Then you looked the other way and I fell to pieces.*
PSALM 30:6–7 MSG

### MORNING

King David knew how easily he could shift his gaze from trusting God toward the trouble God would need to rescue him from once again. Psalm 30 is a glimpse into the heart of a king who often fell into the error of thinking that his personal brownie points made God love him more than most. David kept forgetting he had a wayward heart. This thoughtless combination sometimes led to dark days, sin, and sad psalms.

You can set yourself up for a similar dilemma. When things are going well, you can feel that it means God is blessing and loves you. When things aren't going great, you can think God is upset and withholding blessings. . .

### EVENING

Your personal level of pride and doubt often determines what God's response will be. When you crow like King David and say, "I've got it made. I'm God's favorite," you can expect Him to send a crash course on humility. That's because when you trust in yourself, you'll find yourself doubting Him.

*Dear God, may I come to each moment in life knowing that Your plan for me can be trusted and that there is nothing I can add to it that will improve it. Help me leave pride behind when I follow You.*

# DAY 174

## YOUR HEART COULD BE WRONG

*When the people saw how long it was taking Moses to come back down the mountain, they gathered around Aaron. "Come on," they said, "make us some gods who can lead us."*
EXODUS 32:1 NLT

### MORNING

God invited Moses to come and speak with Him on the mountain. While Moses was gone, the people struggled to continue trusting God. They also struggled to trust Moses.

Finally, they asked Aaron to make a god of gold they could follow instead. It may come as a surprise, but Aaron gave in and made a golden calf, and the people worshipped it. Maybe Aaron thought Moses *wasn't* coming back. Maybe he thought the people would rebel. Maybe he thought he would have to be their new leader.

The people of Israel stopped believing that God had a Promised Land for them and decided they needed to follow their own hearts. God wasn't amused. Neither was Moses. . .

### EVENING

Don't settle for words that make you feel better about sin. Seek God's words. Discover the ways you're breaking God's law. Trust that He forgives and can help you in all future decisions.

*Lord, I want to remember that You're the only God worth following. You've given guidance in the Bible that helps me know what to do and what to avoid. May I refuse to think I can accept only the rules I like or can make up my own rules. Amen.*

# DAY 175

# HOLY BOLDNESS

*For I am not ashamed of this Good News about Christ. It is the power of God at work, saving everyone who believes—the Jew first and also the Gentile.*

ROMANS 1:16 NLT

## MORNING

If Jesus was still physically on earth, and you met Him walking along a street, would you be ashamed to admit you know Him? Imagine living when He was here as a human. He had a lot of enemies—people who felt threatened by His power or who couldn't admit He was more than merely a man. Some admired Him but were afraid to be seen with Him in broad daylight, like Nicodemus, who came to talk to Jesus at night. Have you ever pictured yourself in their place?

We like to think we'd be among His friends, but even those closest to Him were frightened. Think about Peter, one of Jesus' intimate companions. He denied he even knew the Lord when the Roman soldiers whipped Jesus and eventually crucified Him. . .

## EVENING

Everything Jesus did was based on His love for you and me. He came to earth, lived a sinless life, and died a horrible death in our place. But sometimes it is hard to speak up and share the good news of what Jesus has done.

Only those who accept the truth that Jesus is the only way will spend eternity with God in heaven. If we love Him and love our friends, how can we be ashamed to open our mouths to share the gospel?

*Dear Lord Jesus, let me never be ashamed or too timid to tell others about the awesome power of Your love. Amen.*

# DAY 176

# THE BREAD OF LIFE: OUR SUSTENANCE

*Jesus replied, "I am the bread of life. Whoever comes to me will never be hungry again. Whoever believes in me will never be thirsty."*
JOHN 6:35 NLT

## MORNING

Jesus calls Himself the "bread" of life. What is bread? Bread is nourishment for our bodies. When we eat it, one of our body's needs is satisfied.

Your relationship with Jesus is like the bread you eat: It satisfies you and supplies you with what you need. As you draw on that relationship with Him, you'll find your spirit and soul satisfied in a way that nothing else can accomplish.

The interesting thing about bread is that eating it once doesn't fulfill your need for food forever. You eat over and over again to satisfy your body's hunger.

In the same way, your spirit is sustained through coming back to Jesus on a regular basis.

## EVENING

Prayer, worship, reading the Bible, and focusing your thoughts on His goodness and love—all these things are ways you can come to the Father and discover that He is the one who completes your life. When He fills your interests, your love, and your time, you'll find that the material things of this world have no pull on you. Jesus has satisfied your soul.

*Jesus, You are my satisfaction. Today, I will let my spirit and soul be filled with the satisfaction that comes from my relationship with You and nothing else. Amen.*

# DAY 177

## HE'LL TAKE CARE OF IT

*Don't worry about anything; instead, pray about everything. Tell God what you need, and thank him for all he has done. Then you will experience God's peace, which exceeds anything we can understand. His peace will guard your hearts and minds as you live in Christ Jesus.*
PHILIPPIANS 4:6–7 NLT

### MORNING

Worry is a condition of missing faith. Worry unintentionally says that you don't believe God can handle the difficulties you face. Prayer is the intentional refusal to allow worry to hold power over you.

If you're struggling with something or someone, give up on worry. It'll never change the outcome of the time you've invested. Thank God in advance for taking care of things.

An exceedingly wonderful peace is your gift for making a worry deposit with God. You don't have to worry about it, and He won't worry about it. He'll just take care of it.

### EVENING

How often should you worry? Never! When should you stop worrying? Right now! How can you stop worrying? Pray! When can you pray? Right now!

*Dear God, You say I should tell You what I need, so I'm here to say I need to stop worrying. It's easy to think about what's happening right now and the things that could happen. I need faith enough to trust that You've got this. Help me hold on to Your gift of peace by refusing to worry. Amen.*

# DAY 178

## A PEACEFUL HOME

*My people will live in a peaceful settlement,*
*in secure dwellings, and in undisturbed resting places.*
ISAIAH 32:18 NASB

### MORNING

Home is where you should feel safe and most free to be yourself—a place of safety from the outside world. Your home should reflect a strength and quiet confidence that is welcoming to your family, friends, and God.

The atmosphere of your home starts with the people in it. It takes a conscious effort and true discipline to leave the world's cares at the threshold of the front door and stay committed to the pursuit of a peaceful home.

Perhaps you've been running all day and you need to slow down. Take a few minutes before you enter your home and find your focus. Let go of the day; shake off the frustration of school, relationships, and other concerns. Decide to be proactive and peaceful instead of reactive and defensive.

### EVENING

When you enter your home each day, step across the threshold into a place of peace. Put a smile on your face and make a deliberate effort to relax. Speak to your family in a soft, positive, encouraging voice. Make your home a place of peace today.

*Lord, thank You for reminding me to cast off the cares of the day.*
*Help me to bring peace, harmony, and unity into my home. Amen.*

# DAY 179

# GET A LIFE

*In him was life, and that life was the light of all mankind.*
JOHN 1:4 NIV

## MORNING

Do you have a life?

You've probably been asked that more than once. Having a life usually means you have a busy social calendar with lots of places to go, things to do, and friends to meet. The world tells us that those are the things that bring happiness and fulfillment. The Bible defines having a life a bit differently.

In John 14:6, Jesus tells us that He is the way, the truth, and the life. He is our only way to our Father in heaven. Jesus is the light of the world and the only one who can fill us with life. Real life. Deep fulfillment. A life that makes a difference and lasts for eternity.

## EVENING

Do you have the light of Christ living inside you, or do you need to get a life? A place to go, things to do, and people to see don't mean a whole lot at the end of your life here on earth. You will never look back and wish you could have attended one more social event.

Jesus is the only way to eternal life. Make sure you have a life before you leave!

*Dear Jesus, I want You to light up my soul and give me eternal life. Help me to live my life for You. Amen.*

## DAY 180

# HE CREATED EACH UNIQUELY

*The sun has one kind of splendor, the moon another and the stars another; and star differs from star in splendor.*
1 CORINTHIANS 15:41 NIV

### MORNING

People who believe the earth came into being by chance can't fathom a God in heaven who spoke the world into existence and now sustains it. But the redeemed know better. We understand that God not only created everything, but He also keeps it in smooth running order. And everything He does has a purpose.

### EVENING

The sun has one kind of glory and the moon another. Individual stars have yet a different glory. Humans don't even know how many stars exist, but God knows the exact number because He created each one uniquely.

Many people go through life trying to make sense of a supposedly random universe. But we can rest in the knowledge that God isn't fretting or trying to figure it all out. He knows exactly what He's doing.

*Lord of heaven and earth, maker of all things, I worship You! Amen.*

# DAY 181

## A MATTER OF FAITH

*Now faith is being sure we will get what we hope for. It is being sure of what we cannot see.*
HEBREWS 11:1 NLV

### MORNING

*Am I crazy to believe in this?* Has that thought ever run through your mind when you were thinking about the virgin birth, Moses and the burning bush, or the Resurrection?

Logically, these events don't seem to make much sense. After all, each was a onetime incident that no one can re-create. Many people question the truth of these biblical accounts.

In some circles, people have become so doubtful that they try to explain away these phenomena. But such would-be Christians have missed the point, haven't they? Of course none of these events can be explained. It's a matter of *faith*, not intellectual "sight."

### EVENING

As we exercise our faith, even though we can't work out exactly how the miraculous events of the Bible happened, we can begin to see how it's all part of God's plan.

Then we're believing in Jesus.

*Lord, I praise You for being so marvelous and powerful that You boggle my mind. Help me trust in Your power. I want to walk by faith. Amen.*

# DAY 182

## HEARTBROKEN

*The Lord is near to those who have a broken heart.*
*And He saves those who are broken in spirit.*
PSALM 34:18 NLV

### MORNING

Unless you are fond of country music, you don't hear people talking much about broken hearts these days. But they still happen to everyone at least once. You get dumped by someone you really liked. How could you have misread all the signals? How could something that seemed so good turn out to be a nightmare? What did you do?

Most of us turn into hermits for a while, dissecting the failed relationship over and over, trying to figure out what happened. Fortunately, friends put an end to that pretty soon, the unromantic fools. They drag you out of the house or sit in it with you until you go out in self-defense. They tell you to get on with your life, and they fix you up with someone new. They nag you back into emotional health. . .

### EVENING

God's doing a little work on you after a breakup, girl. Unlike your friends, He doesn't nag or fix you up with someone new. He's just there for you when you need Him, and He always understands.

*Father, thank You for comforting me when I go and get my heart broken. I know that if it happens again, You'll be there for me as You always are. Amen.*

# DAY 183

## BE A CHEERFUL WORKER

*"Restrain your voice from weeping and your eyes from tears, for your work will be rewarded," declares the* Lord.

Jeremiah 31:16 NIV

### MORNING

The prophet Jeremiah always said exactly what he was told to say. He wasn't noted for being diplomatic or for worrying about what others would think of his blunt words. In this case, he was saying, "Stop whining and get back to work. You'll get your reward eventually."

But "eventually" doesn't buy things now, and we get impatient waiting for our rewards. We can have instant hamburgers, instant communication, and instant friends. Why not instant rewards?

### EVENING

Jeremiah understood a lot about work. Nobody likes a crybaby coworker who constantly complains about their work and its unfulfilling poverty wage. Those who go about their work cheerfully are much more likely to make a good impression and reap some rewards. Which type of worker would you prefer if you were the boss? Which type are you?

*Father, help me be a cheerful worker who can patiently wait for my reward. Keep me pleasant to be near, not a complainer. Amen.*

# DAY 184

## BLESSED REDEEMER

*For God so loved the world that he gave his one and only Son, that whoever believes in him shall not perish but have eternal life.*

JOHN 3:16 NIV

### MORNING

*Compassion* is "sympathetic consciousness of others' distress together with a desire to alleviate it" (*Merriam-Webster*). Oh, how our God loved us and showed His compassion. He knew we were sinful and were in peril. Our eternal lives were at stake. And He had a plan. He provided a way for redemption.

Despite the fact that we did not deserve His unmerited favor—grace—He gave it to us anyway. He looked down on mankind and desired to bridge the separation between us. He sent His Son, Jesus, to die on the cross for our sins so we might live the resurrected life. Once we've accepted this gift, we can rejoice!

### EVENING

We were in distress, and God came to the rescue. What a mighty God we serve! And how He loves us! The rescuing shepherd came for His flock. He bore what we deserved because He had such compassion. True love, which our Father gives, is eternal. He loved us before we loved Him. What an amazing concept He desires us to grasp! Know today that your heavenly Father loves you.

*Dear Lord, how gracious and loving You are to me! Thank You, Father, for Your arms around me this day. Amen.*

## DAY 185

# LOVE THE UNLOVABLE?

*"Bless those who curse you. Pray for those who hurt you."*
LUKE 6:28 NLT

### MORNING

Do you know anyone like this? Lydia was demanding, incorrigible, and cynical. She manipulated every situation, and if she couldn't, she whined and complained. Gossip was the norm for her, and she would often spread unsubstantiated rumors. Some family members and friends tolerated her shifting moods and bursts of unrestrained anger in an effort to keep peace. Others simply distanced themselves.

So how do we bless those who curse us? Writer Ralph Waldo Emerson once said, "If you would lift me, you must be on higher ground." Christians stand on higher ground. We stand in our faith in Jesus Christ and His Holy Word. We stand on Christ's shoulders to lift others to receive the same saving grace and forgiveness that we embrace.

### EVENING

We *can* bless those who curse or hurt us. Because Jesus based everything He did, and does, on His love for us, how can we do anything less? That doesn't mean we need to befriend every nasty person or accept unacceptable behavior. But it does mean that we are to pray for and attempt to understand and love the unlovable because God loves them.

The Lord never calls us to a task without equipping us to fulfill it. As we pray, He helps us to see that person through His eyes.

*Father, help me look past the person and see the need. Amen.*

# DAY 186

## THE HAND OF RESCUE

*Is anyone crying for help? God is listening, ready to rescue you.*
Psalm 34:17 MSG

### MORNING

A person dangles from a tree root just over the cliff's edge. He shouts for help. If he falls, he'll be injured or killed. He needs to be rescued. Another person hears his cries and makes his way to the edge of the cliff. He offers a hand and pulls the man to safety.

It seems like a simple exchange, but there were decisions to be made. The first man had to recognize his situation and ask for help. The second man had to come close enough to offer help. The first man also had to decide whether he'd trust the second man to help him.

You're the first person, and Jesus is the second. . .

### EVENING

Jesus can rescue you if you cry for help—and if you accept His help. As you learn more about the Lord who reached down and drew you to safety, you'll find a richer and deeper sense of gratitude. The one who rescued you was the only one who could answer your call.

Cry out for help. The Lord is listening.

*Lord, I can't rescue myself from wrong thinking and bad decision-making. Time and again, You've rescued me from spiritual cliffs. May I always accept Your hand of rescue. Teach me how to avoid the cliffs, and help me to remember the mercy I found in You. Amen.*

# DAY 187

## CLOUD AND FIRE TRAINING

*The cloud of the Lord was over the tabernacle by day,*
*and fire was in the cloud by night, in the sight of*
*all the Israelites during all their travels.*

Exodus 40:38 NIV

### MORNING

Moses spoke to the miracle-performing God. He heard God answer in return. God offered to give the people the land He'd promised at the start of their journey. Their refusal to accept it meant that more than a million people would live as nomads for four decades.

They were disobedient, but God invited them back to a place of trust. If they wouldn't trust that He could give them the land He'd promised, then maybe they would learn to trust when God led them using a cloud by day and a pillar of fire by night. . .

### EVENING

For forty years the Israelites watched the cloud and pillar of fire. When they moved, the people moved. They learned to trust God and follow Him.

Maybe you're in the middle of your journey. You might feel that you've blown the early opportunities God had for you. But He's still leading. Each new day brings an opportunity to follow Him. Your real destination has always been toward His plan. You're closer today than you think.

*Lord, I once refused to follow You. Thanks for encouraging me to return from my disobedience. Thanks for considering my life worth the effort. May each decision I make help me follow Your plan. In Jesus' name, amen.*

## DAY 188

# NATURE'S TESTIMONY

*For ever since the world was created, people have seen the earth and sky. Through everything God made, they can clearly see his invisible qualities—his eternal power and divine nature. So they have no excuse for not knowing God.*

ROMANS 1:20 NLT

### MORNING

All of creation testifies to the nature of God. To get to know God, we read the Bible and pray and go to church and do all the normal stuff Christians are "supposed" to do. But have you ever reflected on nature and what it shows you about God?

Try it! What does a sunset tell you about God? Sunsets show me that God has an artistic nature. He loves color and variety. He is a master artist who likes to paint the sky. Sunsets also reveal to me the faithfulness of God. The sun rises and sets—every day, without fail. He is steady. He is faithful. We can always count on Him.

### EVENING

What do you learn about God from nature? What does grass teach you? What about trees, flowers, and ants? The ocean, mountains, and prairies? Lions, cows, and dogs? As you go about your day, take time to observe the nature around you and contemplate what invisible qualities it reveals to you about God.

*God, it's so amazing to think You've hidden a piece of Yourself in every part of creation. Open my eyes to see You in the nature around me. Amen.*

# DAY 189

## VISION IMPAIRMENT

*Jesus said, "My friend, go ahead and do what you have come for."*
MATTHEW 26:50 NLT

### MORNING

Judas may have felt that Jesus couldn't be trusted. There were many in first-century Israel who thought the Messiah would be a savior in a political and military sense. Judas may have followed Jesus because he thought Jesus was *that* Messiah. When Jesus explained that He would die, Judas may have concluded that Jesus wasn't the Messiah and that he'd been misled into following Him.

Judas listened to what Jesus said. But in the end, Jesus' purpose wasn't a match for Judas' ambition. Popular opinion was shifting away from Jesus, and Judas was willing to help the opposition (the religious leaders) find an opportunity to silence Jesus.

Judas handed Jesus over at night. Jesus' other disciples fled the arrest scene. It turned out that Judas was the one who couldn't be trusted. . .

### EVENING

Think about how many people hear the message of love and forgiveness Jesus brought to mankind but are totally unmoved by the good news. Not every encounter with God results in a life change. Sadly, the promise of forgiveness doesn't always inspire trust.

*God, may Your Word penetrate deep into the core of who I am so I become more like You. It's easy to assume that Your plans are meant for those who are smarter, richer, or more famous. You also came for me. Help me keep my eyes focused on You. Amen.*

# DAY 190

## DRINK FROM THE FOUNTAIN

*How exquisite your love, O God! How eager we are to run under your wings, to eat our fill at the banquet you spread as you fill our tankards with Eden spring water. You're a fountain of cascading light, and you open our eyes to light.*

PSALM 36:7–9 MSG

### MORNING

Today's passage is filled with pictures of God's love. His love is defined by wings, banquets, tankards, and cascading light. These may sound like odd examples of love, but keep reading to see how each of these items reveals the heart of a trustworthy God. . .

### EVENING

*Wings*—The psalmist shows a God who shields, shades, and protects. You're always safe when you accept the security of His wings.

*Banquet*—God wants to be clear. His love chooses to meet your needs. He loves you, and your needs are important to Him.

*Water*—You can't live without water. Like water, love offers refreshment and clear thinking.

*Light*—Light doesn't just eliminate darkness. It also allows you to discover things that were hidden in the shadows.

Love God enough to trust Him and gain access to protection, compassion, refreshment, and wisdom.

*Lord, You chose to love me. I can't offer You anything but my heart. You demonstrate love in so many ways that when I accept it, I begin to understand the value of Your protection, care, and wisdom. Help me trust You so I can learn more about Your heart. In Jesus' name, amen.*

# DAY 191

## PLEASE DON'T INTERRUPT ME!

*While Jesus was yet talking, a man came from the house of the leader of the place of worship. This man said to Jairus, "Your daughter is dead. Do not make the Teacher use anymore of His time."*

LUKE 8:49 NLV

### MORNING

Don't you dislike being interrupted? If you're like most people, you hate having to jump from one task to another.

Welcome to Jesus' sphere of ministry. He was continually being interrupted and called to go to another place, to touch another sick person, to minister to another need. In fact, in the story above, Jesus had been deterred from His journey to the house of Jairus by an anemic woman who reached out to touch the hem of His robe. While He talked with her, a runner came and interrupted the conversation, bringing the news that the daughter of Jairus (the leader of the synagogue) had died; there was no need for Jesus to come now, they thought.

Would you have been upset if you had been Jairus? What kind of thoughts were running through his mind? Do you think he was tempted to lash out at the woman who detained Jesus?

### EVENING

Jesus had time for both the runner and the sick woman. He did not work on the schedule of others. He continued to Jairus' home and brought the little girl back to life.

In our lives there will be interruptions, but Jesus showed us that people are more important than a schedule. Taking time to minister to our family, friends, and neighbors is a way that we can follow Him in the commonplace details of living.

*Lord, teach me to accept interruptions and see them as opportunities to identify with You. In Jesus' name, amen.*

# DAY 192

## WITH YOU ALWAYS

*"Go and make disciples of all nations, baptizing them in the name of the Father and of the Son and of the Holy Spirit, and teaching them to obey everything I have commanded you. And surely I am with you always, to the very end of the age."*

MATTHEW 28:19–20 NIV

### MORNING

Jesus made it clear to His disciples that instead of returning to their old jobs, they would be world changers. They weren't to stay home. They were to bring the good news they'd heard to people of every nation. Just as they were discipled by Jesus, so they were to disciple others. They were to lead by example. They had marching orders, and the world was their mission field.

### EVENING

If the disciples had any doubts as to the sanity of this new venture, they were to step forth in courage after Jesus left. The trust they had in Him would enable them to do great things.

You've also been given a big job. Learn; then share what you've learned. Obey; then encourage others to obey. Identify with Jesus; then invite others to trust. The benefit? Jesus said, "I am with you always, to the very end of the age."

*Dear God, help me to remember that every generation needs to hear Your message, and every generation needs ambassadors to share that message. May I use my voice, actions, and life to share the truth that even today You are with Your children. Amen.*

# DAY 193

## HARD-HEART SOIL

*Do not merely listen to the word,*
*and so deceive yourselves. Do what it says.*
JAMES 1:22 NIV

### MORNING

Sometimes we can be the hard-hearted soil Jesus talked about in His first parable, which He called the parable of the sower. He illustrated four responses people have every time the seed, the Word of God, is dispersed to them. A hard-hearted response keeps the seed from penetrating, and Satan steals it. If our hearts are rocky, we have no root and the seed starves and dies. A thorny heart strangles the seedling. If our heart soil is good, the seed is sustained and bears fruit.

### EVENING

We Christians tend to think we are the good soil Jesus described. Yet the point of the parable is doing what God says, not merely hearing it. When we practice God's Word and live by its principles, we will be fruitful, and God will give more seed (truth) for us to respond to (Mark 4:24–25). However, we Christians can also have hard hearts that negate God's truth. Three times in Mark, Jesus even rebuked His disciples for having hard hearts (Mark 6:52; 8:17; 16:14).

Therefore, we must be careful to practice God's truth, not merely to hear it or learn it. What we believe must show up in how we behave.

*Lord Jesus, help me to cultivate my heart so that I have a good response to Your Word and that it will affect what I say and do. May I not negate, neglect, or neutralize Your truth by my careless response, but nurture it instead. I want to live it, not lose it. Amen.*

# DAY 194

## CHANGE THE WAY YOU THINK

*I ask you from my heart to give your bodies to God because of His loving-kindness to us. Let your bodies be a living and holy gift given to God. He is pleased with this kind of gift. This is the true worship that you should give Him. Do not act like the sinful people of the world. Let God change your life. First of all, let Him give you a new mind. Then you will know what God wants you to do. And the things you do will be good and pleasing and perfect.*

ROMANS 12:1–2 NLV

### MORNING

Our feelings, thoughts, and behaviors are intricately connected. Take fear, for example. We "feel" fear before we know we are afraid—our hearts begin to race and our breathing becomes shallow. The thinking follows: *There is danger.* We react based on our thinking. We run or we fight. Our actions are based on the conclusions we draw. Thus, our thoughts are powerful motivators for our behaviors.

In Romans, the apostle Paul challenges us to change the way we think.

### EVENING

Instead of thinking like the people of the world, we are called to interpret our feelings differently. The world says to take care of yourself, you're number one, the power is within you. In Romans, Paul challenges us to think differently. Jesus came to be a living sacrifice, and He beckons us to do the same. We can do this only if God changes us. This passage says that when we think differently, we will behave differently. We will know how to do everything that is good and pleasing to Him. It begins with your thoughts. Turn them over to God.

*Father, please change the way I think so that I will know how to behave in a way that honors You. Amen.*

# DAY 195

## OUR FAITHFUL HIGH PRIEST

*For this reason he had to be made like them, fully human in every way, in order that he might become a merciful and faithful high priest in service to God, and that he might make atonement for the sins of the people.*
HEBREWS 2:17 NIV

### MORNING

Jesus was fully human and yet also completely God. Our minds can't grasp that, but we believe it. If He hadn't been human, He couldn't have impacted society as He did. Even those who don't believe in God admit that Jesus was a person who lived on earth at that point in history. People who haven't put their trust in Him believe in Him the same way they believe in Napoleon or George Washington, but they don't doubt His existence.

Because of His humanity, He had the ability to sin. Don't kid yourself by thinking Jesus couldn't sin. If He hadn't had the potential to sin, He would not have the authority to save us through His death.

### EVENING

Coming as a person equipped Jesus with a unique understanding of what people go through. Even though as God He knew because of His omniscience, as a human He experienced the same things we do. High priests of Bible times made sacrifices to cover sin. Jesus, our faithful High Priest, made the ultimate sacrifice, giving His sinless life to erase our sin—forever. No other figure in history lived a sinless life, died as a criminal, and was resurrected. Beyond that, He still lives and changes lives.

*Lord Jesus, how I love You! I am amazed to think about all You've done for me. You are magnificent!*

# DAY 196

## FREEDOM REIGNS

*For the Lord is the Spirit, and wherever the Spirit of the Lord is, there is freedom.*
2 CORINTHIANS 3:17 NLT

### MORNING

We are free in so many ways because of what Christ did for us on the cross. We are free from death, free from sin, free from guilt, free from shame—and the list goes on. If you have ever felt trapped by someone or something in your life and then were set free, you know that amazing feeling of relief!

That is how living our lives through Christ should feel each day. Freedom reigns in Christ. We can breathe again.

### EVENING

Your past doesn't have to haunt you. The Lord can use it to help change the life of someone else, so don't be ashamed anymore. You are truly free. John 8:36 (NIV) says, "If the Son sets you free, you will be free indeed."

If you are still struggling with thoughts of guilt and shame, ask the Lord to free you from your past, and begin to live a life in which freedom reigns!

*Dear Jesus, thank You for taking away my sin and making me free. Help me to live like I believe that. Amen.*

## DAY 197

# A PERSON OF INTEGRITY

*Love and truth form a good leader; sound leadership is founded on loving integrity.*
PROVERBS 20:28 MSG

### MORNING

If you're a reality television watcher, you've observed many examples of a lack of integrity in the contestants. Honesty falls by the wayside, as it's often every person for himself. The backstabbing, gossiping, putting others down for the benefit of self, and many other actions exhibit a lack of morals.

God wants us to live a life of integrity. Many benefits come as a result of establishing and living by godly morals. One that is mentioned in the book of Proverbs is sound leadership. A good leader has most likely achieved that position because she has integrity. It's a quality that is attractive to those around her, and she will be respected because of her example. She will be known for holding to a strong moral code, treating others in an honorable manner.

### EVENING

Ask God today to help you live a life of integrity. Spend time in His Word and in prayer so that you can develop the godly principles that others will see in you. In doing so, you will be a shining example for Him.

*Dear Father, make me a person of integrity so that I can bring honor to Your name, as well as bring unity to my surroundings. Amen.*

# DAY 198

## IN HIS HANDS

*"So do not fear, for I am with you; do not be dismayed,*
*for I am your God. I will strengthen you and help you;*
*I will uphold you with my righteous right hand."*

ISAIAH 41:10 NIV

### MORNING

On a sunny day in the park, a father held his young daughter upside down. The girl squealed and laughed with delight as her daddy swung her by her ankles, back and forth over the ground. It never occurred to the child that she could possibly be dropped on her head!

Children often express total faith in their parents, believing that as long as they're in their parents' hands, they'll be safe. Kids will enjoy their dads' hair-raising "airplane rides" without the least hesitation—as the girl in the park demonstrated when her father finally lowered her safely to the ground, and she yelled, "Again! Again!"

### EVENING

Imagine how much more we could enjoy our lives if we would simply realize that we are in our heavenly Father's hands. There should be no fear of any accidental drops as long as our Lord has us in His grip. Our Father holds us securely. . .and He will not let us fall.

*Lord, forgive me for sometimes forgetting that I*
*am in Your safe and loving hands. Amen.*

# DAY 199

## DO UNTO OTHERS

*"So in everything, do to others what you would have them do to you, for this sums up the Law and the Prophets."*
MATTHEW 7:12 NIV

### MORNING

Jana and her dad sat in the crowded doctor's office; she was miserable with a head cold and was barely paying attention to her surroundings. If only she could get in to see the doctor and get home and to bed!

She barely noticed the grimacing man across from her until another patient told the nurse, "He's in more pain than I am. Please take him first."

Jana admired the woman, but guilt stabbed her heart. *I never realized he was in such pain,* she thought. *If I had, would I have done the same, even though it meant a longer wait?*

### EVENING

Doing good for others—especially those outside our circle of friends—means tuning in to their needs. Do we block ourselves behind a fake spiritual wall and a "don't touch" mentality? Or do we open ourselves to others, talk to hurting people, and offer them Jesus' help?

After all, that's only a small part of what He gave us.

*Jesus, reaching out is hard when I get boxed into myself. Open my heart and eyes so I can help others. Amen.*

# DAY 200

# PUTTING GOD TO WORK

*Since ancient times no one has heard, no ear has perceived, no eye has seen any God besides you, who acts on behalf of those who wait for him.*

ISAIAH 64:4 NIV

## MORNING

Prayer affects the three realms of existence: the divine, the angelic, and the human. God, angels, and people are subject to the rules of prayer, which God has established. Prayer puts God to work in what is prayed for by His people. Prayer also puts us to work. If we do not pray, God is not sent into action. Prayerlessness excludes God and leaves us at the mercy of our own circumstances. Understanding this, why would we not pray at all times and about everything?

## EVENING

Prayer puts the power into God's hands and keeps it there. Prayer is a privilege. It gives us the ability to ask the God of the universe for action. We should not hesitate.

*Father, thank You for the beautiful and powerful gift of prayer. Prayer puts us in a divine partnership with You. Please help us to remember that we need one another to make prayer the life- and situation-changer that it is. We love how You continue to involve us in Your work. You are amazing, Lord! Amen.*

# DAY 201

## THE RIGHT FOCUS

*Turning your ear to wisdom and applying your heart to understanding—indeed, if you call out for insight and cry aloud for understanding, and if you look for it as for silver and search for it as for hidden treasure, then you will understand the fear of the Lord and find the knowledge of God.*

PROVERBS 2:2–5 NIV

### MORNING

If you've ever lost something—your book, your glasses, or your school papers, for example—you've no doubt searched everywhere. Sometimes when you finally find it, you realize that in your haste, you simply overlooked the very thing you were frantically searching for.

It's all about focus! Even when you're looking in the right direction, you can still miss something because your focus is slightly off. This can be the challenge in our relationship with God.

### EVENING

We can ask God a question and be really intent on getting the answer, only to find that His response to us was there all along—just not the answer we expected or wanted.

Frustration and stress can keep us from clearly seeing the things God puts before us. Time spent in prayer and meditation on God's Word can often wash away the dirt and grime of the day-to-day and provide a clear picture of God's intentions for our lives. Step outside the pressure and into His presence, and get the right focus for whatever you're facing today.

*Lord, help me to avoid distractions and keep my eyes on You. Amen.*

## DAY 202

# KEEP YOUR EYES ON JESUS

*May I never boast except in the cross of our Lord Jesus Christ, through which the world has been crucified to me, and I to the world.*

GALATIANS 6:14 NIV

### MORNING

Stacie went to a great church. She was growing in Christ as she never had before. When she and other members of her church visited other churches, they always mentioned that theirs was the best church around.

One day Stacie's friend Paul, who went to another church, shocked her by asking if she was more attached to her church than to Jesus: "It seems you think your church can never be wrong and that every church should be just like it."

At first she was mad, but later Stacie caught Paul's drift. Nothing should be more important than the Savior in her life. Though they went to different churches, she and Paul were brother and sister in Christ. If she acted as if going to her church was more important than knowing Jesus, she was out of line spiritually.

### EVENING

Support your church; think well of it, but realize that God works through other congregations too. Keep your eyes on Jesus, and you won't go wrong.

*Lord, I don't want churchgoing to get in the way of my faith. Build me up in You, not in a building or way of worship. In Jesus' name, amen.*

# DAY 203

## BRINGING US TO COMPLETION

*Being confident of this, that he who began a good work in you will carry it on to completion until the day of Christ Jesus.*
PHILIPPIANS 1:6 NIV

### MORNING

Remember the old saying "If at first you don't succeed, try, try again"? That's an encouraging statement, but it doesn't tell us how many times we should try. It doesn't tell us when we should throw in the towel and give up.

While there may be an appropriate time to give up on a certain skill or project, we should never give up on people. We should continue to hope, to pray, and to love. After all, that's what God does for us.

### EVENING

No matter how many times we fail, no matter how many times we mess up, we know God hasn't written us off. He's still working on us. He still loves us. He knows our potential because He created us, and He won't stop moving us forward until His plan is completed.

Those of us who have been adopted into God's family through believing in His Son, Jesus Christ, can be confident that God won't give up on us. No matter how messed up our lives may seem, He will continue working in us until His plan is fulfilled and we stand before Him perfect and complete.

*Dear Father, thank You for not giving up on me. Help me to cooperate with Your process of fulfilling Your purpose in me. Amen.*

# DAY 204

## THE BETRAYER

*These are the twelve he appointed: Simon (to whom he gave the name Peter), James son of Zebedee and his brother John (to them he gave the name Boanerges, which means "sons of thunder"), Andrew, Philip, Bartholomew, Matthew, Thomas, James son of Alphaeus, Thaddaeus, Simon the Zealot and Judas Iscariot, who betrayed him.*

MARK 3:16–19 NIV

### MORNING

To betray is to reveal information about a friend or companion to someone who is their enemy. Jesus had twelve disciples, but only one was defined as a betrayer. Judas betrayed Jesus for thirty pieces of silver. He severed his relationship with Jesus and the disciples and separated himself from trust.

There is a reason you appreciate people who can be trusted. They're more likely to give honest answers. They keep private conversations quiet. They know that betrayal removes any shred of trust.

### EVENING

Those who can be trusted are remembered for their integrity and kindness. Those who can't be trusted are usually remembered for their lack of integrity and mercy.

You've probably met both kinds of people. Jesus did too.

*Lord, help me see the act of betrayal the way You do. Help me remember that to betray means to be separated from friends, to make enemies, and to render it much harder to make friends. To betray means that I'm not obeying You. Help me follow Your instructions. Help me remember that You're my friend. Amen.*

# DAY 205

# REDISCOVERED PRAISE

*Why are you down in the dumps, dear soul? Why are you crying the blues? Fix my eyes on God—soon I'll be praising again. He puts a smile on my face. He's my God.*

PSALM 42:5 MSG

## MORNING

When you are facing disappointment, distress, and discomfort, it's easy to think God has abandoned you. You can assume you've been abandoned and forsaken. In those moments, you might conclude that you're on your own.

When you're in the middle of personal pain, God wants you to remember that the story isn't finished. You haven't seen His rescue. You can't understand the plot twists that will be revealed in the next chapter of your story.

It's easy to trust God when everything you want is coming true. But it's easy to abandon trust when struggles drop by.

## EVENING

The psalmist suggests that instead of throwing a pity party on bad days, you should change what you're looking at. When you focus on God's goodness, praise is the result of your redirect in thinking. Remembering God's past faithfulness reminds you that since God never fails or forsakes His people, your present crisis is no match for His ongoing faithfulness. Believe it, and rediscover worship.

*Dear God, I don't know why I'm so easily distracted. I don't know why I can't remember that You're bigger than my worst moments. Help me focus on who You are. Help me recall all You do. Amen.*

## DAY 206

# THE PROMISE

*This letter is from Paul, chosen by the will of God to be an apostle of Christ Jesus. I have been sent out to tell others about the life he has promised through faith in Christ Jesus.*

2 TIMOTHY 1:1 NLT

### MORNING

The apostle Paul realized the moment Jesus Christ revealed Himself that the new life he was granted was not his own doing. Because of his total dependence on Jesus, Paul became a humble, outspoken ambassador for his Lord. When any of us have a revelation that we have nothing without the Lord, all we want to boast about is our dependence on Him.

Paul apparently was thrilled to be counted worthy of being an apostle. He knew that God Himself chose him. What is an apostle? It's more than a disciple, which means a follower. An apostle is described as an advocate, a promoter, a supporter, or a proponent. Apostles went on from discipleship to tell the world about Jesus.

### EVENING

The Bible says we didn't choose God; He chose us. Whether we're chosen with a dramatic encounter like Paul on the road to Damascus or in the quiet of our own home, we are His very own. Everything about our relationship is His doing, not our own. So, when we think of it, there's great joy knowing He selected us to be in His family. All we can do is thank Him and tell others about the wonderful life He makes possible.

*Lord Jesus, I am so privileged, knowing You chose me. I matter to You! Thank You, and show me how to be Your advocate and tell others the fabulous things You've done for me. Amen.*

# DAY 207

## CHRIST AS ADVOCATE

*And if anyone sins, we have an Advocate with the Father, Jesus Christ the righteous.*

1 JOHN 2:1 NASB

### MORNING

An advocate is someone who speaks in support or favor of another person. This is what Christ does for you. There is no logical reason for Him to want or need to defend you. In comparison to what He has done, none of us has done anything in return for Him. It is unfathomable love that He would speak on your behalf to the Father when you sin. Those very sins caused Him such suffering. By earthly standards, one would think that He would want nothing to do with those who sent Him to His death. All you can do is wonder at the purity of His love and thank Him for the utter selflessness He displays on your behalf.

### EVENING

When you sin, go to Christ. There is no one better to be your advocate because there is no one more righteous. Ask Him to intercede for you to the Father. Don't hold back anything from Him.

*Lord, I need You to intercede for me every day. I cannot stand before the holiness of the Father covered in my filthy sins. Take them from me, and be my defense. Your righteousness is my covering. Thank You for loving me so perfectly even though I'm the reason You suffered so intensely. Help me to begin to fathom this kind of love. Amen.*

# DAY 208

## LIVING A COMPLETE LIFE

*It is a good thing to receive wealth from God and the good health to enjoy it.*
ECCLESIASTES 5:19 NLT

### MORNING

You've probably heard the term *workaholic*, but you may be surprised to find that people really can work themselves to death. The Japanese word *karoshi* is translated literally as "death from overwork," or occupational sudden death. The major medical causes of karoshi deaths are heart attack and stroke due to stress.

As you become an adult, it's vital for you to find a balance in your life between hard work and rest. While you will need to earn a living to provide finances to meet your needs, you will also want to pay attention to your physical, mental, emotional, and spiritual needs.

### EVENING

God has promised to supply all your needs, but it takes action on your part. Seeking wisdom for your situation and asking God to direct you to make the right decisions will help you find a well-balanced life that will produce success coupled with the health to enjoy it. It may be as simple as realizing that a vacation is exactly what you need instead of working throughout the year and taking your vacation in cash to pay for new bedroom furniture.

Know when to press forward and when to stop and enjoy the life God has given you for His good pleasure—and yours!

*Lord, as I become an adult, I ask for Your wisdom to help me balance my life so I can be complete in every area of my life. Amen.*

# DAY 209

# FREEDOM

*Exercise your freedom by serving God, not by breaking the rules. Treat everyone you meet with dignity. Love your spiritual family. Revere God. Respect the government.*

1 PETER 2:16–17 MSG

## MORNING

As Christians in the United States, we can be thankful that we live in a free nation. Galatians 5:13 tells us that we are called to be free. We have freedom in Christ because of what He did for us on the cross. It's so important to remember that with this freedom comes great responsibility.

Paul tells us in 1 Corinthians 10:23 (NLV) that "we are allowed to do anything, but not everything is good for us to do. We are allowed to do anything, but not all things help us grow strong as Christians." We must be careful and responsible with our freedom. We must be careful that nothing we do causes harm to anyone else.

## EVENING

Are you a responsible Christian? Is there anything in your life that is causing someone in your life to stumble? Could it be the television shows you watch, the types of movies you frequent, or maybe even your spending habits? Take this to the Lord in prayer and ask Him to search your heart and show you anything that may be hindering another person in their walk with Christ.

*Father, help me to be responsible with my freedom. Please help me to change anything in my life that might be causing someone else to stumble. Amen.*

## DAY 210

# SHUT THE DOOR

*"When you pray, go into a room by yourself. After you have shut the door, pray to your Father Who is in secret. Then your Father Who sees in secret will reward you."*
MATTHEW 6:6 NLV

### MORNING

We all have lists: things to buy, things to do, and even things we want God to do. *Lord, I want. . .God, I need. . .and if You could please. . .*

He meets your needs because He loves you and wants to give you His best. Have you ever wondered what God wants? He wants you—your attention, affection, praise, and worship. He wants to be included in your life.

Prayer isn't just a time to give God our list; it is a time to enjoy each other's company, just as you would if you were to take time with a close personal friend—and that's really who He is. In the busyness of life, we must be careful that our "quiet time" never becomes insignificant because it's limited to the needs we feel we must tell God about. We must remember our most precious desire—just spending time with Him.

### EVENING

Find a moment tonight, shut out the rest of the world, and truly discover how little anything else matters but God. No one knows the path He's chosen for you quite like He does. Let Him point you to the truth and bring about the results He destined for you before the beginning of time.

*Father, forgive me for not taking time to spend with You. Help me to listen and include You in my life at all times. Amen.*

# DAY 211

## SING WITH ALL YOUR HEART

*Worship the Lord with gladness; come before him with joyful songs.*
Psalm 100:2 NIV

### MORNING

Some music sounds good to you—and some is just an irritating noise. But you've probably found out that your "noise" is another person's "sounds good."

Church music is part of the "noise"/"sounds good" debate. If your congregation likes the "oldies and moldies" of Christian music but you like the latest tunes on the Christian music charts, you may be tempted to hold your ears during services. Worse, those slow, dull songs may lull you to sleep.

Chances are, the music you can't stand is favored by your pastor or music leader. Maybe other church members have encouraged the music director to play it. Asking anyone to change it could start World War III.

This psalm doesn't mention the kind of music churches should play—it doesn't specify classical, pop, rock, or even Old Testament–style music. That's because the music isn't important—worshipping God is.

### EVENING

God deserves our praise, no matter what the song is. A joyful heart can always praise Him.

Whether or not your church is tuned in to your music style, sing with all your heart.

*Lord, I want to praise You, not start a war. Thank You for music I enjoy. Let me sing Your praises today. Amen.*

## DAY 212

# YOUR REPUTATION

*So Joseph's ten older brothers went down to Egypt to buy grain. But Jacob wouldn't let Joseph's younger brother, Benjamin, go with them, for fear some harm might come to him.*

GENESIS 42:3–4 NLT

### MORNING

Jacob might never have learned what happened the day Joseph disappeared, but he undoubtedly had some suspicions. Hadn't the favorite son died after he claimed he'd rule over his brothers? Jacob wasn't going to chance losing a second son.

Benjamin's ten brothers had earned themselves a reputation for being untrustworthy—and years after the incident, Jacob remembered it. . .

### EVENING

Getting a reputation isn't hard. People quickly judge your worth based on things you've done and what they've heard about you. Sometimes a reputation isn't deserved. But most often we've earned what we've gotten.

When people look at you, do they see something Jesus would be proud of? As a Christian, your reputation isn't just your own—it belongs to Jesus too. People judge Him by your life.

*I want others to see You in me, Lord, and I don't want to smudge the picture. Make me a trustworthy picture of Your love. Amen.*

# DAY 213

## TIME TO PRAISE

*I will praise you, Lord, among the nations; I will sing of you among the peoples. For great is your love, higher than the heavens; your faithfulness reaches to the skies.*

Psalm 108:3–4 NIV

### MORNING

Some days the praise just floats from your lips to God's ear. Whether it's your school life, social life, or spiritual life, not a cloud troubles your skies. Maybe you've recently had a victory in one aspect of life, and you can't thank God enough.

Or maybe you're up to your ears in troubles, and you're stretched thin spiritually. Every day becomes a challenge. *Praise* seems like a word meant for someone else.

Whether you've just seen God's salvation or you're holding on, depending on it, it's time to praise Him and tell the world of His faithfulness.

### EVENING

Your circumstances may have changed, but God hasn't. His love never left you, and He hasn't forgotten to be faithful. If times are good, you still need Him; if times are rotten, you *know* you need Him even more.

Because you trust Him, tell of His faithfulness. Even if you can't see it yet, it's coming!

*How can I thank You for Your faithfulness, Lord Jesus? Even when I don't see it, I know You're working for my good. Amen.*

# DAY 214

## HUMBLE SERVANT

*Jesus knew that the Father had put all things under his power, and that he had come from God and was returning to God; so he got up from the meal, took off his outer clothing, and wrapped a towel around his waist. After that, he poured water into a basin and began to wash his disciples' feet, drying them with the towel that was wrapped around him.*

JOHN 13:3–5 NIV

### MORNING

Imagine the twelve disciples in the upper room. Among them is the Son of God, with all authority given to Him by the Father. He has come to earth as a man and soon will return to heaven to sit at the Father's right hand. He puts a towel around His waist, pours water into a bowl, and kneels before His disciples. He begins to wash feet—one of the lowliest jobs of that day. The Lord of the universe, the living Word who speaks things into being and commands all things, makes a deliberate choice to get down on His knees and serve others. He handles their dusty feet, getting dirty Himself in order to make them clean.

### EVENING

In word and deed, Jesus teaches the disciples to follow His example. His humility is rooted in the quiet confidence of His relationship with His Father.

Are we willing to make a deliberate step to humble ourselves to serve others? Would we do the lowliest job? Will we enter the messiness of each other's lives?

*Lord, help me to follow Your example. Make me a humble servant. Amen.*

## DAY 215

# HEAVENLY APPRECIATION

*God is not unjust; he will not forget your work and the love you have shown him as you have helped his people and continue to help them.*
HEBREWS 6:10 NIV

### MORNING

Sometimes it seems our hard work is ignored. We sell a record number of lattes at the local coffee shop only to be told that we need to sell more pastries, or we spend days working on a school presentation that the teacher barely acknowledges. Our hard work seems unimportant, and we feel unappreciated.

Unfortunately, our work in the church can often feel the same way. We dutifully assume the role of greeter every Sunday, or we consistently wash communion cups each week. We spend each Sunday afternoon helping with youth group activities, or we volunteer to help fold the newsletter each month. Yet our work seems to go overlooked, and we wonder what the point is of our involvement in the church. . .

### EVENING

When our work for Christ seems to go unnoticed by our church family, we can be assured that God sees our hard work and appreciates it. We may not receive the "church member of the month" award, but our love for our brothers and sisters in Christ and our work on their behalf is not overlooked by God. The author of Hebrews assures us that God is not unjust—our reward is in heaven.

*Dear Lord, You are a God of love and justice.*
*Even when I do not receive the notice of those around me,*
*help me to serve You out of my love for You. Amen.*

# DAY 216

## PRIVATE PRAYER

*After sending them home, he went up into the hills by himself to pray. Night fell while he was there alone.*
MATTHEW 14:23 NLT

### MORNING

Jesus gave us a perfect example of prayer to follow. Not only can we learn *how* to pray from the Lord's Prayer, but we can also discover *where* to pray.

Although there is no magical place where we need to be to talk with Him, we should find a quiet, secluded location. He wants us to focus our thoughts on Him only—not on the television program coming on in fifteen minutes, the ringing telephone, or the household chores that need to be done—just God, and God alone.

### EVENING

Reread today's verse. Jesus went up into the hills. You certainly don't need to go that far—although it can be an option—but your place of prayer should be free of distractions. Night fell while Jesus was there, indicating that it wasn't a hurried time of prayer. He took the time to commune with His Father, giving Him priority.

We can pray at any time and in any place, but it will benefit you and honor God when you follow Jesus' example and find a special place to talk with Him.

*Lord, thank You for listening to me anytime I come to You. Help me to find someplace that can be for just You and me, where I can pour my heart out to You. Amen.*

## DAY 217

# MAKE HIM YOUR TREASURE

*Our holy and glorious temple, where our ancestors praised you, has been burned with fire, and all that we treasured lies in ruins.*

ISAIAH 64:11 NIV

### MORNING

The Jews didn't have a place to worship. Their bright temple lay in ruins. Gone were the golden implements that made worship a pleasure. All they valued lay in ruins.

Come on! Were these guys crazy? What meant so much to them? Stones? Golden bowls and candlesticks? Fine woven hangings?

Or God?

Though their building was ruined, their relationship with God didn't have to be. They couldn't offer blood sacrifices, but God hadn't reneged on the promise of a Messiah who would save them. If only they had trusted Him! If they drew close to God, *He* could become a heart treasure that fire or war engines couldn't destroy and soldiers couldn't carry away.

### EVENING

If you've lost your church building or had to leave a congregation you love, don't let despair overwhelm you. God and His promises stand firm.

Make Him your treasure, and no one can turn your spiritual life to rubble.

*Lord, be the treasure of my life. You're more than buildings or even a group of Christians. I'm part of Your eternal church, made up of those who love You. Amen.*

# DAY 218

## WHAT IS LOVE?

*Love is patient, love is kind. It does not envy,*
*it does not boast, it is not proud.*
1 CORINTHIANS 13:4 NIV

### MORNING

If you're involved in a special romance, do you treat your beloved as someone who's exciting to be around? Probably. But do you also show your honey God's love by living out this verse?

Dating relationships can make emotions run high, but if you're constantly impatient with a date who's never on time or are unkind to one who's having a tough time seeing eye to eye with a family member, you're not reflecting God's love.

God doesn't rewrite the Book so we can act any way we want in our romances. Nowhere does God say we have a right to treat the ones closest to our hearts with less respect than we treat a chance acquaintance or a close friend. When we really love, we treat each other with extra-special gentleness and care.

### EVENING

If you can't treat a date with patience, kindness, and trust, reevaluate things. Your spiritual walk may be slipping. Or perhaps this isn't a person you're suited to, and you'd be better off as "just friends."

*Lord, help me show Your love to anyone I date. Don't let me make my romantic life an exception to Your rules. In Jesus' name, amen.*

# DAY 219

## LOVING WITHOUT THE "IFS"

*[Jesus said,] "This is my command: Love one another the way I loved you. This is the very best way to love. Put your life on the line for your friends."*
JOHN 15:12–13 MSG

### MORNING

Loving unconditionally is loving without the "ifs." The "ifs" are the conditions we place on our gift of love. If you love unconditionally, then the other person doesn't need to do anything but accept your gift.

Loving unconditionally isn't just something for husbands and wives. It's also true in regard to friendships, helping others, or visiting someone.

### EVENING

It seems everyone has love conditions. When you actually do love without demands, someone might say, "I owe you." Even they understand that most people expect something in return. It can be hard to convince them that there's nothing to owe.

God loves us that way. We had nothing to offer God, but He sent Jesus to love us enough to save us (see Romans 5:6). God's love never says, "If you'll just get your life together. If you'd just try a little harder. If you'd just stop being something less than perfect." When we actually accept His love, He cares enough to invite us to a better way of living.

*Dear God, I'm grateful You loved me without any "ifs." I accept Your love, and I ask You to help me share that love with others. May I never place demands as a condition for really loving anyone You created. Amen.*

# DAY 220

## LIVE IN UNITY

*May God, who gives this patience and encouragement,*
*help you live in complete harmony with each other,*
*as is fitting for followers of Christ Jesus.*
ROMANS 15:5 NLT

### MORNING

How does one live in unity with so many different types of people? One friend prefers vibrant, bold colors and has a personality to match. Another friend prefers muted tones, and her demur attitude fits accordingly. One church member might gravitate toward the classical, traditional hymns, while another prefers more contemporary music.

Christians disagree on a lot of issues, and conflicts often result—in and out of the church. Yet we are to exercise the patience and encouragement God provides to help us live in harmony with one another.

### EVENING

Our salvation is based on whom we worship, not where or how we worship. Quibbling over the cut, style, or color of our spiritual clothing causes us to succumb to our fleshly nature rather than God's will for us.

Personal preferences and heartfelt opinions are what make us individuals. Every believer has a gift to share within the body of Christ. If we were all the same, how could we grow and learn? Jesus prayed for unity among the believers. God encourages us to do the same.

*Father, thank You that You give me the ability and power*
*to walk in unity with my brothers and sisters in Christ.*
*I pray for Christian unity. Let it begin with me. Amen.*

# DAY 221

## THE WHOLE TRUTH

*Instead, speaking the truth in love, we will grow to become in every respect the mature body of him who is the head, that is, Christ.*

EPHESIANS 4:15 NIV

### MORNING

When someone gives testimony in a court case, they are sworn in with the question "Do you swear to tell the truth, the whole truth, and nothing but the truth, so help you God?" Sadly, it can take a court case to cause someone to tell the whole truth.

Doctors at the University of Michigan were advised by risk-management executive Richard Boothman and his colleagues to own up to mistakes early. When they chose a more honest approach, the number of malpractice claims fell; they were esteemed by patients for their transparency; legal expenses went down; and patient satisfaction increased. Interestingly, patients seemed to recover faster. . .

### EVENING

Everyone makes mistakes. When we admit them and take responsibility—even asking for forgiveness—we build integrity in our relationships. It also opens doors when we offer grace to others when they make mistakes. Make a choice today to tell the whole truth and build strong relationships in your life.

*Lord, forgive me for the times I have been short on grace or even refused to give it to others. Thank You for Your mercy on my life. Help me to take responsibility when I make a mistake. Please grant me favor with others when I need grace from them. Amen.*

## DAY 222

# GOD'S PROMISES BRING HOPE

*"For I know the plans I have for you, . . .plans to prosper you and not to harm you, plans to give you hope and a future."*
JEREMIAH 29:11 NIV

### MORNING

A sad elderly man, racked by years of physical pain and mental abuse, is shown love and concern for the first time. The result? Hope. A wayward teenage girl is welcomed back home with a compassionate, forgiving embrace from her disappointed yet loving parents. The outcome? Hope. An unappreciated middle-aged woman—consumed with chores, a career, and caring for her two children and an elderly parent—is lifted from despair when friends pitch in to help her. Hope.

Hope and encouragement are precious gifts we can give one another anytime and anywhere. They come in the form of a second chance clothed in a reassuring word; they thrive in the fertile soil of a loving gesture or compassionate embrace.

### EVENING

The writer of the well-known hymn "It Is Well with My Soul" penned those words at the most grief-stricken time of his life after his four children were tragically killed at sea. His undaunted faith remained because he believed in a God who was bigger than the tragedy he faced. God's promises gave him hope and encouragement.

Despite your circumstances, God has a plan for you, one that will give you encouragement and hope and a brighter future.

*Father, may I always say, "It is well with my soul," knowing that Your promises are true and that I can trust You, no matter what. Amen.*

# DAY 223

# DISHONORED

*[Jesus] began teaching in the synagogue, and many who heard him were amazed. They asked, "Where did he get all this wisdom and the power to perform such miracles?"*
MARK 6:2 NLT

## MORNING

The people of Nazareth knew Jesus as the son of Mary. They couldn't see Him as the Messiah. Hadn't He been a playmate for their children? How could this former village boy have the power to heal? And where did He discover such wisdom?

The phrase "You can never go home again" suggests that when you leave home and return wiser and more skilled, there will be those who connect their memories only to someone younger and less wise. The people of Nazareth struggled with that about Jesus.

His former neighbors speculated about Him. You can almost hear them whispering words behind their hands that betrayed envy, malice, and gossip. Jesus was aware that He had no honor in His hometown or in His childhood home.

## EVENING

Jesus faced criticism, so He understands the way you feel when you're criticized. He knows what goes through your mind. So, when you feel left out, gossiped about, or belittled for following God's plan for you, remember that you face each trouble with Jesus.

*God, forgive me when I think You could never understand the things I face. This reminds me that Your Son suffered so that He knows what I'm suffering. Thank You for taking action to connect my pain with Your comfort. Amen.*

# DAY 224

## WHEN BEING HARD IS GOOD AND WHEN IT'S NOT

*When they saw him walking on the lake, they thought he was a ghost. They cried out, because they all saw him and were terrified. Immediately he spoke to them and said, "Take courage! It is I. Don't be afraid." Then he climbed into the boat with them, and the wind died down. They were completely amazed, for. . .their hearts were hardened.*

MARK 6:49–52 NIV

### MORNING

Professional fishermen are a tough bunch. It's hard work, not suited to the lazy or the soft. If you were a fisherman in first-century Israel, you were usually a hardworking guy, made strong by a difficult life. In fact, just about everyone in the ancient world would be considered hardened by today's standards. It was often an unforgiving environment where only the hardy survived. That's when it's good to be hardened. . .

### EVENING

It's not good to be hard when it comes to spiritual lessons. To be dull to the things God has made known about His power and provision is to miss the next lesson. Despite the fact that Jesus had just fed thousands from a handful of food, the disciples were amazed that Jesus was walking on the water.

Are there lessons God has shown you that you haven't taken to heart yet?

*Jesus, help me to remember Your great deeds and to trust You for even more. Let me not be hard of heart. Amen.*

# DAY 225

# BOUNDARY FREEDOM

*[God said to Job,] "Who shut up the sea behind doors when it burst forth from the womb, when I made the clouds its garment and wrapped it in thick darkness, when I fixed limits for it and set its doors and bars in place, when I said, 'This far you may come and no farther; here is where your proud waves halt'?"*

JOB 38:8–11 NIV

## MORNING

God brings order out of chaos. Maybe this is why when someone finally accepts His gift of rescue, they see that life with God makes sense.

He sets ocean boundaries. He gives each season three months. He tells day and night when to start. We feel safe when we know those boundaries are set. It would seem strange for the sun to start shining at night, for winter to show up in summer, or for the ocean to suddenly change locations. . .

## EVENING

Christians exist with boundaries too. When we follow God's limits on our actions, we can feel as if God doesn't want us to have any fun. But the boundaries help us learn God's expectations so we're free to do what we were made to do.

*Dear God, You created birds to fly, not swim. You made snakes to slither, not gallop. You made me to follow You, not to live apart from You. Help me recognize that boundaries are for my good, not to stop me from enjoying good things. Amen.*

# DAY 226

## PRAYER ENGAGEMENT

*Then he returned to his disciples and found them sleeping. "Simon," he said to Peter, "are you asleep? Couldn't you keep watch for one hour? Watch and pray so that you will not fall into temptation. The spirit is willing, but the flesh is weak."*

MARK 14:37–38 NIV

### MORNING

Peter, James, and John followed Jesus to a garden called Gethsemane. These disciples were close to Jesus and probably felt honored to be invited. Like always, Jesus needed to pray. He had one request for His friends: "Watch and pray so that you will not fall into temptation."

They meant well, but as Jesus prayed, knowing He would soon face death, the disciples fell asleep. They'd heard Jesus say that His soul was overwhelmed with sorrow to the point of death, but even these weighty words weren't enough to keep their eyelids open. . .

### EVENING

It's easy to believe that the disciples needed more self-discipline, but how often have we started to pray only to find ourselves tempted to think of other things or perhaps sleep? Prayer is active and necessary, but it's also a place where distractions come easy. Jesus still asks us to pray.

*Lord, I want to be intentional about my prayer life. Seeking You is important in building and keeping my walk with You. Let me accept Your grace but do my best to make conversation with You a regular part of my day. Amen.*

# DAY 227

## PRAYING THE MIND OF CHRIST

*We demolish arguments and every pretension that sets itself up against the knowledge of God, and we take captive every thought to make it obedient to Christ.*

2 CORINTHIANS 10:5 NIV

### MORNING

As Christ followers, we are learning to become like Him in our thoughts, words, and deeds. Part of becoming Christlike is also mastering our minds. Sometimes it is hard to pray because other thoughts interfere with our ability to listen closely to what God is saying. This is a favorite trick of Satan's—getting us to think about our to-do list instead of what God is trying to tell us.

By reading and praying scripture and using positive statements in our prayers that claim what God has already said He will do for us, the mind of Christ is being activated in us. By taking captive every thought, we learn to know what thought is of God, what belongs to us, and what is of the enemy.

### EVENING

Recognize, take captive, and bind up the thoughts that are of the enemy, and throw them out! The more we commune with God, fellowship with Him, and learn from Him, the more we cultivate the mind of Christ.

*Lord, help me identify the thoughts that are not Your thoughts and purge them. I know that soon Your thoughts and not the enemy's will be the ones that I hear. In this way, I will hear You more clearly so I may be an obedient disciple. Amen!*

# DAY 228

# WHO REALLY NEEDS THE LESSON?

*She begged him to cast out the demon from her daughter. Since she was a Gentile, born in Syrian Phoenicia, Jesus told her, "First I should feed the children—my own family, the Jews. It isn't right to take food from the children and throw it to the dogs." She replied, "That's true, Lord, but even the dogs under the table are allowed to eat the scraps from the children's plates."*

MARK 7:26–28 NLT

## MORNING

Jesus was a shrewd teacher. He didn't teach only the person in front of Him. Often, He was also teaching those who were standing around observing and scrutinizing Him. The disciples wanted this woman to go away because she was an embarrassment, a Gentile excluded from the promise of a Jewish Messiah.

For the disciples' ears, Jesus intentionally compared her to a dog—and a few Jewish heads must have nodded. *Yeah, that's right. She's not one of us.* But the mother was undeterred, and because of her faith, this "dog" received the miracle she asked for!

## EVENING

What a lesson to the disciples: A "dog" with faith is better than a man with a Jewish last name who does not have faith.

Faith is the only thing that impresses God. No family history or heritage matters, nor the denomination or church you grew up in. Faith alone puts you in touch with the Savior.

*Father, count me a dog if necessary,*
*but a dog of faith. In Jesus' name, amen.*

# DAY 229

## DID HE REALLY JUST SAY THAT?

*A man in the crowd answered, "Teacher, I brought you my son, who is possessed by a spirit that has robbed him of speech. . . . I asked your disciples to drive out the spirit, but they could not." "You unbelieving generation," Jesus replied, "how long shall I stay with you? How long shall I put up with you? Bring the boy to me."*

MARK 9:17–19 NIV

### MORNING

It's hard to imagine Jesus getting exasperated with people who needed His help; but in this passage, Jesus is clearly annoyed—with everyone, including His disciples, the father of the mute boy, and the whole of Jewish society.

And it's not the only time Jesus became impatient with people's lack of faith. Consider this statement: "If that is how God clothes the grass of the field, . . .how much more will he clothe you—you of little faith!" (Luke 12:28 NIV). Or ponder this incident: "Jesus appeared to the Eleven as they were eating; he rebuked them for their lack of faith and their stubborn refusal to believe those who had seen him after he had risen" (Mark 16:14 NIV).

### EVENING

Jesus can be known only by faith—even back then, when standing in His physical presence. How are you responding to Him today? Are you responding in faith, or are you causing Him to be "amazed at [your] lack of faith" (Mark 6:6 NIV)?

*I pray, O God, as the father of this boy did. Help me overcome my unbelief. Amen.*

# DAY 230

## WHO IS THE REAL WINNER?

*"So the last will be first, and the first will be last."*
MATTHEW 20:16 NIV

### MORNING

When trees leafed out as spring came to Brad's rural community, the teen began early morning training rides for the upcoming bike races. In the past, he had always won first place.

"What do you like best about these races?" a local reporter had asked him.

Brad grinned. "Winning—and the good-looking girls!"

However, when the new season began, the judges handed the first-place trophy to David, who topped thirty-five miles per hour in some parts of the route. A frowning Brad received second.

David's recumbent bike was not like Brad's road bike. Its pedals were out front instead of underneath the rider, making it faster. It should have been in a different racing class because no ordinary racer could compete.

At home, Brad cried with disappointment, "No fair!". . .

### EVENING

Like Brad's story. . .in a parable told by Jesus, the workers of a field all started at different times of the day, and all were paid the same wage at the end of the day. The earliest crowd protested loudest. Jesus ended His parable with "Don't I have the right to do what I want with my own money? Or are you envious because I am generous?" (Matthew 20:15 NIV).

Jesus is teaching us about grace. Some people are faithful followers from the cradle. Others accept Him at death. Yet He offers all His gift of forgiveness and a winning ticket to heaven. Praise God for all His latecomers.

*Jesus, we thank You for giving us victory. Amen.*

# DAY 231

## BLESSED ARE THE PERSECUTED

*"Blessed are those who are persecuted because of righteousness, for theirs is the kingdom of heaven. Blessed are you when people insult you, persecute you and falsely say all kinds of evil against you because of me. Rejoice and be glad, because great is your reward in heaven, for in the same way they persecuted the prophets who were before you."*

MATTHEW 5:10–12 NIV

### MORNING

Believers should expect persecution. Depending on where and how you live, the persecution you experience may be great or may be miniscule. In many parts of the world, brothers and sisters in Christ are being denied jobs, food, and justice because of their faith. They are in danger of losing their families, homes, and freedom for Jesus' sake. Still, they cling to the Savior and share the good news of His salvation. They trust that He will accomplish the justice that they cannot (Romans 12:19).

If, in contrast, your family possesses power, money, or safety, don't feel guilty. God has given you exactly what you have so you can bless the worldwide body of Christ.

### EVENING

No matter our situation, we can all go before the Father and plead for our brothers' and sisters' faith to be strong and for their persecutors to know Jesus' salvation! Ask the Spirit to prompt your heart to pray and to give to share Christ's kindness with your precious fellow members of the body of Jesus.

*Jesus, thank You that You are near to me and that You are near my faraway brothers and sisters. Please move my heart to pray for those who persecute Your church. Amen.*

# DAY 232

## CRISIS OF FAITH

*After summoning two of his disciples, John sent them to the Lord, saying, "Are You the Coming One, or are we to look for another?"*
LUKE 7:19 NASB

### MORNING

Christians are not exempt from becoming disillusioned with God or questioning their relationship to Him. We can learn how to handle those doubts by looking at John the Baptist. His life purpose was to point people to Christ, and his ministry was wildly successful (Matthew 3:5). However, in what must have been the most exciting time of John's life, he suddenly found himself in prison. How could he fulfill his mission there?

As he continued to suffer, his expectations crashed. *If I'm the messenger sent to proclaim the Messiah, why am I locked up? If Jesus is really the Promised One, why doesn't He rescue me?* He sent two of his followers to ask Jesus point-blank, "Are You the Messiah or not?"

### EVENING

Jesus hardly ever answered a question directly, so He did not say, "Tell John to remember when he baptized Me and heard God's voice speak to him." Instead, Jesus sent them back with Isaiah 35:3–7. He wanted John to consider the evidence based on scripture, not on his thrilling experiences. John needed to discover for himself that Jesus' miracles were fulfilling the Old Testament prophecies about the Messiah.

So it is with us. When we doubt, we need to look to scripture, not to emotional events. The evidence is in what God has said, no matter how we may feel.

*Lord Jesus, when suffering makes me doubt You, remind me to run to Your Word and respond by believing it. Amen.*

# DAY 233

## DEEP ROOTS

*"They will be like a tree planted by the water that sends out its roots by the stream. It does not fear when heat comes; its leaves are always green. It has no worries in a year of drought and never fails to bear fruit."*

JEREMIAH 17:8 NIV

### MORNING

Watering your garden doesn't seem difficult, but did you know you can train a plant to grow incorrectly just in the way you water it? By pouring water from the hose for only a few moments at each plant, the root systems become very shallow. They start to seek water from the top of the soil, and the roots can easily be burned in the summer sun. By using a soaker hose, the water slowly percolates into the ground, and the plants learn to push their roots deeper into the soil to get water.

### EVENING

The prophet Jeremiah talked about a larger plant, a tree. A tree needs deep roots to keep it anchored in the ground, providing stability. The roots synthesize water and minerals for nourishment and then help to store those elements for a later time. Our deep spiritual roots come from reading God's Word, which provides stability, nourishment, and refreshment.

*Father, I do not want to wither in the sun. Help me to immerse myself in Your Word. When I do, I sink my spiritual roots deeper into life-giving soil and drink from living water. Help me to be the fruitful follower of You that I am meant to be. Amen.*

# DAY 234

# THE SIMPLE THINGS

*In him our hearts rejoice, for we trust in his holy name.*
PSALM 33:21 NIV

## MORNING

Think about the simple pleasures in everyday life—that first sip of a latte in the morning, waking up to realize you still have a few more minutes to sleep, or putting on fresh, warm clothes right out of the dryer on a cold winter morning. Perhaps it's a walk along the beach or a hike up the mountains into the blue skies that gives you a simple peace.

God knows all the simple pleasures you enjoy—and He provides them for your delight.

## EVENING

When the simple things that can come only by God's hand fill you with contentment, He is pleased. He takes pleasure in you. You are His delight. Giving you peace, comfort, and a sense of knowing that you belong to Him is a simple thing for Him.

Take a moment today and step away from the busyness of life. Notice and fully experience some of those things you enjoy most. Then share that special joy with Him.

*Lord, thank You for the simple things that bring pleasure to my day. I enjoy each gift You've given me. I invite You to share those moments with me today. Amen.*

# DAY 235

## IRRITATING THE LORD

*People were bringing little children to Jesus for him to place his hands on them, but the disciples rebuked them. When Jesus saw this, he was indignant. He said to them, "Let the little children come to me, . . .for the kingdom of God belongs to such as these. Truly I tell you, anyone who will not receive the kingdom of God like a little child will never enter it."*

MARK 10:13–15 NIV

### MORNING

Because God is loving and patient, it may seem hard to understand how Jesus could get so irritated with His disciples—but He did. The definition of *indignant* is "feeling or showing anger or annoyance at what is perceived as *unjust treatment*." And denying children access to the Messiah was about as unjust as it got. It was completely contrary to Jesus' heart for people.

The surest way to irritate the Lord is to stand in the way of people coming to Him.

### EVENING

Jesus reserved His harshest criticism for those who interfered with salvation, saying, "Woe to you, teachers of the law and Pharisees, you hypocrites! You shut the door of the kingdom of heaven in people's faces. You yourselves do not enter, nor will you let those enter who are trying to" (Matthew 23:13 NIV).

When the way to God is blocked by religious systems and prejudices, true believers should be indignant like He was.

*O Lord, let me always make the way open for those who are seeking You. Amen.*

# DAY 236

# GOD'S GRASSHOPPERS

*But the men who had gone up with [Caleb] said, "We can't attack those people; they are stronger than we are." And they spread among the Israelites a bad report about the land they had explored. . . . "We saw the Nephilim [giants] there. . . . We seemed like grasshoppers in our own eyes."*

NUMBERS 13:31–33 NIV

## MORNING

The journey from Egypt to the Promised Land was roughly two hundred miles. On the way there, God forged a collection of slave families into a nation that would trust Him. For a little more than a year, He guided them through faith-building experiences. He provided manna, gave laws, tested them in battle, and displayed His power over and over.

But the Israelites were slow to learn to trust Him. They complained and rebelled at every hardship, even talking of stoning Moses and returning to Egypt.

Finally, on the edge of the Promised Land, only two of the twelve spies believed they could enter. The rest complained that they were only "grasshoppers" compared to the "giants" of Canaan. . .

## EVENING

God always knew that His people would face giants. When you look at yourself, you *should* see nothing more than a grasshopper—a grasshopper with the promises of a faithful God. He will take you into the land, and you will rejoice in *His* victory.

*Father, thank You for allowing a "grasshopper" to live in Your power and promises. Amen.*

# DAY 237

## THE DNA OF SIN

*Only fools say in their hearts, "There is no God." They are corrupt, and their actions are evil; not one of them does good! God looks down from heaven on the entire human race; he looks to see if anyone is truly wise, if anyone seeks God. But no, all have turned away; all have become corrupt. No one does good, not a single one!*

PSALM 53:1–3 NLT

### MORNING

Evil is one of the hardest concepts to discuss with nonbelievers. Even if they're willing to acknowledge that evil exists in some form, they claim that it's not something that comes from within and is expressed outwardly; it's something outside ourselves that only a few choose. Even so, "evil" behavior is often excused: a lack of education, environmental conditions, mental disorders, poor parenting. . .any source but our own inherent corruption.

Believers understand that the flesh is corrupt. But sometimes Christians don't acknowledge their dilemma for what it is. They embrace a Savior but often make excuses for their corrupt actions. . .

### EVENING

At times Christians make almost as many excuses for sin as the "fools" who say there's no God to sin against.

But to acknowledge Christ is to happily acknowledge weaknesses and take hold of His power and His gift of freedom as children of God.

*Father, help me to openly acknowledge my sin and moral failures and my need for Your redemption. Amen.*

# DAY 238

## FACING THE DARK

*The leading priests and Pharisees had given Judas a contingent of Roman soldiers and Temple guards to accompany him. Now with blazing torches, lanterns, and weapons, they arrived at the olive grove. Jesus fully realized all that was going to happen to him, so he stepped forward to meet them. "Who are you looking for?" he asked. "Jesus the Nazarene," they replied. "I AM he," Jesus said. (Judas, who betrayed him, was standing with them.)*

JOHN 18:3–5 NLT

### MORNING

He came into this world under a cloud of suspicion; the townspeople of Nazareth never did quite believe Mary's story of an angelic visit and a miraculous pregnancy. When He came into His own area, they said, "Isn't this man the carpenter's son?" His enemies taunted and threatened Him and tried to make Him look bad. They ultimately came after Him, using one of His followers to do the dirty work of betrayal.

On that black night in the garden of Gethsemane, Jesus faced them all. He stepped out into the light of their torches and asked who they wanted (though He already knew). Then He faced the darkness and went forward. In a few hours, He would win the victory, wresting the keys of hell and the grave from Satan and completing our redemption.

### EVENING

You and I will never face what Jesus did, but we will be called to step forward to meet terrifying challenges. In that moment, we can know that He will give us the courage to conquer in His name.

*Dear Father, I want to face the darkness with courage. Please give me strength to step forward and conquer. In Jesus' name, amen.*

## DAY 239

# A GATHERING OF FRIENDS

*Six days before the Passover celebration began, Jesus arrived in Bethany, the home of Lazarus—the man he had raised from the dead. A dinner was prepared in Jesus' honor. Martha served, and Lazarus was among those who ate with him.*

JOHN 12:1–2 NLT

### MORNING

Do you think Jesus had fun? Do you think He enjoyed downtime with friends?

We aren't told much about the social life of Jesus outside the realm of ministry, but these verses give a little insight. From this and other references in the Gospels, we are quite sure that this home in Bethany was one in which Jesus was a frequent guest. This sibling trio of Martha, Mary, and Lazarus seems to be close to the Teacher.

Martha felt comfortable enough to ask Him to prod Mary to help her in the kitchen. Mary sat at His feet and poured precious ointment on His feet in an act of adoration. When Lazarus was sick and near death, the sisters sent a message to Jesus telling Him, "Lord, the one you love is sick" (John 11:3 NIV). . .

### EVENING

Jesus believed that friendships were important. It seems He took time to cultivate these relationships. If we are to follow His steps, we must not try to go through life alone. We must joyfully accept those whom God brings into our lives to encourage us, strengthen us, and gladden us. We must gather often with friends.

*Lord, thank You for my good friends. Help me to be one as well. Amen.*

# DAY 240

## JUST LIKE JESUS

*Follow God's example, therefore, as dearly loved children and walk in the way of love, just as Christ loved us and gave himself up for us as a fragrant offering and sacrifice to God.*

EPHESIANS 5:1–2 NIV

### MORNING

It's been said that imitation is the highest form of flattery. When others want to be like us, it means they admire us. When we imitate God, we show Him we admire Him and long to be like Him.

A small, dearly loved child might share that she wants to be just like her mommy when she grows up. She dresses in high heels, puts on lipstick, and practices walking and talking like her mother. If given the opportunity to answer the phone, she might even mimic her mother's intonations when saying hello. She does this because she adores her mother, because she sees in her mother everything good and worthy and admirable.

The Bible tells us that God is love. And when we imitate Christ, we become living, breathing examples of that love.

### EVENING

When we act more Christlike, we begin to look more like Him as we take off our own self-centered thoughts and dress up in His clothing and adopt His way of thinking. Then something miraculous happens. We begin to take on a family resemblance to God, and we more fully experience the other aspects of His character: joy, peace, patience, kindness, and goodness. When we imitate God, He transforms us into His image and pours out His blessings on our lives.

*Dear Father, I want to be just like You.*
*Help me to love the way Christ loves. Amen.*

# DAY 241

## LIFE ISN'T FAIR!

*So he took Joseph and threw him into the prison where the king's prisoners were held, and there he remained. But the Lord was with Joseph in the prison and showed him his faithful love. And the Lord made Joseph a favorite with the prison warden.*

Genesis 39:20–21 NLT

### MORNING

Joseph didn't look for trouble—it just seemed to find him. First, his brothers sold him into slavery. Then his master's wife lied about him and got him tossed into prison.

*If Joseph was favored by God so much, why wasn't his life smooth?* we're tempted to ask. He didn't deserve what he got, especially not from Potiphar's wife.

The hard fact is that the wicked of this world don't live in a vacuum—they inhabit the earth along with Christians, and sometimes Christians get hurt by their wrongdoing.

### EVENING

When evil people bring harm to Christ followers, we cry out, "Life isn't fair!" And we're right—it isn't. But it wasn't fair, either, that Jesus had to come to earth for unbelievers and die to save them.

Are you ready to be treated unfairly for Him?

*Lord, life isn't fair sometimes, but I still love You and want to serve You—even if it means getting mistreated by someone who doesn't know You. Amen.*

# DAY 242

## LIVE IN HIS LOVE

*Walk in the way of love, just as Christ loved us and gave himself up for us as a fragrant offering and sacrifice to God.*

EPHESIANS 5:2 NIV

### MORNING

Have you ever stored a Bible in a musty cellar? If you have, you know that the next time you use it had better *not* be in Bible study. No one will want to sit anywhere near you.

But the worst thing you could do isn't pulling out your smelly Bible—it's never pulling out your Bible at all.

Longtime Christians who never read the Word smell too. These Christians who dress up their coffee tables with their Bibles but never open them won't love others the way Jesus does either.

### EVENING

Even using a "stinky" Bible every day helps you become more like the Master. Because the more you live in His love, the more you can smell like Jesus, who gave Himself as a "fragrant offering" to God the Father.

*Jesus, I don't want to be a stinky Christian.*
*Keep me in Your Word every day. Amen.*

# DAY 243

# HE WON'T LET YOU DOWN

*I tell you that Christ has become a servant of the Jews on behalf of God's truth, so that the promises made to the patriarchs might be confirmed.*

ROMANS 15:8 NIV

## MORNING

Everyone has been hurt at one time or another by a broken promise. When that happens, it is best to forgive and go on. People are just people. They mess up. But there is one who will never break His promises to us—our heavenly Father. We can safely place our hope in Him.

Hebrews chapter 11 lists biblical characters who placed their trust and hope in God and weren't let down. Do you think Noah was excited about building an ark? Surely Sarah and Abraham hadn't planned on parenting at their ages. Daniel faced the lions' den knowing that his God would care for him. We can find encouragement from their examples, knowing that their faith in the God who had come through for them time and again wasn't misplaced. They did not grow weary and lose heart. They knew He was always faithful.

## EVENING

We choose to place our hope in God's promises. We won't be discouraged by time—God's timing is always perfect. We won't be discouraged by circumstances—God can change everything in a heartbeat. We will keep our hearts in God's hand, for we know He is faithful.

*Lord, I choose this day to place my trust in You, for I know You're the one true constant. Amen.*

# DAY 244

## EVERYDAY WAYS

*The heavens tell of the glory of God;*
*and their expanse declares the work of His hands.*
PSALM 19:1 NASB

### MORNING

Another day had come and gone. It wasn't a special day—not that Janet knew of anyway. She sat in her backyard and watched the sun set. Glorious shades of orange melded with yellow and bright red, all artfully meshed at the edges with a now navy-blue sky. It was unlike any sunset she had ever seen. *God showing off again*, she mused.

As she thought about it, no two sunsets were ever the same. The sun went down in a slightly different location along the horizon each day at a slightly different time depending on the season. The color variations were never exactly the same, as if an artist had painted them. But then, a great artist did paint them. Every day. Something new.

### EVENING

Tonight, think about how deeply God must love you and every one of His children to give us a fresh work of art in the sky every day of our lives. Many duties and burdens may fill our days, and He loves us during all of it, enough to provide beauty and wonder all along the way.

*Father, thank You for Your everyday ways. Let the wonder of Your creation continue to deepen our understanding of Your great love for us. Amen.*

# DAY 245

# THE JOY OF YOUR SALVATION

*You forgave the guilt of your people—*
*yes, you covered all their sins.*
Psalm 85:2 NLT

## MORNING

In today's Old Testament verse, the writer understood that humankind could never atone for its own sin—God would need to take it away from His people and cover it so that it would no longer be remembered. In this particular instance, the writer was referring to when God's people were brought back from Babylonian captivity.

Can you think of a time when you had to deal with the consequences of your sin—a time in which you felt far from God but then experienced a complete restoration the way this writer did? How did you express the joy you felt? Did you tell others? Write about it? Sing about it? Worship? Dance for joy? Any of these responses would be appropriate.

## EVENING

If you can't think of a time when you had to deal with the consequences of your sin and then were able to celebrate God's faithfulness, you're probably not looking hard enough. As David prayed in Psalm 51:12 (NIV), "Restore to me the joy of your salvation."

*Lord, my sin is a burden to me. It's heavy, and it weighs me down. But You are a forgiving God, and I trust in You to completely pardon me. Amen.*

# DAY 246

## SPIRITUAL EARS TO HEAR

*"My sheep hear My voice and I know them. They follow Me. I give them life that lasts forever. They will never be punished. No one is able to take them out of My hand."*

JOHN 10:27–28 NLV

### MORNING

When the Jews asked Jesus if He was the Christ, He spoke plainly to them, also telling them that they were not of His sheepfold. If they were part of His flock, they would have followed Him rather than questioning Him.

His sheep know His voice—it has a ring of truth to it for the converted heart. It has *the* ring of truth to it. If anyone has spiritual ears to hear, let them hear.

### EVENING

The voices around you might be loud, making demands on your time and calling you to work, volunteer, serve—or even escape to a nearby lake for a weekend fishing excursion. You hear all of them and often respond accordingly.

But do you still hear Jesus' voice when He calls out or whispers to you? Or has it been a while? If you aren't tuned in to His Word, it's time to set aside some time to focus on Him above all else.

*Lord Jesus, my spiritual ears aren't always in tune with You. I often place a higher value on the voices of others than on Yours. Forgive me, Lord. Draw me close. Speak to me. I want to hear from You. Amen.*

# DAY 247

# THE BASIN

*It was just before the Passover Festival. Jesus knew that the hour had come for him to leave this world and go to the Father. Having loved his own who were in the world, he loved them to the end.*

John 13:1 NIV

## MORNING

Jesus' actions seemed as absurd as seeing the president checking coats at a restaurant, the owner of a pro football team running down the field for a touchdown, or the owner of a car company on call to change a customer's flat tire.

It was a time that's often referred to as the Last Supper. Jesus knew that He would be betrayed, yet He assumed the role of a servant by wrapping a towel around His waist and carrying a basin of water. He humbled Himself, and He washed and dried the feet of His disciples one by one—even those who objected. . .

## EVENING

Perhaps Jesus knew that the disciples would need the memory of how He would demonstrate the need to serve, care, and love in tangible ways. The work of redemption was close, the cross waiting, and His disciples would soon spread the news of how Jesus led by serving, lived by dying, and forgave through personal sacrifice—and He never asks us to do something He was unwilling to do.

*None of us are worthy of Your love, Lord. I've done nothing to earn the care You provide, but I see by Your example that I'm to serve, care, and love. The depths to which You love mankind overwhelm me. May I never view others as beyond Your love or beyond my ability to serve. Amen.*

# DAY 248

## MY TRUTH, MY FREEDOM

*Jesus said to the people who believed in him, "You are truly my disciples if you remain faithful to my teachings. And you will know the truth, and the truth will set you free."*

JOHN 8:31–32 NLT

### MORNING

Throughout scripture, slavery is used as a metaphor to explain our relationship to sin. Sin holds us in bondage. On our own, we are powerless to break its chains, just as the Israelites were powerless to escape from the Egyptians. The good news of the gospel is simple: God made a way to free us. In John 14:6, Jesus declares that He is the way, the truth, and the life. In Romans 5:8, Paul explains that Jesus (the truth) died for us while we were still enslaved to sin. Romans 6:22 says that because of this, we are free from the power of sin. We are free to do the things that make us holy and allow us to spend eternity with Him.

### EVENING

Remaining faithful to Jesus' teachings will lead to knowledge of the truth. The truth sets us free—free from sin and bondage; free from pride, selfish ambition, and darkness. The truth gives us freedom from fear, from the unknown, from anxiety and waste. The freedom Christ brings allows us to experience joy and peace beyond anything we could ever know. Have you taken hold of the freedom that is yours in Christ?

*Dear Lord, I am awed and amazed by the truth of Your Word. You alone are truth, and I confess with my mouth that You are my Lord and Savior. Without You, my end was certain death, eternal bondage to sin and despair. Thank You for the joy and the freedom that come from You. Help me to live no longer as slave, but as Your child, with all the freedom You provide. Amen.*

# DAY 249

## ON A MISSION

*"The Spirit of the Lord is on Me. He has put His hand on Me to preach the Good News to poor people. He has sent Me to heal those with a sad heart. He has sent Me to tell those who are being held that they can go free. He has sent Me to make the blind to see and to free those who are held because of trouble. He sent Me to tell of the time when men can receive favor with the Lord."*

LUKE 4:18–19 NLV

### MORNING

Do you have a personal mission statement? Do you know what your purpose is? Do you have a plan for the way you are living your life?

Many organizations today have mission statements to define their guiding principles and plot the practices they put into place.

Jesus had a mission statement. He said in John 6:38 (NLV) that He came to do the will of "the One Who sent Me."

### EVENING

One day while reading the scripture in a synagogue in Nazareth, Jesus defined His mission—to heal the brokenhearted, proclaim liberty, give sight, release the oppressed, and preach God's kingdom at hand. Jesus lived His earthly life with that focus; His earthly life was zeroed in on this mission, His Father's business.

Each of us should know our mission in life. Ultimately, it is to love God and others. Yet He has given us unique gifts and a particular setting with which to accomplish this. Today, take a little time to put into words the specific mission to which God has called you. Then, like Jesus, go and fulfill it.

*Father, thank You for calling me and gifting me for Your purpose. Clarify that mission in my mind today. In Jesus' name, amen.*

# DAY 250

## NOT ALONE

*When Jesus saw her weeping, and the Jews who had come along with her also weeping, he was deeply moved in spirit and troubled.*

John 11:33 NIV

### MORNING

Christ is compassionate. When we are hurting, He hurts. Our tears affect Him.

Yet many of those who claim to belong to Him show little compassion. Oh, it's easy to show kindness and concern for people who live across the globe. We can save and send our allowance money or drop off our old clothes at a donation center and feel we've done our part. Yet Christ offered face-to-face, in-the-flesh compassion when He saw that His friend Mary was hurting. He hurt with her. Then He did something to ease her pain: He raised her brother from the dead.

### EVENING

We can't all raise people from the dead, and that's not the point of this passage. The important thing is that Jesus hurt with His friend, and He did what He could to help. When people around us are hurting, we should respond as Jesus did. We should hurt with them and do what we can to ease their pain. Sometimes that means sending a card or offering to help with some chores. Sometimes it's just sitting with those people, holding their hands, and weeping with them.

When we're hurting, it helps to know we're not isolated. We can show compassion to others by doing what we can and letting them know they're not alone.

*Dear Father, thank You for showing me compassion when I'm hurting. Help me to be compassionate to others. Show me practical ways to share Your love. Amen.*

# DAY 251

## FRUITFUL LIVING

*But the Holy Spirit produces this kind of fruit in our lives: love, joy, peace, patience, kindness, goodness, faithfulness, gentleness, and self-control. There is no law against these things!*

GALATIANS 5:22–23 NLT

### MORNING

We've all had those days. Frustration grows. Resentment surfaces. Anger brews. Our day is not going according to our plan. We might as well be beating our heads against the wall. What's the problem?

Because we are human, we tend to want to rely on ourselves to fix our problems. It's a constant battle. The apostle Paul describes this wrestling match in Romans 7:19 (NIV): "For I do not do the good I want to do, but the evil I do not want to do—this I keep on doing." Paul asks in verse 24, "Who will rescue me from this body that is subject to death?" His answer? Jesus Christ!

### EVENING

If we're having the worst day, we need to recognize the root of the problem. Frustration, resentment, and anger are red flags. They are by-products of our sinful nature, proving that we've bypassed the help and peace God offers. We want life to go according to our plan and agenda, but God's way is so much better. Jesus came to rescue us from ourselves. He came to enable us to walk in the Spirit by yielding control to Him. Once we do that, our lives will produce the spiritual fruit God wants us to grow. It's a better way to live!

*Dear Lord, help me realize when I am walking in the flesh. May I yield to You so that I reap spiritual fruit. Amen.*

# DAY 252

## CONQUER THAT MOUNTAIN

*"I am the Lord your God, who teaches you what is best for you, who directs you in the way you should go."*
Isaiah 48:17 NIV

### MORNING

Life is full of ups and downs—mountain and valley experiences. There are times when you can get stuck or grow frustrated trying to conquer one specific mountain. Maybe you find yourself facing the same obstacle for the second or third time. Sometimes those mountains can present very difficult lessons to learn, so you climb them again and again, trying to understand something about yourself that is vital to reaching your next level of life.

If you feel like you're repeating the same lesson, go deep into your heart and ask yourself the hard questions. *Why am I climbing this mountain again? What did I miss? What do I need to know or learn before I can go to the next level?* Then ask the Lord to give you answers and show you things you might have missed.

### EVENING

God gave you a life to fulfill with a specific purpose to complete. He wants to see you moving forward. With your heart and mind open, ready to receive clear direction, you can conquer the mountain this time! You have an amazing destiny to achieve.

*God, I ask for Your wisdom and guidance in my life. Help me to see whatever it is I've missed, and help me to follow Your direction in all things. Amen.*

# DAY 253

## CREATIVE FITNESS

*Young people, it's wonderful to be young! . . . But remember that you must give an account to God for everything you do. So refuse to worry, and keep your body healthy.*
ECCLESIASTES 11:9–10 NLT

### MORNING

"I know I should work out, but the gym is just so boring!" Rebekah said as she held up her sweatpants and tank top. She wanted to be healthy and take care of the body God gave her. Yet she also despised hitting the treadmill for thirty minutes while staring at the television.

Going to the gym is great for some people, but for others it can be overwhelming, boring, or even too expensive to keep their interest. Luckily, there are plenty of other options for staying fit. Instead of hitting the gym, find a local hiking or biking trail and spend some time enjoying the beautiful world God created. Or take a class in martial arts, dance, or Pilates. Some local churches may even offer fitness courses for their members, so check the bulletin. Team sports like soccer, softball, or basketball are also great options and are often organized through churches, businesses, or local recreation centers.

### EVENING

If you're having trouble staying motivated to exercise regularly, try this: Create your own workout. Simply put on your favorite Christian radio station and dance. . .or clean your room to some inspirational music. It makes working out less of a chore and gives you some quality time with God.

*Dear Lord, I want to take care of the body You gave me. Help me to find creative and enjoyable ways to stay fit while honoring You in the process. Amen.*

# DAY 254

## PLEASING GOD

*His pleasure is not in the strength of the horse, nor his delight in the legs of the warrior; the LORD delights in those who fear him, who put their hope in his unfailing love.*

PSALM 147:10–11 NIV

### MORNING

Americans value achievement. We measure our country by its various accomplishments. Scientific discovery, space exploration, technological advancement, and world economic and political power all attest to the hard work and achievement of people building a nation.

As individuals, we measure our days by how much we get done. We take pride in checking items off our to-do lists. We email on our handheld devices while sitting in the waiting room, and we talk on our phones while walking on the treadmill in an effort to maximize our time so we can get more accomplished in a day. . .

### EVENING

God does not place value on our achievements. He does not measure our days by how much we get done. He is not delighted by our efficiency or our excellence. That is pretty hard to believe, because our culture places such value on self-reliance. What pleases Him is our worship of Him. He wants our reverent fear, our wonder and awe at His great power and steadfast love. He desires our dependence. He enjoys our hope when we are looking to Him to meet all our needs.

*Great God, who gave Your Son for all my sins, help me to remember that I do not have to perform for You. You have redeemed me and made me Your own. You desire my worship and my hope. Amen.*

# DAY 255

# AN ACCEPTED REJECT

*He was despised and rejected—a man of sorrows,*
*acquainted with deepest grief.*
Isaiah 53:3 NLT

## MORNING

Each person has something they really want in life. It's simple, really. They want to be accepted. They want to be loved.

However, rejection always brings its two best friends—sorrow and grief. These traits cause us to hold back and refuse to interact with others because we're afraid that the cycle of rejection will happen all over again, so we risk loneliness in an effort to stop rejection. . .

## EVENING

We're never happy when we're rejected, and somehow we assume that any rejection is God's way of saying we don't matter.

We miss all the evidence that proves something else. God loved us enough to send His Son to rescue us from sin. He cared enough about us to make a way for us to be His friends. He saw something special in us that allowed Him to offer a hope for our future. We are not rejected by God. We are loved. We are accepted. We are His family.

*Dear God, You have always accepted me. You made me and knew who I would become. Your commands shape me into who You want me to be, and You love me. You never reject me from coming to You. Thanks for being patient. Amen.*

# DAY 256

## SECURITY OF LOVE

*"The thief comes only to steal and kill and destroy; I have come that they may have life, and have it to the full."*
JOHN 10:10 NIV

### MORNING

Do you think you're valuable to anyone? We each have a seed of insecurity inside us that grows up and bears fruit when we don't want it to. It's like a voice whispers, "Hey, you're still not good enough." This voice is the thief who wants to destroy our lives. Our enemy doesn't want what's good for us. He may tempt us with small changes in thinking, or he might attempt to convince us that we aren't worth anything.

We should be willing to recognize that we're insecure in our thinking—but totally secure in God's love and grace.

### EVENING

God came to bring us a full life. He came prepared to bless us with all kinds of spiritual blessings. We find all the security we need in being His child. All our failures mean very little when compared to knowing Him and accepting the security of His love.

*Dear God, there are times when I want to know if I really have value to anyone. Your words say that You created me, love me, and have a future for me. I'm accepted by You. Help me live in the joy of Your acceptance. Help me thrive in the hope of Your promises. Amen.*

# DAY 257

## PRIDE CAUSES STRIFE

*Where there is strife, there is pride,*
*but wisdom is found in those who take advice.*
PROVERBS 13:10 NIV

### MORNING

"Mr. Milton drives me crazy," Tim admitted to a classmate. "Every other day, he's criticizing my work. I almost snapped back at him."

Criticism isn't easy to take. At first, your mind wants to snap back with explanations and countercriticisms. *Well, if I'd had enough time. . . If I'd been given the right information. . .*

Maybe your objections are true, but giving a sharp answer won't help others appreciate your efforts. Pride can get in the way of good work.

### EVENING

When you are criticized, take a good look at the critique. *Were* you sloppy? *Could* you have done better? What would have helped you improve? Don't start with excuses; look at it from your teacher's point of view. Would *you* like your work if you were in charge?

If you've made mistakes, learn from them. Turn the critique into advice that helps you do better.

*I know I'm not perfect, God, but sometimes it's hard to admit it to others. Keep our communication clear so pride can't lead us into quarrels. Amen.*

# DAY 258

## FOLLOW THE RIGHT LEADER

*He also told them this parable: "Can the blind lead the blind? Will they not both fall into a pit?"*
LUKE 6:39 NIV

### MORNING

What an interesting description Jesus gave us in this parable! You can easily see this pair ending up in a pit because neither can see the road.

Sometimes we're no better than these foolish men. Without even thinking of it, we hang on to a person who's going in the wrong direction. By the time we realize we've been following others rather than God, we're on the edge of a crater.

Do you want to know if you will end up in a spiritual hole? Look at the people you follow. Are they filled with peace and serving God, or are they running their own show, constantly dissatisfied with life?

### EVENING

Since you'll end up much like the people you follow most, be sure the people you imitate are worth following. Do they do what the Bible says is right? Are they honest and loving?

In the end, make sure you're following the greatest leader—Jesus. His paths don't go into pits.

*Lord, I want to be a leader who won't bring others into a pit. Guide me this day to walk in Your footsteps. Amen.*

## DAY 259

# LINKING HEARTS WITH GOD

*"You will receive power when the Holy Spirit comes on you; and you will be my witnesses. . .to the ends of the earth."*

ACTS 1:8 NIV

### MORNING

God knows our hearts. He knows what we need to make it through a day. So, in His kindness, He gave us a gift in the form of the Holy Spirit. As a counselor, comforter, and friend, the Holy Spirit acts as our inner compass. He upholds us when times are hard and helps us hear God's directions. When the path of obedience grows dark, the Spirit floods it with light. What revelation! He lives within us. Therefore, our prayers are lifted to the Father, to the very throne of God. Whatever petitions we have, we may rest assured they are heard.

### EVENING

We can rejoice in the fact that God cared enough to bless our lives with the Spirit to direct our paths. God loves the praises of His people, and these praises revive the Spirit within you. If you are weary or burdened, allow the Holy Spirit to minister to you. Seek the Holy Spirit and His wisdom, and ask Him to revive and refresh your inner self. Place your hope in God and trust the Spirit's guidance, and He will never let you down.

*Father God, how blessed I am to come into Your presence. Help me, Father, when I am weak. Guide me this day. Amen.*

# DAY 260

## GIRLFRIENDS

*Two people are better off than one, for they can help each other succeed. If one person falls, the other can reach out and help. But someone who falls alone is in real trouble.*

ECCLESIASTES 4:9–10 NLT

### MORNING

Lauren had been hurt by girls in middle school and high school. Her experiences included name calling and backstabbing at the expense of her heart. She chose to hang out with the guys as much as she could and threw herself into work to put herself through college. She promised herself she'd never trust another female.

Years went by, and she found herself in a counseling session with a woman who came to be both a mentor and a friend. She led Lauren to the Lord, and He began to connect her to other women who genuinely cared about her. Through the love of these other women, she began to see herself in a new way. She opened her heart to those the Lord directed her to connect with. She needed women to speak truth into her life, and those women also needed to hear what Lauren had to share.

### EVENING

If you've been hurt by girls who pretended to be your friends, know that God wants you to have friends—ones who will love you like He does and who will pray for you.

*Lord, show me the friends that You want to put into my life. Help me to be the friend to others You desire me to be. Amen.*

# DAY 261

## AHHH. . .REFRESHMENT!

*"For in six days the LORD made the heavens and the earth, . . .but he rested on the seventh day. Therefore the LORD blessed the Sabbath day and made it holy."*
EXODUS 20:11 NIV

### MORNING

Wendy looked forward to four days at the campground with her friend's family. No school, church, or household chores. Her plans included sleeping in and sitting by the fire, soothed by its crackling and glow, admiring God's creation in the woods.

Until Wendy stopped for this breather, she was unaware of her deep need for stillness. Month after month, she had pushed herself, filling every day with school and activities, shutting out God's voice. Even Sundays had become a chance for her to get caught up. What she really needed was to stop and rest.

### EVENING

God knew we'd run ourselves ragged. He commands us to rest—for our own good! The truth is that it's difficult to be still and focus on God. There are so many other things competing for our attention. But connecting with Him in spirit is essential for a fruitful life that honors Him. We can't hear Him if there's always a television, cell phone, computer screen, or just busyness in the way. He is worthy of our time. Resting and communing with Him is the best way to spend a Sunday.

*Father, help me to rest on Sunday, quieting myself and being freed from the need to always be doing something. Still me that I might experience Your presence and be refreshed by our time together. Amen.*

# DAY 262

## ASK FOR JOY

*Make the soul of Your servant joyful, for to You, Lord, I lift up my soul.*
PSALM 86:4 NASB

### MORNING

The psalmist buried a nugget in this verse, showing us the source of joy and how to be joyful. All we must do is ask, and then look to God to make us glad.

So often we get stuck in frustration, depression, ingratitude, or anger. We go about our days feeling defeated, without the hope and joy the scriptures promise us. But have we asked our Lord for joy? Have we lifted our souls to Him?

Psalm 16:11 (NASB) tells us, "In Your presence is fullness of joy." When we draw near to God, confessing our sin and our need of Him, we are met by His mercy, His forgiveness, and His perfect love that casts out all fear. In the presence of that love, our joy is found, regardless of our circumstances. He is a father. He desires to love and care for His children.

### EVENING

Just as you want to run to your parent when you are hurt, our heavenly Father longs to hear your voice crying out to Him. Sure, He already knows your need; but He also knows there is benefit for each of us in the confession, in crying out to Him. When we hear ourselves verbally lifting our souls to Him, we are reminded of our need of Him. Confession is good for the soul.

*Father, help me to lift my soul to You, the source of joy. Only You can make me rejoice. Forgive my pride that keeps me from confessing my sins. Draw me into Your loving presence, where there is fullness of joy. Amen.*

# DAY 263

## WHAT'S IN YOUR HEART?

*Delight yourself in the Lord: and He will*
*give you the desires of your heart.*
Psalm 37:4 NASB

### MORNING

What is it that you most desire? Is it a successful sports career or your own car? Do you wish for someone to date or maybe just to spend some fun time with? It really doesn't matter. What does matter is that you are fully committed to God. When that is the case, the desires in your heart will be the ones He places there. He will grant them because they honor Him.

Too many times we look at God's promises as some sort of magic formula. We fail to realize that His promises have more to do with our own relationship with Him. It begins with a heart's desire to live your life in a way that pleases God. Only then will fulfillment of His promises take place.

### EVENING

The promise in Psalm 37:4 isn't intended for personal gain—although that is sometimes a side benefit. It is meant to glorify God. God wants to give you the desires of your heart when they line up with His perfect plan. As you delight in Him, His desires will become your desires, and you will be greatly blessed.

*Lord, I know You want to give me the desires of my heart.*
*Help me live in a way that makes this possible. Amen.*

# DAY 264

## FREEDOM OF RELIGION

*Blessed is the nation whose God is the Lord.*
Psalm 33:12 NASB

### MORNING

We don't have a state religion because our forefathers, who lived under one, experienced it as oppressive, limiting individual freedom. While it might be efficient to have one religion for all, we just won't line up like sheep going through a gate. It's not in our character. We're a nation of fence jumpers.

Were our forefathers great examples of godliness? Probably not. They broke the same commandments we do, just as often as we do. The fact that the press didn't follow them around with a telephoto lens probably helped their reputations, though. . .

### EVENING

It would be inaccurate to say that our country follows the Lord God today and is blessed because of it. As a political unit, it doesn't, but as individuals, we can. Those who prize religious freedom are still free to be as good as they can be, to apply religious principles to their own lives anytime they want to, and to build a nation where the Lord God is free to reign in *their* hearts.

*Father, thank You for the many freedoms we enjoy in this country. Help us build a righteous nation, one person at a time. In Jesus' name, amen.*

# DAY 265

## RESPECT YOUR OPPONENTS

*The wolf will live with the lamb, the leopard will lie down with the goat, the calf and the lion and the yearling [fattened calf] together; and a little child will lead them.*

ISAIAH 11:6 NIV

### MORNING

When playing sports, we often use phrases like "going to war" and terms like "enemies." And in some small sense, both are accurate descriptions. Giving anything less than 100 percent harms our testimony. But seeing opponents as enemies can also lead to disrespect and clouded emotions that can spill onto the field of play.

Isaiah spoke of a future time when the wolf would live with the lamb and the leopard would lie down with the goat, the calf, the lion, and the fattened calf—all against their original nature. But the coming Christ child, whom Isaiah prophesied, would one day change their nature and bring peace to situations in which savagery once reigned.

### EVENING

How might you be able to change the tone of the recreational sports you play? Can you simply "live" with your opponents in a competitive but respectful way? How different would your team or league be if you were to speak highly of opponents before, during, and after a competition?

*Lord, help me to model Your peace every time I step onto the field of play. Amen.*

# DAY 266

## NO REGRETS

*Remember your Creator in the days of your youth,*
*before the days of trouble come and the years approach*
*when you will say, "I find no pleasure in them."*
ECCLESIASTES 12:1 NIV

### MORNING

The teen years are full of promise. You can't wait to drive and have your own car. You look ahead to your future with excitement and imagine the adventure and independence of college. Your future is a blank canvas, and you can be anything or do anything you want!

What most teens *don't* realize is how your choices now can drastically affect your future. One simple choice now can have consequences for the rest of your life that you never imagined.

### EVENING

Ask a teen mom how bright her future looks. Ask a high school senior who drove drunk and killed someone in a car accident. Many teens and college students who live the wild life while they are young come to regret it when they're older.

But if you remember your Creator and stay committed to Him now, you're setting yourself up for success—both now and later! Instead of looking back with regrets and feeling like you've wasted parts of your life, you can look back with peace and happiness and feel abundantly blessed at all the Lord has given you.

The choice is yours—starting now.

*God, help me to make wise choices so I don't have any regrets when I'm older. I want to be committed to You and not dabble in the empty pleasures of the world. Amen.*

# DAY 267

## THE POWER OF GOD'S LOVE

*Above all, love each other deeply,*
*because love covers over a multitude of sins.*
1 PETER 4:8 NIV

### MORNING

Let's face it—we're human. As Christians, we try to follow the teachings of Christ but fall short. Periodically, our actions take the course of a runaway train. Maybe a brother tested your patience, and your intolerance of his behavior ignited you to lash out in anger. Perhaps a sister in Christ took the credit publicly for some good work you did in private, and you seethe. Or maybe someone falsely accused you and you retaliated.

Every believer is flawed, and too often we fail miserably. Peter—endowed with a few flaws of his own—admonished the church to love one another intensely. He, above all, had learned the power of repentance and forgiveness, having denied Christ three times after the Roman soldiers apprehended Jesus. Yet Peter was one of the first to see Jesus after His resurrection, and it was Peter who first reached Jesus on the Sea of Galilee. There, the Lord commissioned Peter to feed His sheep. After Jesus' ascension, Peter—the spokesman of the apostles—preached the sermon that resulted in the conversion of approximately three thousand souls (Acts 2:14–41).

### EVENING

Christ's love forgives and disregards the offenses of others. His love covers a multitude of sins. That's the power of God's love at work. Love resurrects, forgives, restores, and commissions us to reach others for the kingdom.

*Jesus, teach me to love rather than to judge. Amen.*

# DAY 268

## THE CROWN OF LIFE

*Blessed is a man who perseveres under trial; for once he has been approved, he will receive the crown of life which the Lord has promised to those who love Him.*

JAMES 1:12 NASB

### MORNING

Stephen is known as the first Christian martyr. Stoned to death for preaching Christ unashamedly, he entered heaven and saw Jesus standing at the right hand of God. Stephen stood up for Jesus, and Jesus stood up to welcome him home to heaven! Stephen endured a great trial. He paid a high price—his life. Stephen received the crown of life that day as he entered the glory of heaven. In fact, did you know that his name means "crown"?

### EVENING

As you face temptations and trials in your life, be encouraged. Realize that Christ followers through the ages have endured persecution. The temptations you face have been struggles for believers for centuries. The good news is that the Bible tells us that God will always provide a way out when we are tempted. Look for that way! Cling to that Christian support system when you are tempted to stray from God. Make necessary changes that will help you defeat Satan's desire that you fall into his traps. One day you, like Stephen, will receive the crown of life!

*Father God, in the name of Jesus, I will stand against Satan's schemes. I will not give in to temptation. I love You, God. Amen.*

# DAY 269

## POWERFUL PRAYING

*Therefore confess your sins to each other and pray for each other so that you may be healed. The prayer of a righteous person is powerful and effective.*
JAMES 5:16 NIV

### MORNING

When someone we know well, someone we admire and respect, talks to us about something, we usually listen. But if a different person—someone we don't know well or who hasn't earned our respect—talks to us about the same thing, we may not listen with the same intensity. We tend to listen more to people we respect. And when the people we admire ask us for something, we'll often bend over backward to give them what they want.

God is the same way. When we have God's approval, when we live with integrity and faith, He listens to us. But when we consistently make poor choices and disregard God's guidance, He may not take our prayers as seriously.

### EVENING

God will never take His love from us, no matter what; He will always listen when we ask for help out of our sin. But if we want our prayers to hold extra power, we need to live righteously. When we have God's approval on our lives, we can also know we have God's ear about all sorts of things. When we walk in God's will, we have access to God's power.

*Dear Father, I want my prayers to be powerful and effective. Help me to live in a way that pleases You. Amen.*

# DAY 270

# LOVE LEADS TO OBEDIENCE

*God sticks by all who love him, but it's all over for those who don't.*
PSALM 145:20 MSG

## MORNING

Scholars point out that Psalm 145 is one of the "alphabetical psalms" in which each verse (except one, in this case) starts with a sequential Hebrew letter and is ordered alphabetically. This is believed to have been done to aid children so they could memorize and sing it, planting the truth of God deep in their hearts.

As they reached today's verse, Hebrews would have known the importance of loving God. They would have known that loving God is more than mere lip service. Love leads to obedience. Verse 6 of 2 John (MSG) says, "Love means following his commandments, and his unifying commandment is that you conduct your lives in love. This is the first thing you heard, and nothing has changed."

## EVENING

In Luke 6:46 (NIV), Jesus asks a large group of His disciples, "Why do you call me, 'Lord, Lord,' and do not do what I say?" You cannot separate love for God and obedience to Him. Take inventory of your life, comparing your actions to the commands of God. You will never obey Him perfectly, but your desire to obey should be obvious.

*Lord, I know I fall short of Your commands every day. The closer I examine my heart, the more disobedience I see. But my ultimate desire is to obey You. Amen.*

# DAY 271

## THE FLOW OF NATIONS

*In the last days the mountain of the LORD's temple will be established as the highest of the mountains; it will be exalted above the hills, and all nations will stream to it.*

ISAIAH 2:2 NIV

### MORNING

The news is full of reports of torture, abuse, and war. Humankind often doesn't treat each other very well. It's nearly too much to bear in big doses. And it's difficult not to wonder if the world is void of hope. It won't always be this way though.

Isaiah saw a vision in which the Lord's house, which many believe to be the church (the people of God), shall be established on this earth, exalted above the hills (for the gospel shall reign supreme above all else), and all nations shall flow unto it like a mighty river.

### EVENING

Imagine some of the most hostile nations on earth bowing the knee to Jesus. Imagine the sweet sound of the gospel rolling off the lips of once-distant lands. Imagine the darkness being pushed back by the flood of light. Don't lose hope, no matter what you see going on around the world right now. It won't always be like this.

*Lord Jesus, I confess to allowing the events of this world to dictate my mood sometimes, but this verse brings me so much hope as I consider Your faithfulness. Amen.*

# DAY 272

# A WANT AND NEED LIST FOR GOD

*[Jesus said,] "This, then, is how you should pray: 'Our Father in heaven, hallowed be your name, your kingdom come, your will be done, on earth as it is in heaven.'"*

MATTHEW 6:9–10 NIV

## MORNING

*Dear God,*

*Please give me eggs, milk, flour, potatoes, pasta, snow boots, wool socks, ski passes for our family, and a metal snow shovel. Thanks for everything. P.S. You're the best!*

*Love, Justin*

Jesus modeled a pattern for a prayer. It wasn't a lengthy list of needs and wants like Justin's, or a memorized Lord's Prayer; Jesus addressed His Father, our Creator, with thanks and praise. That is the way He suggested we begin. Jesus placed God's will and kingdom first. Then He asked for daily needs and forgiveness.

## EVENING

"Forgive us our debts, as we also have forgiven our debtors" (Matthew 6:12 NIV). This verse highlights the importance of coming to the Lord with a repentant heart. God has forgiven our debt of sin, and Jesus paid it forward.

Jesus taught that before giving an offering at the altar, "First go and be reconciled to them; then come and offer your gift" (Matthew 5:24 NIV).

People always have multiple needs, but our greatest needs are God's kingdom and Christ's love.

*Jesus, we thank You for teaching us honor and respect for You and Your Father, God. Amen.*

# DAY 273

# THE HAND OF GOD

*"For I am the LORD your God, who takes hold of your right hand and says to you, Do not fear; I will help you."*
ISAIAH 41:13 NIV

## MORNING

If there is a Bible verse you need to have handy in times of trouble, this is it! Post it on your fridge; write it on a sticky note to tack up on your bulletin board; commit it to memory so that the Spirit of God can bring it to mind when you need to hear it most.

Psalm 139 tells us that God created us and knows everything about us. He knows when we sit and when we get up, and He knows every word that's on our tongue before we speak it. Psalm 139:7–10 tells us that no matter where we go, God's hand will guide us and hold us.

## EVENING

Heading to the emergency room? Repeat Isaiah 41:13 and remember that God is holding your hand. Afraid of the future? Stop worrying and trust the God who loves you and has great plans for you. Facing a problem that you cannot possibly bear? Take hold of God's mighty hand and believe that He will help you.

*Father God, help me not to fear. Take hold of my hand and guide me. I put my faith and trust in You alone. Amen.*

# DAY 274

## GRACE ACCEPTED

*But because of his great love for us, God, who is rich in mercy, made us alive with Christ even when we were dead in transgressions—it is by grace you have been saved.*
EPHESIANS 2:4–5 NIV

### MORNING

Have you ever been wrongly accused of something or completely misunderstood? Have the words of your accusers struck your heart, making you feel like you have to make it right somehow, but no amount of reasoning with them seems to help?

If anyone understands this situation, it's Christ Himself. He was wrongly accused and misunderstood, yet He offered unfathomable grace at all times. And He still offers it today.

### EVENING

Christ's amazing grace reminds us that we are to aim to offer the same to our accusers and those who misunderstand us. We will be misunderstood when we try to obey and follow God in a culture that runs quite contrary to the ways of Jesus in many ways. Our job is to first accept God's grace and then offer it up to others as lovingly as we can. Like Christ.

*God, help us to continually accept Your grace through Christ and reflect You by offering that same grace to others. Amen.*

# DAY 275

# LIKE LITTLE CHILDREN

*One day some parents brought their children to Jesus so he could touch and bless them. But the disciples scolded the parents for bothering him. When Jesus saw what was happening, he was angry with his disciples. He said to them, "Let the children come to me. Don't stop them! For the Kingdom of God belongs to those who are like these children. I tell you the truth, anyone who doesn't receive the Kingdom of God like a child will never enter it."*

MARK 10:13–15 NLT

## MORNING

Have you ever heard a child pray from their heart? Not just a memorized prayer that they repeat before lunch but a real, honest prayer? A four-year-old boy prayed this: "Dear God, I really don't like all the bad dreams I've been having. Will You please make them stop?"

His prayer was so pure and honest. He prayed, believing that God would listen to his prayer and do something about it. He wasn't afraid to say how he really felt.

This passage in Mark tells us that no matter how old we are, God wants us to come to Him with the faith of a child.

## EVENING

God wants us to be open and honest about our feelings. He wants us to trust Him wholeheartedly, just like little kids do.

Adults sometimes play games with God. They tell God what they think He wants to hear, forgetting that He already knows their hearts! God is big enough to handle your honesty. Tell Him how you really feel.

*Father, help me come to You as a little child and to be more open and honest with You in prayer. Amen.*

# DAY 276

## THIS WAY!

*How gracious he will be when you cry for help! As soon as he hears, he will answer you. . . . Whether you turn to the right or to the left, your ears will hear a voice behind you, saying, "This is the way; walk in it."*

ISAIAH 30:19, 21 NIV

### MORNING

Sometimes making decisions seems like playing hide-and-seek with God. He hides—and we have to seek! But Jesus always wants you to find Him.

You won't get very far in hide-and-seek if all you do is stand in one spot. You have to search. You can pray and pray and pray when you need God's direction, but you also have to get a move on. Take some action! Move a little to the left. Rats, a closed door. Okay, how about to the right? Oh, an open one! Okay, what's through here? . . .

### EVENING

If you aren't sure which summer job to accept, pursue all your options until you feel God guiding you to the right one. Are you unsure which spring sport to play? Try out for soccer *and* track, and see which one brings you more joy and peace.

Finding God's will shouldn't remain an unsolved mystery. The magi followed a star. Moses saw a burning bush. Elijah heard a whisper. Look around you. What clues is God giving you?

*Lord, thanks for always guiding me. Help me move in the right direction by opening and closing doors and giving me peace when I make the right decision. Amen.*

# DAY 277

## LOVING FRIENDS

*But Ruth replied, "Don't urge me to leave you or to turn back from you. Where you go I will go, and where you stay I will stay. Your people will be my people and your God my God."*

RUTH 1:16 NIV

### MORNING

The story of Ruth and Naomi is inspiring on many levels. It talks of two women from different backgrounds, generations, ethnicities, and even religions. Rather than being obstacles to loving friendship, these differences became invisible. Both women realized that their commitment, friendship, and love for each other surpassed any of their differences. They were a blessing to each other.

### EVENING

Do you have friends who would do almost anything for you? A true friendship is a gift from God. Those relationships provide us with love, companionship, encouragement, loyalty, honesty, understanding, and more! Lasting friendships are essential to living a balanced life.

*Father God, thank You for giving us the gift of friendship. May I be the blessing to my friends that they are to me. Please help me to always encourage and love them and to be a loving support for them in both their trials and their happiness. I praise You for my loving friends! Amen.*

# DAY 278

## COME, LORD JESUS!

*It will happen in a moment, in the blink of an eye, when the last trumpet is blown. For when the trumpet sounds, those who have died will be raised to live forever. And we who are living will also be transformed.*

1 CORINTHIANS 15:52 NLT

### MORNING

In today's verse, the church is promised resurrection. A trumpet will sound, the dead in Christ will rise to be transformed into a resurrected body, and those who are living will be transformed. This is the great promise of Christianity. Jesus will return for His church in the most glorious event since the day He willingly died for you on the cross.

### EVENING

Knowing that the final trumpet can sound at any minute, it's time to get busy doing kingdom work, leaving the foolish pursuits of this world behind.

*Lord Jesus, I look forward with great anticipation to the final trumpet. As I live with the resurrection in mind, may it shape every decision I make and every action I take. Amen! Come, Lord Jesus.*

# DAY 279

## THE LEAST

*For I [Paul] am the least of all the apostles. In fact, I'm not even worthy to be called an apostle after the way I persecuted God's church. But whatever I am now, it is all because God poured out his special favor on me—and not without results. For I have worked harder than any of the other apostles; yet it was not I but God who was working through me by his grace.*

1 CORINTHIANS 15:9–10 NLT

### MORNING

Paul's background wasn't a secret. Before his conversion, he persecuted the church. He watched approvingly as Stephen was stoned (Acts 22:20). It's no wonder Paul considered himself the least of the apostles. But the grace of God changed him.

It's difficult to have an inflated ego when you have such a checkered past. Maybe that's your story too. Surely you did things in the past that you regret, but if you've called on the name of the Lord for salvation, you've tasted the same grace of God that Paul is talking about in this passage.

### EVENING

Do you consider yourself the least of the people at your church? What about in your Bible study? Maybe you have been around the church long enough that your ego has become inflated. Paul had quite the religious background (see Philippians 3:3–6), but he had no confidence in his postconversion flesh. Nor should any Christian.

*Lord, apart from Your grace, I am nothing—a worm among worms. With Your grace, I am redeemed, but I am still among the least in Your kingdom. For I know my own heart too well to believe otherwise. Amen.*

# DAY 280

## GOD IS NEAR

*Where can I go from your Spirit? Where can I flee from your presence? If I go up to the heavens, you are there; if I make my bed in the depths, you are there.*

PSALM 139:7–8 NIV

### MORNING

David's questions in today's verses might make it seem as if he actually wanted to find a way to separate himself from God, but that wasn't true. Earlier in the psalm, he listed many of the ways that God was close to him. David was making the case that God is everywhere and always sustains His people.

That's not to say that His people don't hide from Him or pull away from Him during times of sin or hardship. But the great news is that He's never far away. You can trust that about Him. Does this provide great comfort to you, or does it strike fear in your heart? The truth is, it should probably do a little of both.

### EVENING

You can't hide from God, but despite your sin, He sees you through the lens of Christ.

What can you do to be more aware of His presence in your everyday activities? How might becoming more aware of His presence change your routines and further your sanctification process?

*Father, I can't escape Your presence. I praise You for being such a personal God that You never leave me alone. You love me too much to abandon me. Amen.*

## DAY 281

# PROCLAIMING THE LORD'S DEATH

*For whenever you eat this bread and drink this cup,*
*you proclaim the Lord's death until he comes.*
1 CORINTHIANS 11:26 NIV

### MORNING

Communion is the most somber of celebrations because the church looks back on what Christ did for us, recognizing that our sins led to His death while also recognizing that His death led to our redemption. So Christians of all denominations take communion in faith, and the mere act proclaims the Lord's death to a lost and dying world.

Why proclaim His death? Because He's the Lamb of God who takes away the sin of the world by laying down His life as the ultimate sacrifice. Nothing else shows the world that the church is different—set apart for God's use—more than when we proclaim the Lord's death.

### EVENING

Regardless of how often your church celebrates communion, stir yourself up to earnestly desire to be there to partake in it. It's a glorious opportunity to wipe your slate clean and start fresh while also encouraging unbelievers who might be seated around you to do the same the next time they have an opportunity. If they see that the church is serious about its sins, perhaps they'll be inspired to be so as well.

*Lord Jesus, I look forward to the next time my church offers communion. I'll be faithful to examine myself, to confess my sin, and to proclaim Your death until You return. Amen.*

# DAY 282

## CALM DOWN

*He got up, rebuked the wind and said to the waves, "Quiet! Be still!" Then the wind died down and it was completely calm.*

MARK 4:39 NIV

### MORNING

It's been said that life is what happens when you're planning something else, and life is lived in a world of chaos and confusion. For Jesus' disciples, this was evident when they were in a boat during a storm. Waves rushed over and into the boat. The disciples had heard the stories. Men died in storms like this.

Somehow Jesus slept through the panic at the back of the boat. The disciples apparently didn't want to bother Jesus, so they tried to manage on their own. When they finally determined they couldn't, they woke Jesus from sleep. However, instead of asking for help, they accused Him: "Don't you care if we drown?" (Mark 4:38 NIV).

Had they really been with Jesus such a short time that they hadn't observed His compassion?

### EVENING

Why do we accuse God of not helping when we've refused or neglected to ask? This story ends with Jesus calming the storm with three words. These words weren't incantations or spells; they were words of authority. The one who mastered the storm also created the water, clouds, and wind and is Master over all things.

*I like to be in control. I want to prove I don't need as much help as others. Failure follows me all the days of my life. When I am struggling to hold on, remind me to accept Your helping hand. May I trust You with my past, present, and future. Thanks for always taking care of me. Amen.*

# DAY 283

## SPOKEN

*In the beginning was the Word, and the Word was with God, and the Word was God. He was with God in the beginning.*

JOHN 1:1–2 NIV

### MORNING

Saint Francis of Assisi is commonly (and incorrectly) quoted as saying, "Preach the gospel, and if need be use words." However, this is not the biblical example. This godly man knew the importance of intertwining word and deed. Even a quick look through the Gospels and the book of Acts shows the importance of words, which were then verified by miraculous works.

More importantly, Jesus is identified as the Word, who became flesh and lived among us. God chose to reveal Himself through the written and spoken word. He endowed humans with this gift apart from the rest of creation. Jesus and His followers did many wonderful things, but their actions were put into context when they talked to others about God's plan.

### EVENING

Good deeds need to be accompanied by a reason. Who gives the strength and compassion for doing good? Jesus always pointed back to the Father. Christians may not always have occasion to speak, but they should always be ready so that God may get the glory and not man. Paul asks, "How, then, can they call on the one they have not believed in? And how can they believe in the one of whom they have not heard? And how can they hear without someone preaching to them?" (Romans 10:14 NIV). Our words may often seem inadequate, but Christians speak with the living breath of God.

*Eternal Word, guide me to speak Your truth and to know the beauty and power of words that come from You. Amen.*

# DAY 284

## NEVER FORSAKEN

*About the ninth hour Jesus cried out with a loud voice, saying, "Eli, Eli, lema sabaktanei?" that is, "My God, My God, why have You forsaken Me?"*
MATTHEW 27:46 NASB

### MORNING

This point marks the lowest depth of Christ's suffering. At this moment, all the sin of mankind was piled on Jesus, the sacrificial Lamb. The Father turned His face away because in His holiness, He could not bear to look on it. Jesus was completely and utterly alone. For Him, it wasn't just as if someone whom He loved had abandoned Him. In the Trinity, the Father and Son are one and the same. So what happened to Christ on the cross was a mystery and a sorrow that we cannot fathom.

### EVENING

Think about what Christ was willing to suffer to save you. The depth of His love for the people who were responsible for His death is incomprehensible. He deserves your utmost gratitude and service. Because of what Christ went through, you will never have to utter that same agonizing cry. Those who have been covered by the sacrificial blood of Christ will never be forsaken by God. He has redeemed you and presented you blameless before the Father.

*Lord, I will never understand the depth of Your suffering. But help me to comprehend even the slightest bit of the depth of Your love for me. Help me to recognize every day that I was bought with a price and am free only through Your sacrifice. Amen.*

# DAY 285

## THE MAIN THING

*For what I received I passed on to you as of first importance: that Christ died for our sins according to the Scriptures.*

1 CORINTHIANS 15:3 NIV

### MORNING

I like the way the apostle Paul referred to this message as being of first importance—that Christ died for our sins. Stop and think about that. Nothing is more important in the eternal scheme of things than for each of us to come to grips with that truth. It must be deeper than merely something we know in our minds. We must let it sink in and put down roots into our hearts.

Before Paul could pass the message on, he had to receive it. The testimony of his conversion is incredible. He had been a zealous Pharisee who studied the Hebrew scriptures since his youth. He was convinced that Jesus was an imposter and that everyone who believed in Him was breaking Jewish laws. Paul traveled throughout the region arresting Christians wherever he found them until God stepped in, stopped Paul's rampage, and sent believers to teach him the truth.

### EVENING

Paul received the gospel immediately when he finally listened; from that point on, he was on fire with the message that Christ died for our sins. Not only did Paul become a powerful missionary and evangelist, but his letters make up a large portion of the New Testament. His words continue to change people's lives even after two thousand years.

*Heavenly Father, thank You for the good news that Christ died for our sins. It is extremely important for me to pass it on to the people in my life. Amen.*

# DAY 286

## NO FEAR

*"When you pass through the waters, I will be with you; and when you pass through the rivers, they will not sweep over you. When you walk through the fire, you will not be burned; the flames will not set you ablaze."*

ISAIAH 43:2 NIV

### MORNING

Can you imagine standing at the edge of the Mississippi River and having the waters part so you could walk across on a dry riverbed? To call it a miracle would be an understatement.

Scripture tells us over and over of God's mighty acts. He parted the Red Sea so thousands of Israelites could cross on dry land. Daniel spent the night in the company of hungry lions and emerged without a scratch. Three of his friends were unscathed after time spent in a blazing furnace.

These are more than Sunday school stories. They are real miracles performed by *your* God.

### EVENING

God's miracles were not included in scripture merely for dramatic effect, because God's power wasn't just for the Israelites, Daniel, and Shadrach, Meshach, and Abednego. One of the reasons God recorded His mighty acts was so we would have the assurance that His power is available to us as well. When you are facing what seems to be impossible odds, return to God's Word. Recount His marvelous deeds. Then remember that this promise in Isaiah is *yours*.

*Heavenly Father, when I am facing an impossible task, help me to remember all the miracles You have performed. Thank You for the promise that this same power is available to me whenever I need it. Amen.*

# DAY 287

## LEARNING AS WE GROW

*"But I am only a little child and do not know how to carry out my duties."*
1 KINGS 3:7 NIV

### MORNING

When babies are born, they cannot do anything for themselves; they cannot walk or talk or feed themselves. As children grow, they slowly begin to learn new skills, like sitting up, crawling, and walking. Later, children will be expected to put their toys away, make their beds, dry the dishes, or walk the dog. But children do not innately know how to perform these duties—they must be learned.

When King David died, Solomon became the king of Israel. Just like a child who does not yet know how to put away his toys, Solomon confessed that he did not know how to carry out his duties as king of Israel. Instead of sitting down on his throne in despair, though, Solomon called on the name of the Lord for help. . .

### EVENING

As Christians, we are sometimes like little children. We know what our duties as Christians are, but we do not know how to carry them out. Just like Solomon, we can ask God for help and guidance in the completion of our responsibilities. God hears our prayers and is faithful in teaching us our duties, just as He was faithful to Solomon in teaching him his.

*Dear Lord, thank You for being willing to teach me my Christian responsibilities. Help me to learn willingly and eagerly. Amen.*

# DAY 288

## EQUIPPED FOR THE TASK

*[May God] equip you with everything good for doing his will, and may he work in us what is pleasing to him.*
HEBREWS 13:21 NIV

### MORNING

God knew that Paul the apostle would face hard times in his life. This distinguished, well-educated Pharisee went through an intensive training period for more than seven years, living obscurely in his hometown. God equipped Paul because He knew the price he would pay for following Christ: He was lashed five times, beaten three times with rods, stoned once, shipwrecked three times, adrift alone in the sea a night and day, robbed, rejected by his own countrymen, hungry, cold, naked, and resigned to a relentless thorn in his flesh. Through it all, many Gentiles came to know Jesus.

### EVENING

Hopefully, we aren't being equipped for a rigorous life like Paul's. But whatever He's called us to do, He will give what we need to accomplish it. You may not feel you are equipped, but God keeps His promises. Scripture plainly states He's given you everything good for carrying out His work. When you are discouraged in ministry and you want to quit, remember that He promises to work in you what pleases Him. The Spirit empowers us, making us competent for our tasks.

*Lord, help me to draw on Your resources that I might be fully equipped for accomplishing Your tasks. Work in and through me to touch the lives of others as only You can do. Amen.*

# DAY 289

## GET COMFORT—PASS IT ON

*All praise to God, the Father of our Lord Jesus Christ. God is our merciful Father and the source of all comfort. He comforts us in all our troubles so that we can comfort others. When they are troubled, we will be able to give them the same comfort God has given us.*

2 Corinthians 1:3–4 NLT

### MORNING

The Bible says, "In this world you will have trouble" (John 16:33 NIV). God promised that difficulties would be normal. That may sound like a promise we'd be happy to see God fail to keep. We don't like to worry, fear, or struggle. The good news is we don't have to.

God is described as merciful. He offers comfort whenever the struggles come. He may not shield us from trouble, but He does give us a place to rest in the middle of the trials we face.

### EVENING

In times of testing, we grow, we're stretched, and we learn a lot about ourselves and others. When God comforts us, it becomes our responsibility to comfort others and help them find God, the ultimate source of comfort.

We often ask why we have to go through difficulties, but if we accept that everyone struggles, then we may ask the new question "What do You want me to learn?"

*Dear God, because You love us You provide comfort. Help me remember that compassion demonstrates love. Amen.*

# DAY 290

## STAY IN SPIRITUAL SHAPE

*All athletes are disciplined in their training. They do it to win a prize that will fade away, but we do it for an eternal prize.*
1 CORINTHIANS 9:25 NLT

### MORNING

Do you work out to keep your body in decent shape? It takes a lot of determination and effort, but you keep at it because you know it will result in a longer, healthier life. Of course, in time your body will still fail, no matter how hard you train. There's no way around that, but you do everything you can to put it off a little longer.

What about your spiritual training? Do you give an equal amount of time and energy to that?

### EVENING

Do you study the Bible, your spiritual training manual, and obey its commands? Do you take advantage of the personal trainers who are willing to help you at no charge? When you get in spiritual shape, do you help others with their training?

Physical training can take you only so far. Spiritual training is for eternity.

*Lord, don't let me ignore the fitness of my soul, which is far more important in the long run than the fitness of my body. Amen.*

# DAY 291

## KEEP YOUR MIND STRAIGHT

*Don't copy the behavior and customs of this world, but let God transform you into a new person by changing the way you think. Then you will learn to know God's will for you, which is good and pleasing and perfect.*

ROMANS 12:2 NLT

### MORNING

The world is full of amateur tailors trying to make us fit into their patterns, even if they have to squeeze and push us into them. If we don't fit, they will claim it's not because their pattern is wrong but that something's wrong with us.

Some friends think a weekend without getting drunk is a waste of time. If they can't convince you to come along, they'll find someone else to spend time with, because you obviously don't fit in.

If you have your mind straight, this won't bother you. You wouldn't wear a way-too-small pair of jeans, so why should you try to be something you aren't?

### EVENING

You're not stamped out of a mold—you're an individual with your own mind. Don't let anyone convince you that you need to conform to their pattern.

*Father, thank You for helping me set my own priorities. Give me the strength to resist those who want me to ignore my values and adopt their own. Amen.*

# DAY 292

## BE COURAGEOUS

*"This is my command—be strong and courageous! Do not be afraid or discouraged. For the* Lord *your God is with you wherever you go."*

Joshua 1:9 NLT

### MORNING

We all spend a lot of time being terrified. It's true that there's plenty out there to scare us, but not nearly as much as the news reports or movies would seem to indicate.

You can't let yourself be paralyzed by fear or become a prisoner of terror. You need to take some precautions, but you have a life to lead.

### EVENING

In scary times, it helps to remember that God is always with you, urging you to be strong and courageous. Find a balance between caution and trust that will allow you to live a full, satisfying, and reasonably safe life.

*Father, thank You for Your comfort and protection, which give me the confidence I need to lead a full life in a world that is never perfectly safe. Amen.*

# DAY 293

## MY WILL FOR YOUR WAY

*You will show me the way of life, granting me the joy of your presence and the pleasures of living with you forever.*
PSALM 16:11 NLT

### MORNING

It's possible to think that if God is all you have, then you don't really have much. Some people think it's like choosing a library over a roller coaster. They feel that God just isn't exciting enough to allow Him to influence every part of their life. What if they spend time with God and miss out on something fun?

Surrendering to God means your perspective will change. You'll discover a secret that will surprise you. Every amazing experience you've ever had won't satisfy you the way God can. Every experience has a beginning and end. You'll get tired of each new experience. God always comes through.

### EVENING

God invites us to really live life with Him. That life comes with joy-filled satisfaction, encouraging us to put everything else lower on our priority list. Experiences can make us happy, but only God can bring joy; and in His presence, you'll always find a greater satisfaction you didn't know was possible.

*Dear God, I could never have a greater life than the one I can have as Your child. Help me seek and find satisfaction in You. Help me surrender my will for Your way. Amen.*

# DAY 294

## BREATH OF LIFE

*He heals the brokenhearted and bandages their wounds.*
PSALM 147:3 NLT

### MORNING

As a result of sin, every person on earth is born into a fallen world. The sinful condition brings hurt and heartache to all—those who serve the Lord and those who don't. The good news is that as a child of God, you have a hope and eternal future in Christ. Jesus said, "I have told you all this so that you may have peace in me. Here on earth you will have many trials and sorrows. But take heart, because I have overcome the world" (John 16:33 NLT).

### EVENING

When your life brings disappointment, hurt, and pain that are almost unbearable, remember that you serve the one who heals hearts. He knows you best and loves you most. When the wind is knocked out of you and it feels as if there is no oxygen left in the room, let God provide you with the air you need to breathe. Breathe out a prayer to Him and breathe in His peace and comfort today.

*Lord, be my breath of life today and always. Amen.*

# DAY 295

## MEMORY COLLECTOR

*"Each of you is to take up a stone on his shoulder. . . to serve as a sign among you. . . . These stones are to be a memorial to the people of Israel forever."*
JOSHUA 4:5–7 NIV

### MORNING

Shortly after Linda moved out of her parents' house, her mother presented her with a box. When Linda opened it, she was surprised to discover a stash of memorabilia from her past. Photos, ticket stubs, ribbons, dried flowers: Each had held a special significance to Linda during her school years. Memories of people and events long forgotten came flooding back to her as she picked up each cherished item.

We often save items from special events as a way of preserving priceless memories. This is also an important biblical concept. In fact, God instructed the Israelites to do the same thing to remember His faithfulness to them.

### EVENING

Just as the Israelites built altars as a way of remembering God's provision and deliverance, so can we. Has God blessed you through a word of encouragement from a friend, a special provision in a time of need, or just the right scripture verse at just the right time? Consider finding a tangible way to remember these blessings. Make a treasure box for your spiritual milestones, just as you do for your physical milestones. Keeping these memories fresh is one way to find encouragement during times when we need it most.

*Father, help me to look for tangible ways to remember Your faithfulness to me. Amen.*

# DAY 296

## HOLDING ON TO HOPE

*"In this world you will have trouble.*
*But take heart! I have overcome the world."*
JOHN 16:33 NIV

### MORNING

Images on television sometimes convince us that evil triumphs over good. War. Hunger. Poverty. Domestic disputes. Random acts of violence. Drugs.

Seeing the world's brokenness can leave us discouraged. And we Christians do not find ourselves immune from that brokenness. Divorce, racism, and greed pervade our congregations as they do our communities. Some days it is hard to see the difference between how the world lives and how we live: in fear.

This should not be. Christ tells us to hold on to the hope we have in Him.

### EVENING

God's Word tells us to "take heart" because the trials of this world have already been won, the evil has already been conquered, and He has already overcome the world. Do you live your life as though you trust His words, or do you live in doubt?

Live your life as a statement of hope, not despair. Live like the victor, not the victim. Live with your eye on eternity, not the here and now. Daily remind yourself that you serve a powerful and gracious God, and decide to be used by Him to act as a messenger of grace and healing to the world's brokenness.

*Lord, forgive my doubts. Forgive me for growing discouraged*
*and not placing my full trust in You. May I learn to trust*
*You better and to live my life as a statement of hope.*

# DAY 297

## REPAY LOVE WITH LOVE

*"The* L*ORD your God is with you, the Mighty Warrior who saves. He will take great delight in you; in his love he will no longer rebuke you, but will rejoice over you with singing."*

ZEPHANIAH 3:17 NIV

### MORNING

What's your first reaction to today's verse?

"Who, me?" It's a little mind-boggling, isn't it? The Lord wants to save you from your enemies, just as He did for David. He takes delight in you—you make Him smile. When you're upset, His love will calm you. And when you come to Him, He will sing a song of joy.

The Bible's not talking just about a group of people, either. It's talking about *you,* with all your fears and all your faults.

### EVENING

With all the billions of people in this world, all the stars in the sky, and all the other forms of life here or elsewhere, God is not too busy for you. When you fall in love, God is happy with you. When you suffer, He suffers. When you laugh, He laughs.

How do you repay love like that? The only way you can—with love.

*Father, thank You for Your unbounded love. I know I am unworthy, but I am so grateful that You care so much for me. Amen.*

## DAY 298

# SUCCESS LEADS TO HARDER WORK

*"From everyone who has been given much, much will be demanded; and from the one who has been entrusted with much, much more will be asked."*
LUKE 12:48 NIV

### MORNING

Who would complain if they suddenly found themselves rich or were promoted to positions of responsibility? Not too many of us. Everyone loves the idea of a windfall, but the truth is, your work has just begun when you see your dreams fulfilled. . .

### EVENING

When you have nothing, no one expects very much from you. Someone who stocks shelves is not expected to worry about the quality of the merchandise or the foreign exchange rate, but if a shelf stocker is suddenly put in charge of purchasing, he has to scramble to learn everything that goes with the new job and how to handle his new responsibilities.

None of that is bad or to be avoided as long as you realize there's no such thing as a free lunch. Success comes from hard work and leads to even harder work.

*Father, help me remember that it'll be a long time before I can rest on my laurels in this world. The more I have, the more will be required of me. Amen.*

## DAY 299

# GOD DOESN'T GIVE UP

*For I know that nothing can keep us from the love of God. Death cannot! Life cannot! Angels cannot! Leaders cannot! Any other power cannot! Hard things now or in the future cannot! The world above or the world below cannot! Any other living thing cannot keep us away from the love of God which is ours through Christ Jesus our Lord.*

ROMANS 8:38–39 NLV

### MORNING

A lot of things try to separate us from God. We trip on our own sins or over the feet of those we're walking with. We get "too busy" to attend church or too "educated" to trust the Bible. We often forget about God's love in our daily lives, turning to it only when we find ourselves in trouble. Our memory is pretty short, and God seems far away.

Yet none of this or anything else in all creation makes God give up on us.

### EVENING

God's love is always there for us, in good times or bad, in success or failure, in sin or sanctity. We can always go home to Him, no matter how far we stray.

You may have given up on yourself, but God hasn't. Accept His constant love and forgiveness, no matter how undeserving you feel.

*Father, I often feel unworthy of anyone's love, especially Yours. During these times, remind me that You will never give up on me. Amen.*

# DAY 300

## A GOOD NAME

*A good name is to be chosen instead of many riches.*
*Favor is better than silver and gold.*
PROVERBS 22:1 NLV

### MORNING

Life offers us a lot of opportunities to cheat and get away with it. Creative cheaters can bluff their way into a good grade on a report, class presidency, or extra servings at lunch, and they seem to get away with it most of the time.

When they do, it's not always because they're so clever that no one notices. Sometimes the people around them are perfectly aware of the cheating going on, but for reasons of their own, they look the other way. But they usually know who's a cheat, and they would never trust those people with much that is of value. . .

### EVENING

The next time you're tempted to cheat a little, ask yourself if it's worth the consequences. What would you prefer to see on your tombstone? "Here lies an honest woman" or "She was successful, but. . ."?

*Father, there are many ways to get to the top. Help me*
*choose the ones that earn me the respect of others,*
*even if the path is a little longer and harder. Amen.*

# DAY 301

## A CONTINUAL FEAST

*The cheerful heart has a continual feast.*
PROVERBS 15:15 NIV

### MORNING

Ellen finished shopping with a friend and was in a foul mood. It lasted through afternoon errands, dinner, and kitchen cleanup. Finally, the truth dawned on her: She felt terrible because her friend, who never seemed happy, had complained through their entire outing.

Ellen vowed to back off on shopping with her friend, instead keeping their communication to short phone calls or texts. *I can pray for her*, she thought. *But I don't have to spend a lot of time with her.*

Our choice of companions has much to do with our outlook. Negativity and positivity are both contagious.

### EVENING

The writer of Proverbs says that "the cheerful heart has a continual feast," so it's safe to assume that a grumpy heart will feel hungry and lacking instead of full.

While God calls us to minister to those who are hurting, we can do so by making wise choices. The next time someone complains, ask them to pray with you about their concerns. Tell them a story of how you overcame negativity or repaired a relationship. You could help turn their day around, and you won't feel like you've been beaten up afterward.

*God, help me be a positive influence on my friends and family. Give me wisdom and the unwavering hope that comes from Christ so that I may share Your joy with others. Amen.*

# DAY 302

## A GOOD MORSEL

*Taste and see that the LORD is good;*
*blessed is the one who takes refuge in him.*
PSALM 34:8 NIV

### MORNING

Parents must sometimes encourage children to eat foods they may not even want to try. This may be because of the way it looks or smells or because they've gotten the notion it's just not going to be tasty. Having more life experience, adults know that not only does it taste good, it is also good for them.

The world gives the idea to nonbelievers that God isn't worth a taste. The world emphasizes self-focus, while the Lord says to put others before yourself and to put God before all. In reality, walking and talking with God is the best thing you can do for yourself.

### EVENING

As you walk with God—learning to pray, lean on Him, and operate in His will—you are storing up treasures for yourself in heaven. In the world, you are demonstrating the love of Christ and being an influence to get others to taste of the Lord.

Like so many foods that are good for us, all it requires is that first taste, a tiny morsel, which whets the appetite for more of Him. Then you can be open to all the goodness, all the fullness of the Lord.

*Lord, fill my cup to overflowing with Your love so that it pours out of me in a way that makes others want what I have. Amen.*

# DAY 303

## LOVE MADE PERFECT

*There is no fear in love. But perfect love drives out fear, because fear has to do with punishment. The one who fears is not made perfect in love. We love because he first loved us.*

1 John 4:18–19 NIV

### MORNING

It's good to fear God, isn't it? God is awesome and fierce in His power. Yet, while we need to have a healthy respect for God, we don't need to be terrified of Him. At least, not if we really love Him.

We who truly love God with all our hearts and souls have nothing to fear, for we know He loves us even more. We know that although He may allow us to walk through some difficult things, His plans for us are always good. When we love God, His love is made perfect in us. Our love for God causes His love for us to reign.

### EVENING

It's only when we choose not to love God that we need to fear Him; although God's patience is long, He is a just God. He will not let the guilty go unpunished. When we love God with our lives, there's no need for punishment. When we love God with our lives, we love others and put their needs ahead of our own. And that, dear friends, is how His love is made perfect in us.

*Dear Father, thank You for loving me. I want to love You with my life and honor You with my actions. Amen.*

# DAY 304

## LOOK WHO IS CHEERING YOU ON!

*Therefore, since we are surrounded by such a huge crowd of witnesses to the life of faith, let us strip off every weight that slows us down, especially the sin that so easily trips us up. And let us run with endurance the race God has set before us.*

HEBREWS 12:1 NLT

### MORNING

Liam's pastor asked him to help make phone calls to the parents of the younger children in the church. The pastor needed Liam's assistance because many of the older kids in youth group had been hit by a wave of the flu, which had left the group extremely shorthanded. He knew this would be difficult for Liam, but he encouraged him to step outside his comfort zone anyway.

Computers, Liam understood; people. . .not so much! Liam felt a wave of nausea pass into the pit of his stomach. He took a deep breath and tried to press through it. He bowed his head and asked God for strength. . .

### EVENING

Perhaps there are things that you must do that are outside your comfort zone. Remember that you have a crowd of faithful witnesses cheering you on. God's strength is perfect to get you through whatever you must face.

*Lord, there are things that I have to do that really worry me. When I am called upon to do those things, please fill me with Your strength and give me confidence to trust that You will help me do what I need to do. Amen.*

# DAY 305

## BE HAPPY!

*Blessed are those who act justly, who always do what is right.*
PSALM 106:3 NIV

### MORNING

Did you know that the Greek word for *happy* is the same one for *blessed*? It sounds strange to us because we think *happy* refers to an emotional state. The truth is that neither of these words means anything emotional but instead refers to the recognition that everything good or fortunate that happens to us is a gift from God.

In our world today, some people might think that a mistake on a report card in their favor would make it okay to not say a word about the error. But a true Christ follower would not look at this kind of situation as a good or fortunate event. We would find happiness and blessedness in bringing such an error to the attention of the teacher. Our happiness is being honest and doing what is right, because that happiness is the promised spiritual reward.

### EVENING

Because we want to be blessed by God, to be a happy follower of Him, we will seek to always do what is right.

*Gracious and heavenly Father, thank You for Your blessings each and every day. I am thankful to be Your follower. When I am tempted to do something that would displease You, remind me that You will bless me if I act justly. My happiness will be a much better reward. In Your name, amen.*

## DAY 306

# DANCING WITH THE SPIRIT

*Since we live by the Spirit, let us keep in step with the Spirit.*
*Let us not become conceited, provoking and envying each other.*
GALATIANS 5:25–26 NIV

### MORNING

I love to dance! In middle school my dad surprised me with two-stepping lessons. It's a country dance that requires partners, so every week Dad and I had a date and learned to two-step. Dancing with a partner is far different than dancing solo. As girls, we have to follow the guy's lead. When I didn't follow Dad's lead, we'd trip and stumble over each other and mess up the dance moves. But when I stayed in step with him, we sailed across the dance floor doing all kinds of fun spins and twists. . .

### EVENING

Living by the Spirit is a lot like dancing. You have to follow His lead. If you try to go your own way, you'll trip and stumble through life. But if you let the Spirit lead, seeking His guidance and listening to His prompts in your spirit, you'll sail much more smoothly.

Are you taking charge of your life—making your own decisions and going your own way? What's one thing you can do today to allow the Holy Spirit to direct your life?

*God, I want to dance beautifully with You. Help me submit to You today and learn to do things Your way so we dance well together. Amen.*

# DAY 307

# NEW BELIEVERS

*Then he said to his disciples, "The harvest is plentiful but the workers are few. Ask the Lord of the harvest, therefore, to send out workers into his harvest field."*
MATTHEW 9:37–38 NIV

## MORNING

The Bible tells about a woman named Lydia who, unlike many women of her time, was a merchant. She sold expensive purple cloth. Lydia worshipped the true God of Israel, but she had not yet become a believer in Christ.

One day Lydia and others gathered near a river just outside the city of Philippi. It was the Sabbath, and the apostle Paul and several of his companions were in town teaching the people about Jesus. They went down by the river and talked with the women there. While Lydia listened to them, God opened her heart to receive the message of Christ. Lydia believed and was baptized. Then she persuaded Paul and his companions to stay at her home for a while. This was the beginning of Lydia's service for the Lord. The Bible suggests that her home became a meeting place for believers.

## EVENING

Encouragement is important to new believers. After Lydia accepted Christ, she was eager to learn more about Him. Paul and his companions agreed to go to her home, where they encouraged her in her faith. Perhaps you know a new believer who could use your encouragement. Think of ways you can help them today.

*Dear Lord, who can I encourage today?*
*Show me a new believer who could use my help. Amen.*

# DAY 308

## START YOUR DAY WITH GOD

*Listen to my voice in the morning, Lord. Each morning*
*I bring my requests to you and wait expectantly.*
Psalm 5:3 NLT

### MORNING

Mornings are hard for a lot of people—especially night owls who get more done in the evening. And verses like this one can tend to make night owls feel like they aren't as spiritual as those who get up early to be with God.

The reality is that God wants to be the very center of your life. He doesn't want to be merely at the top of your priority list—just another box to check off each day. He wants your heart and attention morning, noon, and night. You won't get more points with God if you read ten Bible verses before your morning cup of tea.

### EVENING

How can you start your day with God even if you haven't gotten up hours earlier for devotions? As you wake up in the morning, thank the Lord for a new day. Ask Him to control your thoughts and attitude as you make the bed. Thank Him for providing for you as you toast your bagel. Ask that your self-image be based on your relationship with Christ as you get dressed and brush your teeth. Continue to pray as you go to school. Spend time in His Word throughout the day. End your day by thanking Him for His love and faithfulness.

God wants a constant relationship with you, and He is available and waiting to do life with you twenty-four hours a day.

*Dear Lord, thank You for the gift of a new day. Help me be aware of Your constant presence in my life. Amen.*

# DAY 309

# UNSTOPPABLE

*God told the serpent: "Because you've done this, you're cursed, cursed beyond all cattle and wild animals, cursed to slink on your belly and eat dirt all your life. I'm declaring war between you and the Woman, between your offspring and hers. He'll wound your head, you'll wound his heel."*

GENESIS 3:14–15 MSG

## MORNING

Nothing is beyond God's control. Even at the Fall, when His brand-new creation was ruined by the serpent's deception and Adam and Eve's disobedience, God immediately announced His prophetic plan to redeem His people—the seed (Jesus) who would crush the serpent and release mankind from sin and death. Nothing catches God off guard.

Satan's whole game plan is based on upsetting God's redemptive plan. Time and time again, Satan failed—even going back as far as Cain killing his brother, Abel. Other examples are when Pharaoh and later Herod killed babies. And when Jesus allowed His hands to be nailed to the cross, Satan thought he had won, but "the one who rules in heaven laughs. . . . For the Lord declares, 'I have placed my chosen king on the throne'" (Psalm 2:4, 6 NLT).

## EVENING

Adam and Eve fell because they didn't trust God. They saw in the serpent's questions a reason to doubt that God was looking out for them. They fell for what today is a common concern—the fear of missing out. God doesn't promise you everything that is good, but He freely gave you His very best in Jesus Christ.

*Even in the worst times, God, You are still sovereign, and Your Word is still being fulfilled. No enemy can ruin Your plans for the world or for my life. Amen.*

## DAY 310

# THE WITNESS OF OBEDIENCE

*So Noah did everything exactly as God had commanded him.*
GENESIS 6:22 NLT

### MORNING

Noah trusted that when God in His power told him to build a ship, he had better get cracking. And people gave Noah a hard time about it. He spent a century building a huge floating boxcar hundreds of miles from the nearest ocean, and his neighbors were asking questions—mocking what they feared or didn't understand.

Yet Noah's obedience was a witness to all. Peter later called him a "preacher of righteousness" (2 Peter 2:5 NIV)—not because he literally preached but because his faithful work of building the ark was a daily warning that the world was doomed. Every day his plodding obedience shouted a warning to people. . .

### EVENING

Amid ridicule and a long wait, Noah would've taken comfort in David's words: "I lay down and slept, yet I woke up in safety, for the LORD was watching over me. I am not afraid of ten thousand enemies who surround me on every side" (Psalm 3:5–6 NLT).

When the world's bad news or your own hardships threaten to overwhelm you, sleep soundly, knowing that your God is sovereign and is watching over you.

*When I obey You, Jesus, I can rest peacefully, knowing that You have my back here and now and my future in the palm of Your nail-scarred hands. Amen.*

# DAY 311

## LET GOD CHOOSE

*But let all who put their trust in You be glad. Let them sing with joy forever. You make a covering for them, that all who love Your name may be glad in You.*

Psalm 5:11 NLV

### MORNING

There's waiting on God, and then there's just waiting. You have an idea, and even though you're pretty sure it came from God, you're still waiting to act. There are always more reasons to wait—such as uncertainty about support or timing—and only one reason to move. But is God telling you "Go" enough? You'll never know until you take that first step.

When God calls you to follow Him, you won't know all the steps and stops along the way. All He told Abram was to "go to the land that I will show you" (Genesis 12:1 NLT). All you know for sure is that God will lead you step-by-step as you obey.

### EVENING

After some ups and downs, Abram eventually learned to trust God. When he and Lot parted company after a land dispute, Abram let his nephew choose the territory he wanted—but really, Abram was letting God choose for him. And whereas Lot chose Sodom, God came to Abram and gave him the rest of the land "as a permanent possession" (Genesis 13:15 NLT). God knows best, so let Him be Himself. You won't regret it.

*God, You will take care of me in ways I can't imagine when I trust You to give me Your best. Amen.*

# DAY 312

## WISE WORDS

*"Let your yes be YES. Let your no be NO.*
*Anything more than this comes from the devil."*
MATTHEW 5:37 NLV

### MORNING

Part of being trustworthy is being a person of your word. It's a lost value at a time when almost everyone feels like they must lie at least a little bit just to get by. And in a broken world, you must look to God as your anchor for what is true and right. To be a person of your word, first you must be a person of God's Word.

God's living Word cuts through the shifting morality and offers clarity (Hebrews 4:12). Even when an issue isn't specifically addressed, the Bible directs you to timeless principles that not only guide you but offer you a brighter path forward (even if in the world's eyes, it's a narrower, more challenging road).

### EVENING

James wrote, "Do not merely listen to the word, and so deceive yourselves. Do what it says" (James 1:22 NIV). A person for whom God's Word is their bond will stand out. When people ask you why you're like you are, you can tell them it's because you're trusting your words to God, who called you to a higher standard and helps you live up to it.

*Father, help me to believe what I say I believe,*
*trusting that Your unchanging and eternal Word*
*will help me to speak and act wisely. Amen.*

# DAY 313

## WITH YOUR WHOLE HEART

*Teach me your way, Lord, that I may rely on your faithfulness;*
*give me an undivided heart, that I may fear your name.*
Psalm 86:11 NIV

### MORNING

Some days we feel pulled in every direction by our responsibilities and worries. Then, when God asks us in His Word to love Him with all our hearts, minds, and strength, we're tempted to throw up our hands. "Look at me! I'm scattered all over the place! How am I supposed to keep this all together?"

During Jesus' arrest and trial, Peter's heart, usually so fervent for his Messiah, was divided by fear. Even though he had been one of Christ's closest disciples, he quickly denied any association with his Master. When he realized what he'd done, Peter wept bitter tears. Yet, after His resurrection, Christ forgave and restored Peter, even commanding Peter to continue His work once He ascended (John 21:15–19).

### EVENING

We may long to love God fully but find our hearts are divided by fear or lack of trust. We might love our school, families, or hobbies more than we love Him. Christ's restoration of us is no less amazing than His conversation with Peter on the shore. Though we may struggle to give Him all our hearts, He continues to love us unfailingly. It is His love that transforms us.

Our Savior calls us to live in hope, trusting in His goodness and His ability to heal our divided hearts. By His mercy and grace, He makes us whole!

*Father, help me pray as the psalmist prayed, believing that Your Spirit can knit my divided heart together in love for Jesus. Amen.*

# DAY 314

## SUFFICIENT GRACE

*And He has said to me, "My grace is sufficient for you, for power is perfected in weakness." Most gladly, therefore, I will rather boast about my weaknesses, so that the power of Christ may dwell in me.*

2 CORINTHIANS 12:9 NASB

### MORNING

No one likes to admit they are weak physically or spiritually. Human nature tries to hide it. Yet God has a plan in using these weaknesses. The apostle Paul had a limitation, a thorn in the flesh, which he begged the Lord to take away. Three times he pleaded for this illness to be taken away from him. Paul then heard the voice of Jesus and understood. Jesus was not going to take this thorn away. It existed because of humankind's fall into sin. He would, however, give Paul strength to endure.

### EVENING

Only when we see our own shortcomings do we realize how large God's grace is. We humble ourselves and recognize Jesus' strength as the only power that can help. When we focus on Jesus, we can boast in our suffering because we know it is being used to mold us. God's redemption is at work using the results of the Fall and of man's disobedience to draw creation back to Himself. The weaknesses do not have power over us. Jesus' power rests in us. The treasure is in overcoming and in having done so through complete surrender to His grace and in perfect fellowship with His power.

*All-sufficient Grace, empower me to remember that when I am weak, it is then that I am strong through Jesus. Amen.*

# DAY 315

# HE WAS TEMPTED

*For since He Himself was tempted in that which He has suffered,*
*He is able to come to the aid of those who are tempted.*
HEBREWS 2:18 NASB

## MORNING

Remember that when Christ was on earth, He had a human nature just like yours. This means that sin was just as enticing to Him as it is to you. Yet He did not sin. Don't brush over the fact that Christ was tempted and yet remained sinless. This means that the temptation itself is not sin. So don't allow yourself guilt over feeling tempted. Instead, recognize that Christ was in that same place, and throw yourself onto His mercy and grace to help you *resist* that temptation.

## EVENING

It's worth noting that Christ did not come to earth in His perfect nature as God. He would not have been able to experience this world and all its heartaches and temptations as we experience it. Though He was still God, He came in human nature. This means that He absolutely understands when you come to Him with your struggles. As the verse states, He is able to come to your aid because He knows what it's like. So ask Him to help you and to give you the strength to resist sin as He did.

*Lord, You know exactly what it feels like to be tempted. So I come to You, not hiding my struggles, but laying them before Your feet. Please give me the strength to stand up against temptation. In Jesus' name, amen.*

# DAY 316

## STANDING FIRM

*"Be quiet!" said Jesus sternly. "Come out of him!" The impure spirit shook the man violently and came out of him with a shriek.*

MARK 1:25–26 NIV

### MORNING

Most children's Bible storybooks portray Jesus as a gentle, peaceful soul. That is an accurate portrayal but not a complete one. While Christ was certainly kind and compassionate, He was also a powerful force to be reckoned with. He was very strong when He needed to stand against injustice.

It's not possible to show complete compassion if we're not able to hold ground when necessary. After all, how can we stand for what's right if we can't stand against wrong? How can we rescue others and ourselves from unfairness if we allow those who are being unfair to plow right over us?

Becoming like Christ requires us to be forceful at times. It means putting ourselves in the line of fire, and even taking a few hits, but not backing down.

### EVENING

The key to knowing when to show softness and when to flex our spiritual muscles is love; all of Christ's actions were driven by love. God's kind of love doesn't manifest itself in a wimpy pushover, but in a disciplined soldier. When we have both gentleness and forcefulness in our arsenal, and know when to use each, we are well on our way to becoming Christlike warriors.

*Dear Father, help me to be stern and stand my ground when I need to. Teach me when to be forceful and when to be gentle. Let all my actions be driven by love. Amen.*

# DAY 317

## VOICE OF CHEER

*For they all saw Him and were afraid. At once Jesus talked to them. He said, "Take hope. It is I, do not be afraid."*
MARK 6:50 NLV

### MORNING

There are many voices in our world. They call to us promising pleasure or wealth or importance. Sometimes they invite us to seek revenge or inflict pain or tell us that we're worthless and urge us to destroy ourselves.

The only voice in the world that is totally "for" us is the voice of Jesus. He calls to us above the clamor of our world and speaks truth—He loves us, He died for us, and He offers us hope and eternal life.

### EVENING

Christ's voice is a voice of cheer. In the darkest times of life, He offers hope, peace, and forgiveness. The disciples' little boat was being tossed by huge waves and they were about to drown; then they saw a figure walking on the water—they were sure it was a ghost. However, when they heard His voice, they knew everything was going to be all right.

So it is today. The addict in the crack house, the drunk in the gutter, the drug pusher in the stairwell, the businessman with his greed, the mother with her fatigue—whatever blackness surrounds us, His voice breaks through and brings us hope.

God has given us voices as well. We can reflect Jesus by being voices of cheer, pointing the way to the only hope for us all—the Savior.

*Thank You, Jesus, for being the voice of cheer. Let me reflect You to my world. In Your name, amen.*

# DAY 318

## OBEDIENCE

*Even though Jesus was God's Son, he learned obedience from the things he suffered.*
HEBREWS 5:8 NLT

### MORNING

Imagine your little sister playing at your mom's feet in the kitchen. The stove is hot, and your mom says repeatedly not to touch it. "Ouch," Mom says. "Don't touch." The little one looks at Mom's face with wonder and a smile. Silly Mom, what is she saying? The gleaming white stove is a temptation. What could possibly be the harm? She reaches up her tender, pink-skinned fingers, and then sudden pain surges through her body. Her hand recoils in agony. From that day forward, she avoids the stove, never needing another reminder.

Pain gets our attention. The wise one learns from pain, changes her behavior, makes corrections, and changes her ways.

### EVENING

Our desire to avoid pain can be a powerful teacher and can protect us from suffering. Even Jesus learned obedience from the things He suffered. His hunger pangs in the wilderness sharpened His focus to His Father. Pain refined Him, and it refines us. When we learn to embrace pain and suffering and diligently learn the lessons they have to teach us, we will become obedient and more like Christ.

*Father, it's hard for me to see pain as a gift. I hate suffering. Yet I understand there is a purpose for pain and suffering. I understand Your desire to use them in my life to shape and refine me. Help me to accept them graciously and to learn from them how to be more like You. Amen.*

# DAY 319

## ANOTHER PROMISED GIFT

*[Jesus said,] "I will ask the Father, and he will give you another advocate to help you and be with you forever—the Spirit of truth. The world cannot accept him, because it neither sees him nor knows him. But you know him, for he lives with you and will be in you."*

JOHN 14:16–17 NIV

### MORNING

When we hear the term *God the Father*, we might think of His work in the Old Testament, envisioning stories of Abraham, Moses, and Noah. When we hear of Jesus, we may think of the New Testament, envisioning stories of the disciples, those He healed, and Easter. How do we think of the Holy Spirit?

It shouldn't be a surprise that most people are unsure how the Holy Spirit works. They hear the name associated with God, but what/who is He? . . .

### EVENING

Jesus promised the arrival of the Spirit and referred to Him as an advocate. He would be "God with us" when Jesus returned to His Father. One way to think of the Holy Spirit is "one who comes alongside." He was sent to help. When you think of the Holy Spirit, think of your story. More than a conscience, the Holy Spirit speaks biblical truth and encourages us to be courageous as we walk with God.

*My story always seems to merge with Your story. I am who I am because Your hand has been a part of my journey from the beginning. You give me life, hope, salvation, and a purpose for my tomorrow. Your Spirit leads, even when I don't recognize His work. Thanks for the story You're still writing for me. Amen.*

# DAY 320

# STEADFAST HOPE

*We have this hope as an anchor for the soul, firm and secure.*
HEBREWS 6:19 NIV

## MORNING

Have you ever been on a boat that was drifting? The feeling of rocking with the waves is hypnotic, and the boat can move much farther than you anticipated because it lulls you into complacency. In our spiritual lives, we can become complacent when things go well, not pursuing the things of God or seeking Him in prayer.

The author of the letter to the Hebrews describes hope as an anchor for our soul. An anchor for a ship holds it steady and in place, keeping the craft from moving too far from its set course. Without this hope, we become hypnotized by the world's temptations, and we can move away from the main purpose of life: to know Jesus and make Him known.

However, when we continually seek Christ, God gives us hope that holds us steady, even when storms threaten to rock our faith.

## EVENING

The comforting presence of the Holy Spirit keeps us strong. If you've ever experienced devastating grief after you came to Christ, you may have experienced something supernatural and unexplainable: peace in the middle of deep sorrow. This is the hope that holds us secure: that we are not alone, our suffering is for a season, and we will see all things made right one day in the kingdom of heaven.

*Jesus, thank You for the resurrection hope You provide.*
*It makes my mind, heart, and soul steady and strong*
*when the winds of circumstances blow. Amen.*

# DAY 321

## HOLD TIGHT TO HIM

*Reverently respect* G*OD*, *your God, serve him,*
*hold tight to him. . . . He's your praise! He's your God!*
DEUTERONOMY 10:20 MSG

### MORNING

Deuteronomy 10:20 holds three commands and an eternal truth we can apply to our everyday lives. The first command tells us to live with respect for our God. Several times God's Word states that reverent fear or respect for the Lord is the beginning of wisdom and knowledge.

The second command tells us to serve Him. That is our purpose here on earth: to serve and worship the Lord.

The third tells us to hold tight to Him. This command makes the verse so much more personal. God is our loving Father who wants to comfort us and hold us throughout life—through the good and the bad.

### EVENING

Deuteronomy 10:20 ends with a reminder that God is our praise. He is a good and loving God worthy of our affection. James 4:8 tells us that if we draw near to God, He will draw near to us. So hold tight to the Lord and experience His presence in your life.

*Dear Father, help me to live with respect for You in all areas of my life. I want to serve You with all my heart. Thank You for wanting to draw near to me as I hold tight to You. Amen.*

# DAY 322

## WORTHWHILE SUFFERING

*Yet what we suffer now is nothing compared*
*to the glory he will reveal to us later.*
Romans 8:18 NLT

### MORNING

At times the things you endure for the cause of Christ will bring a great deal of suffering. Family, friends, and acquaintances will not understand the decisions you make or the convictions you hold dear. This is especially true if the situation directly involves them. They might mock or reject you. They might try to inflict feelings of guilt. There are many ways they might react, and few are pleasant.

Determine today to stand strong in your convictions. God's ways are the right ways even when you don't understand them. You might suffer for a while, but think of the rewards that are coming.

### EVENING

It might be hard to determine God's will in some circumstances. It's true that universal things that God expects from all believers are revealed in His Word. However, issues specific to your own life are sometimes harder to determine. You might think you know what He wants, but someone you love—at times even another believer—has other ideas. These differing convictions can be confusing and discouraging. That is why it is so important to stay close to God. He will guide and bless you in His time.

*Lord, sometimes I suffer as I try to do Your will. It hurts,*
*but I know You make all things beautiful in Your time. Amen.*

# DAY 323

# THE TRUTH ABOUT THE HOLY SPIRIT

*"Then I will ask My Father and He will give you another Helper. He will be with you forever. He is the Spirit of Truth. The world cannot receive Him. It does not see Him or know Him. You know Him because He lives with you and will be in you."*

JOHN 14:16–17 NLV

## MORNING

To some Christians, the Holy Spirit is a mystery. To others, He is a frightening part of the Trinity. And even for adult believers, the Holy Spirit is often misunderstood.

Jesus called the Holy Spirit a comforter, helper, and friend. In Acts, the Messiah-promised Spirit fell on the early church with power. He made the new Christians bold, authoritative, and fearless. And the Spirit longs to do the same for us.

## EVENING

Are you lonely? Let the Holy Spirit be a friend to you. Are you grieving? He will comfort you. He can guide you to the perfect scriptures for your grief, and He will pray to the Father for you when you don't have the words. Do you want to make a difference for Christ? Pray for the Spirit to give you opportunities to share your faith with seekers.

Our Father wants to make the Spirit less of a mystery. Jesus longs for you to understand the one who came to be with the church after He ascended to heaven. And instead of frightening you, the Holy Spirit wants to be as much of a second nature to you as your next breath.

Will you let Him?

*Father, thank You for providing the Holy Spirit. Make me aware of His promptings and help me to understand the Spirit's dealings with me. Amen.*

# DAY 324

## RELEASING YOUR WORRIES

*"Look at the birds of the air; they do not sow or reap or store away in barns, and yet your heavenly Father feeds them. Are you not much more valuable than they? Can any one of you by worrying add a single hour to your life?"*

MATTHEW 6:26–27 NIV

### MORNING

God loves you so much. You are His precious child, created in His image. He longs for you to find rest in Him. Over and over in His Word, He reminds you that you do not need to worry. He calls you to cast your cares upon Him because He cares for you. He offers a special peace that the world cannot give. He vows that He has plans to prosper and not to harm you. He says you are His sheep and He is the good shepherd. He does not want you to worry.

Worry is a human thing. It is not of God. As Matthew 6:27 points out, worry cannot add a single hour to your life. It is, in other words, pointless and a waste of time.

### EVENING

Rest right now. Calm your mind and heart before God. Consciously release to Him all the worries that you cling to so tightly. Ask your Father to take care of you as He does the birds of the air and the flowers of the fields. He made you. He knows just what you need.

When your mind begins to race, remember that God has you in the palm of His hand. Don't worry. God is good.

*Father, take the worries that I am burdened by today. Give me rest. In Jesus' name, amen.*

# DAY 325

## A ROARING FIRE

*For the word of God is alive and active. Sharper than any double-edged sword, it penetrates even to dividing soul and spirit, joints and marrow; it judges the thoughts and attitudes of the heart.*

HEBREWS 4:12 NIV

### MORNING

The world is filled with books on every topic and in many languages. You can find pages at your fingertips on a computer keyboard and can explore volumes of information that provide you with entertainment and knowledge, but only the Bible—the Word of God—can truly speak to you.

No matter what you are facing, there is always something in the Bible to help you find your way. There is simply no other book like it. Other books can encourage, inspire, and motivate, but the Bible gives life. The Word of God can fill you with strength, sustain you in battle, and uphold you during the darkest days you'll ever face.

### EVENING

Maybe for you the fire of God's Word starts out as a small glowing ember. You could read for days, and then suddenly you stumble upon that verse—those amazing words—written so many years ago that seem written specifically to you. You know it the moment the Word comes alive as it ignites your heart. It comforts you, provides an answer to the questions you've been asking, and consumes you with a hunger for the truth.

*Lord, I want to read Your Word and hear Your voice as it speaks to me. Ignite me with a passion for the Bible. Amen.*

# DAY 326

## GENUINE ARTICLE

*"Whoever speaks on their own does so to gain personal glory, but he who seeks the glory of the one who sent him is a man of truth; there is nothing false about him."*

JOHN 7:18 NIV

### MORNING

Amy is solid and true. She isn't swayed by the opinions of others or what's in style. She doesn't have to always be the center of attention. Knowing the job is done for God's glory is enough. Is she stiff or boring? On the contrary—she's refreshing! There is nothing fake about her. She has the freedom to be herself, to be who God created her to be. She is liked and respected for her strength of character, which is actually Christ shining through her.

### EVENING

Recognition, achievement, money, fame—that's what matters to many people. While there is nothing wrong with these, how they're obtained does matter. Self-promoters push their way through. They can be shallow and a pain to be around. Christ promoters are secure in not having to receive accolades. This brings freedom and an authenticity that, in the long run, outshines the self-absorbed heart. By focusing on Christ and the glory He deserves, we allow God to touch others as well as produce in us an enriched life as a person of truth.

*God, sometimes I find I am promoting myself rather than giving You the honor. All of life is about You. May that be obvious in my words and actions. Help me to be all I am created to be because You are foremost in my heart. Amen.*

# DAY 327

## DID YOU HEAR. . . ?

*Though some tongues just love the taste of gossip, those who follow Jesus have better uses for language than that.*
EPHESIANS 5:3 MSG

### MORNING

Our tongues can sing the highest praises of someone or destroy them—all in the matter of a few seconds. And once those negative words slip past our lips, there is no way to erase them, no matter how much we wish we could.

Have you ever been a victim of gossip? It hurts when we hear what someone has said about us! The words can tear us up inside. A close friendship can easily be ruined as a result of breaking a trust.

One more question to consider: Have you ever spread gossip? You may have thought it harmless, perhaps even sharing it only as a "prayer request." However, the words you spoke may have injured someone deeply. . .

### EVENING

Before speaking, take a moment to consider whether what you are about to say would be considered gossip. Those few seconds could spare a lifetime of grief!

If you have given your life to Jesus, your whole body is His—including the tongue. Commit it to Him, and ask Him to help you to control the words that come from your mouth. Remember, "Those who follow Jesus have better uses for language than [gossip]."

*Dear heavenly Father, please guard my tongue so I won't be guilty of spreading gossip. Help me to seek forgiveness if I have and to be forgiving when gossip is spread about me. Amen.*

# DAY 328

## PERMISSION TO TURN YOUR BACK

*"Repent of your sins and turn to God,*
*so that your sins may be wiped away."*
ACTS 3:19 NLT

### MORNING

It doesn't take much skill to sin, and it only gets easier.

Doing the wrong thing can seem empowering. Wearing the wardrobe of a rebel can appear to offer independence, but it never does. The choice to sin is actually inviting our enemy to influence future decisions.

God knows that the end result of sin is death, which is why He gives us access to life.

### EVENING

We're restored in our relationship with God when we turn from the easy choice to sin to the life-affirming choice to obey. Repentance requires turning away from the choice to sin.

Sometimes we want to be forgiven, but we don't want to stop making the same sinful choice. We ask God to forgive, but we keep looking at and entertaining the same sinful choices.

The choice to turn away can seem hard. You have an emotional attachment to sin. God wants to change your mind. Repentance is your positive response to His desire to restore you to life.

*Dear God, there are times I don't want to do the right thing. You offer forgiveness, but You want me to turn my back on the easy choice and follow You. Help me listen for Your voice, read Your words, and follow Your plan. Amen.*

# DAY 329

## CHOOSE THE RIGHT PATH

*The fear of the Lord is the beginning of wisdom. All who obey His Laws have good understanding. His praise lasts forever.*

PSALM 111:10 NLV

### MORNING

We all need to feel respected. Unfortunately, respect is hard to earn when you're young. If you haven't been in the club very long, almost no one will bother to listen to your good ideas, let alone act on them. Some members will even steal your ideas, taking the credit that rightfully belongs to you! What should you do?

Two paths lead to respect, and the one you choose determines your future—so choose carefully. The first path comes most naturally. You watch your back, strike before you're struck, and butter up the right people until you've clawed yourself to the top. . .

### EVENING

What's the second path to respect? Follow the principles laid down by the Lord. This is not the easy way. It's not a shortcut, and at times it doesn't even seem to work. But it will soon give you self-respect—the first step on the path to success.

*Father, help me choose wisely when I come to life's crossroads. Give me wisdom to choose the Lamb's path rather than the tiger's. Help me be someone who's respected for the way I live rather than for the damage I can do. Amen.*

# DAY 330

## FINANCIAL WISDOM

*When God gives someone wealth and possessions, and the ability to enjoy them, to accept their lot and be happy in their toil—this is a gift of God.*
ECCLESIASTES 5:19 NIV

### MORNING

Your parents probably have no more spare cash than you do. After all, your living expenses are less than theirs at this point, and they're trying to save up for retirement. Your father may have been downsized a few times, your brothers and sisters have taken their share for educational expenses, and pension plans aren't what they used to be.

That doesn't mean you can't go to your parents for help now or in the future. Maybe they're still housing and feeding you. Or maybe you'll have gotten your own place but are having trouble making the rent. Whatever your situation, if you have a job, you need to pay at least some of your own way—maybe even cut out some of the frills. Mom and Dad have already done that.

### EVENING

There's no need to pity your parents or suffer from guilt when you need help. They consider you a good investment, and you haven't disappointed them. You are their gift from God—and their gift to God.

*Lord, I'm not sure how financially secure my parents are these days, but I need to learn to handle my own money wisely. Amen.*

# DAY 331

## THE INSTRUCTION BOOK

*How can a young person stay on the path of purity? By living according to your word.*
PSALM 119:9 NIV

### MORNING

Finding time to read is hard, but why not dig out your copy of the Bible and put it where you'll see it every day? It has everything you need. It has plenty of action and suspense, not to mention memorable characters. If you run into something you don't understand, you can flip the page and find a new subject. If you're dealing with a problem in your life, the answers to it are in the Bible. Plus, it can be read in short spurts. You can read a whole psalm while the bread is toasting.

### EVENING

Reading the Bible will teach you how to live according to God's wishes. You can't be a good person without knowing what a good person does. Invest in a concordance, and you'll be able to find everything the Bible says about whatever subject interests you. Then you'll know what God wants you to do. Life *does* come with an instruction Book.

*Father, when I have a question about what I should do in a certain circumstance, remind me that all Your answers are there for me in Your Word. Amen.*

## DAY 332

# SHOW RESPECT AND GENTLENESS

*Always be prepared to give an answer to everyone who asks you to give the reason for the hope that you have. But do this with gentleness and respect.*
1 PETER 3:15 NIV

### MORNING

Christians should be rich in hope, secure in the blessings they see ahead. Even when times are tough, they have faith in the future.

This confuses people. "You just lost your job? How can you smile?" "Your car's been totaled? How can you be so calm?" When people have known you for a while and see that you *consistently* react with hope, they will be impressed and truly want to know how you do it.

### EVENING

When asked about your hope, you don't have to give a long theological answer. Be gentle. Since you probably already know these people, you can tailor your answer so that you show respect for their beliefs.

You've sat around and discussed sports teams, life on other planets, and the latest music. The rules are the same here. Don't be concerned when people seem truly interested in gaining a little hope for themselves.

*Father, give me wisdom when people ask me about my faith. Help me answer their questions with gentleness and respect, bringing glory to You. Amen.*

# DAY 333

# RESPONSIBLE CONDUCT

*Pay careful attention to your own work, for then you will get the satisfaction of a job well done, and you won't need to compare yourself to anyone else. For we are each responsible for our own conduct.*

GALATIANS 6:4–5 NLT

## MORNING

Once you graduate and go out into the world, peer pressure lessens—though you will always have some pressure from the groups to which you belong, whether work, church, or social groups. At this point in life though, you have more groups to choose from and their demands are more moderate, so you have more freedom. You have the chance to "reinvent" yourself. A shy high school student can choose to speak out in a new group. A follower can become a leader, or a leader can decide to take a break.

## EVENING

Now is the time to become the person you've always thought you could be. Carefully choose the groups with which you want to associate. Assume responsibility for your own actions and take pride in the way you live, "for we are each responsible for our own conduct."

*Lord, now that I have the freedom to be whoever I want to be, help me make wise choices. I want to live a life I can be proud of, and I know You have something special in mind for me. Amen.*

## DAY 334

# SERVE WHOLEHEARTEDLY

*Serve wholeheartedly, as if you were serving the Lord, not people.*
EPHESIANS 6:7 NIV

### MORNING

Young people are noted for their vitality and enthusiasm. God likes that attitude so much that He promises to reward those who show that kind of wholeheartedness in their work, doing it as if they were working for Him instead of for their bosses.

Unfortunately, age and experience seem to take the edge off our enthusiasm. Some jobs just don't reward it. At first, employers welcome enthusiasm, but then it begins to annoy them. Like too much sugar, enthusiasm can become—well—just *too much*. . .

### EVENING

How do you strike a good balance of just enough versus too much enthusiasm? Look at someone older than yourself, someone well respected and successful at work, and see how that person operates. You'll see she's thorough in her work, quiet and humble, but when she speaks, people listen. They know that in her own quiet way, she's working wholeheartedly.

She probably started off just like you, but she was able to rein herself in until she learned her job. If you too can learn to harness your energy productively, you'll be on your way to success.

*Father, show me how to channel my enthusiasm into solid work that pleases both my employer and You. Amen.*

# DAY 335

## WELL-LAID PLANS

*You can make many plans, but the LORD's purpose will prevail.*
PROVERBS 19:21 NLT

### MORNING

There's nothing wrong with making plans, but ultimately, all our plans depend on the will of God—and sometimes His will and ours are not the same. He knows when our plans won't get us where we should be, so sometimes He puts a roadblock in front of our carefully thought-out path and nudges us in another direction—while we mutter and complain about the detour. . .

### EVENING

Just because scripture tells us that "the LORD's purpose will prevail," this doesn't mean we shouldn't plan at all and leave everything to God. That would be aimlessly wandering around without purpose. We must be flexible in our planning though, aware that several roads may lead us where we want to be. We may not be able to see far enough ahead to plan the route, but God can, and His plans for us will never fail.

*Lord, be patient with all my plans and dreams, even the ones You know won't work out the way I think they will. You've given me this need to look ahead, so it must be a good thing. Now give me the faith to trust You when everything falls apart, knowing You will lead me onto the right path for my life. Amen.*

# DAY 336

## GOOD INTENTIONS DO COUNT

*Let us cleanse ourselves from everything that can defile our body or spirit. And let us work toward complete holiness because we fear God.*

2 CORINTHIANS 7:1 NLT

### MORNING

Unless you plan to live the life of a hermit, this verse is going to give you problems. We live in a thoroughly contaminated world where it's difficult to be even a little holy, let alone perfectly holy.

Start with the most important fact though: Your sins have *already* been forgiven.

### EVENING

How do you thank someone for saving your life now and forever? By trying to be what He wants you to be. No, you are not going to do it perfectly. Yes, you will still sin. But you will steer clear of situations that God disapproves of. You will treat your body as the holy temple of God, who lives in you. You will treat others the way you want to be treated. It's a start, anyway, and this is one case where good intentions *do* count.

*Father, I can never live my life in total holiness, but I can show my thankfulness and reverence for You in many ways. Help me live my life in a way that will reflect Your glory and mercy and eternal love. In Jesus' name, amen.*

# DAY 337

## HELP MY UNBELIEF!

*"What do you mean, 'If I can'?" Jesus asked. "Anything is possible if a person believes." The father instantly cried out, "I do believe, but help me overcome my unbelief!"*
MARK 9:23–24 NLT

### MORNING

This story in the New Testament tells of a man who brought his demon-possessed son to Jesus for healing. First, he asked the disciples to drive out the demon, but they could not. Then he said to Jesus, "But if You can do anything, take pity on us and help us."

The man had his focus on his problem instead of on Christ. He was thinking about how long his son had been possessed and the great damage that had been done. He wasn't convinced that Jesus could do anything about it. But Jesus corrected the man and showed him that anything is possible through Christ.

### EVENING

Are you facing hard times right now? Does your faith feel a little weak? When you are tempted to let your problems get the better of you and you feel that your faith isn't strong enough to overcome, pray for God to change your thinking from doubt to firm faith in Christ. And remember, when you are weak, He is strong!

*Heavenly Father, my problems seem too big for me to handle right now. I trust You, and I want to believe that You are bigger than anything I'm facing. Help my unbelief! Amen.*

# DAY 338

## SOUND ADVICE

*Perfume and incense bring joy to the heart, and the pleasantness of a friend springs from their heartfelt advice.*

PROVERBS 27:9 NIV

### MORNING

Did you ever ignore unwanted advice, such as "You know, I think if you'd only cut down on chocolate, you could lose that extra ten pounds" or the backhanded approach: "I don't care what others think—you're a wonderful person"?

When someone who knows or cares little about you offers criticism, it is offensive. Yet the Bible emphasizes that constructive criticism, offered in love, is a pleasant perfume. In fact, the scriptures instruct us to beware of flattery and embrace godly correction.

### EVENING

Receiving and giving criticism is risky business, but both are necessary elements to our Christian growth. Although we may shudder at first, loving criticism lessens tunnel vision and serves as a springboard to positive changes.

As for the unwanted advice from self-appointed counselors? Ignore it!

*Father, thank You for friends who care enough to season their suggestions with love. Amen.*

# DAY 339

# A FOREVER PASSWORD

*If we are children of God, we will receive everything He has promised us. We will share with Christ all the things God has given to Him.*
ROMANS 8:17 NLV

## MORNING

In today's high-tech society, passwords are required for so many things in our lives, including bank ATMs, computer settings, and bill paying. These passwords identify the user and are intended to keep others out of our business.

Rejoice. Because God loved us so much, He gave us an eternal password: Jesus. Once we acquire this password through salvation and set our hope in Him, we become heirs with Christ. Children of the King. Precious saints. These are names given to us by the Father to set us apart from the world because of His great love.

## EVENING

Unlike the security passwords for business, this password given by Christ can never be compromised. We are safe and secure in the Father's arms and able to access His promised gifts. Open your Bible and discover all that is available to you as a believer: eternal life, provision, and blessing upon blessing. Then praise Him for His wondrous love. His awesome care. Jesus. That's the most important word you'll use. As a child of the King, you have rights to so much through your special relationship and kinship. What a blessing it is to know that Jesus is the password to the kingdom of God!

*Heavenly Father, thank You for Your everlasting love. I will store the password You have given me in my heart, for all eternity. Amen.*

## DAY 340

# WAITING FOR THE STORM TO PASS

*You do not know about tomorrow. What is your life? It is like fog. You see it and soon it is gone. What you should say is, "If the Lord wants us to, we will live and do this or that."*

JAMES 4:14–15 NLV

### MORNING

Summer monsoon seasons in Tucson, Arizona, can bring a haboob—a violent, desert dust storm. Dust forms a high wall with winds up to thirty miles per hour. The storm can last up to three hours. People respond differently to the storms. Some drivers try to press through with extremely low visibility. Others wait it out.

One individual, Dex, shared with a friend, "When my parents and I got caught in the haboob last night, instead of trying to move through it, we decided to enjoy it. We stopped, went to a movie, ate dinner out, and made it home before 10 p.m." . . .

### EVENING

The storms of life are always going to come. The next time you see a storm on the horizon, choose to have a little fun while you are waiting for the storm to pass!

*Lord, sometimes I get lost in the storm. I'm looking at the damage the storm can do instead of looking to You. Help me to rest in Your peace and have a little fun while waiting for the storm to pass. Amen.*

# DAY 341

## NO GREATER LOVE

*For God so loved the world that he gave his one and only Son, that whoever believes in him shall not perish but have eternal life. For God did not send his Son into the world to condemn the world, but to save the world through him.*

JOHN 3:16–17 NIV

### MORNING

Probably the most memorized passage of scripture, John 3:16 is the gospel in one sentence. We memorize it at an early age, so our ears become accustomed to hearing it. But have you allowed it to completely change your life?

God didn't send Jesus to condemn us! He came to save us by giving up His life for ours. John 15:13 (NLT) says, "There is no greater love than to lay down one's life for one's friends." That is the very foundation of Christianity. As author C. S. Lewis said, "Christianity, if false, is of no importance, and if true, of infinite importance. The only thing it cannot be is moderately important."

### EVENING

The next time you recite John 3:16 or listen as this verse is being read aloud, allow the words to truly seep into your soul once again. Thank God for His amazing gift of life and His unfailing love for us.

*Heavenly Father, thank You for the cross and its infinite importance in my life. Thank You for making a way for me to know You and live eternally with You. I give my life fully to You. Teach me how to live for You. Amen.*

# DAY 342

## SECOND CHANCES

*"I, even I, am he who blots out your transgressions,*
*for my own sake, and remembers your sins no more."*
ISAIAH 43:25 NIV

### MORNING

How many of us have hung our heads low, knowing we really messed up—wishing we could redo that homework assignment, take back the unkind words that leaped from our mouths without thinking, or even pull back that email message right after we clicked SEND? We've all done something we wished we could undo. Often, we think we have failed not only ourselves but also God. . .

### EVENING

The Bible is full of people whom God used even though they made mistakes. Moses had an anger problem. Saul (later Paul) was harmful to Christians before becoming a great apostle. Jacob was deceptive. The wonderful thing about our faith is that we serve a God of second chances. Not only is He willing, but He wants us to confess our sins so He can forgive us. Sing praises for the wonderful blessing of starting over!

*Gracious and heavenly Father, we are grateful that we serve a God of second chances. In fact, You give us more than two chances, and You don't keep score. We are all prodigals, and we need to feel Your love and forgiveness. Thank You for loving me enough to not give up on me. You are still with me! Amen.*

# DAY 343

## GOD AS FATHER

*"I am the Living One; I was dead,*
*and now look, I am alive for ever and ever!"*
REVELATION 1:18 NIV

### MORNING

When we think of God as our Father, many times we naturally compare Him to our own father. But our earthly fathers aren't perfect, and that can create misperceptions about God. So what does the Bible say Father God is like?

He is the Creator of everything (see Acts 17:24–29) and the sovereign ruler of all nations (see 1 Timothy 6:15). He is a holy judge who deserves respect and reverence (see 1 Peter 1:15–17; Ephesians 2:1–3). He demands justice for our sins but also provides loving mercy through offering His own Son to take our punishment (see Romans 3:24–26). He loves us and takes pleasure in us and lavishes us with His blessings (see Ephesians 1:3–14). He is faithful (see 1 Corinthians 1:9) and passionate about restoring our relationship with Him (see John 3:16).

### EVENING

What does the term *Father* mean to you? How much does your relationship with your earthly father affect your relationship with your heavenly Father? Is your view of God unbalanced? After learning what the Bible says about God as Father, how does your perception of Him need to change?

*Father God, Your role as holy judge makes me approach You with reverent respect. But Your compassion, mercy, and love overwhelm me. You are mighty and powerful, yet You love fervently. Thank You for loving me! Amen.*

# DAY 344

## HAVE YOU THANKED SOMEONE TODAY?

*They have been a wonderful encouragement to me, as they have been to you. You must show your appreciation to all who serve so well.*

1 CORINTHIANS 16:18 NLT

### MORNING

Have you thanked your pastor, friends, or family who have encouraged or helped you just when you needed it?

Paul wrote to the Corinthian church and explained that Stephanas and his family were the first converts in Achaia and that they devoted themselves to serving others. He reminded them that when Stephanas, Fortunatus, and Achaicus arrived in Corinth, they supplied whatever needs the people had and they "refreshed my spirit and yours" (1 Corinthians 16:18 NASB).

When true believers serve, they serve from the heart rather than from an inward desire for outward praise. This is what Stephanas did, yet Paul still prompted the church to show appreciation for God's servant and what he did for them.

### EVENING

Do you ever feel taken advantage of? Do you work hard and receive little to no recognition? As God's servants, we work because we love Christ; yet an occasional display of appreciation is always. . .well, appreciated. That's what Paul communicated. "Hey guys, let's encourage our brothers by showing our appreciation to them for all they did for us!"

Paul's suggestion holds true today. Thank someone who has refreshed your spirit. It will encourage them and you to keep persevering on life's pathway.

*Lord, encourage me to show my appreciation to those who have touched my life with Your love and grace. Amen.*

# DAY 345

## LOVING THROUGH OUR ACTIONS

*He has shown you, O mortal, what is good. And what does the Lord require of you? To act justly and to love mercy and to walk humbly with your God.*
MICAH 6:8 NIV

### MORNING

The beautifully wrapped gift box was thrust in the direction of Brent's date. He hoped that the gift of an expensive necklace would make the proper impression on Lily. Although they had been seeing each other for a while, Brent kept heaping gifts on her, hoping that she would fall in love with him.

How many of us have thought a similar thing about our relationship with God? If we're good enough, God will bless us richly. If we pray the right way or make sure we go to church every Sunday, He will make things go our way. Is this the right way to impress our Father?

### EVENING

The prophet Micah names three great acts of love for God and fellow man that will glorify God: to be righteous and fair to everyone, to show kindness freely and willingly to all, and to live humbly in a conscious fellowship with a sovereign King. Our motives should be to please Him through the legitimate gift of selfless service to Him and our fellow man.

*Gracious Father, thank You that You love me just as I am and that there is nothing I can do that can make You love me more! May I continue to serve You by selfless service to others. Amen!*

# DAY 346

## REST FOR YOUR SOUL

*"Come to me, all you who are weary and burdened, and I will give you rest. Take my yoke upon you and learn from me, for I am gentle and humble in heart, and you will find rest for your souls. For my yoke is easy and my burden is light."*

MATTHEW 11:28–30 NIV

### MORNING

Jesus says, "Come to me." Just as He invited the little children to come to Him, Jesus calls us to come to Him and bring all our burdens and lay them at His feet. He wants to help. He wants to relieve the load we're carrying.

A yoke is a harness placed over an animal or set of animals for the purpose of dragging something or carrying heavy equipment. Jesus liked to use visual imagery to get His meaning across. Can't you just picture all the burdens you are carrying right now strapped to your back like an ox plowing a field? Now imagine yourself unloading each one onto Jesus' shoulders instead. Take a deep breath.

### EVENING

Jesus tells us many times throughout the Gospels not to worry. Worrying about something will never help you. Worry makes things worse and causes burdens to seem larger. Worry clutters your soul. Jesus wants us to find rest in Him. Hear His gentle words rush over you: "Come to me." Find rest for your soul.

*Jesus, thank You for taking my burdens. I give them fully to You. Help me not to take them back! I want the rest and peace that You are offering. Amen.*

# DAY 347

## HAND HOLDERS

*As long as Moses held up his hands, the Israelites were winning, but whenever he lowered his hands, the Amalekites were winning. When Moses' hands grew tired, they took a stone and put it under him and he sat on it. Aaron and Hur held his hands up—one on one side, one on the other—so that his hands remained steady till sunset. So Joshua overcame the Amalekite army with the sword.*

Exodus 17:11–13 NIV

### MORNING

How do you view your pastor? Do you see him as the cheerleader of your congregation, trying to motivate his members to be better Christ followers? Perhaps the teacher? Maybe even the ultimate decision maker? The truth is that some pastors feel that they are expected to be all things to all people and to do it with perfection. . .

### EVENING

Today's scripture shows that Moses was an ordinary (but called) person trying to do a huge job by himself. No one could be expected to hold their hands up for the duration of a battle. Moses needed help. One way we can help our pastors in the work they have been given is by the power of consistent prayer for them personally, for their families, and for their ministry.

*Father, our pastors are precious to us. Yet we know they have been given big assignments with sometimes unrealistic expectations. Remind us to keep our pastors, their families, and their ministry in prayer. It is one way we can hold their hands high to You. Amen.*

# DAY 348

## THANK YOU FOR FRIENDS

*Be careful then, dear brothers and sisters. Make sure that your own hearts are not evil and unbelieving, turning you away from the living God. You must warn each other every day, while it is still "today," so that none of you will be deceived by sin and hardened against God. For if we are faithful to the end, trusting God just as firmly as when we first believed, we will share in all that belongs to Christ.*

HEBREWS 3:12–14 NLT

### MORNING

The writer of the book of Hebrews laid out a clear battle plan when it came to retaining a strong belief and trust in God. What was his plan? Keep your mind from all kinds of deception, and do everything to keep your heart from being hardened. Keep in contact with other Christians who feel comfortable pointing out any red flags in your behavior.

### EVENING

It's easy to get defensive when someone points out your flaws. No person likes to think they are failing. But you're asked to accept such candid observations from other Christians.

Trust is something God requires of you. He wants you to finish your journey well. Christ-following friends can help you stay focused on the finish line.

*Lord, it's a gift to find a Christian friend who can see failings in my life that I've missed and who loves me enough to point them out. Remind me why trusting Your rebukes through godly friends is wiser than trusting the praise of fools. Amen.*

# DAY 349

# AN INVITATION TO TRUST

*"When the time is ripe, I'll free your tongue and you'll say, 'This is what God, the Master, says: . . .' From then on it's up to them. They can listen or not listen, whichever they like."*

EZEKIEL 3:27 MSG

## MORNING

God had a message for a people determined to rebel. Ezekiel was one of several prophets God used to ensure that the people had every opportunity to turn away from the things they had done. He wanted them to have a mindset that matched His own. Ezekiel was bold in sharing the message because it came from God, was honest, and contained an invitation to trust.

## EVENING

God knows it's hard to fully trust someone who offers no choice. Maybe you've heard people make decisions for others and then say, "Trust me. This is for your own good." The decision might *be* good, but forcing it on someone doesn't generally cause them to trust—only to go along with it.

Ezekiel spoke God's truth, but the people had to decide for themselves if they'd trust. As today's verse says, "It's up to them. They can listen or not listen, whichever they like."

God has a message for you. He asks you to accept it, but receiving His truth will require trust.

*Dear God, You have given me a mind to think with. Help me to do so. You've given me an invitation to trust. Help me believe. You've given me a choice. Help me choose wisely. In Jesus' name, amen.*

# DAY 350

## MEANT FOR MORE

*Our people have to learn to be diligent in their work so that all necessities are met (especially among the needy) and they don't end up with nothing to show for their lives.*

TITUS 3:14 MSG

### MORNING

The life of a Christ follower is identified by action. When you work, it means you can help those in need. Christians demonstrate love to others by being generous. They demonstrate they're trustworthy when they provide for their families. They do the hard things because they know that the work they do is done for God.

Today's verse isn't one you should use to promote self-reliance. You still need to depend on God for everything, but when you're an adult, He'll give you a job to help you be productive. Your salary will help provide for your family. That same effort can benefit others who can't work.

### EVENING

God has a plan for your life, and you can show your trust in that plan by taking the necessary action to finish well. Whatever plan God has for your life will also impact others. You serve a relational God. Money never advances God's objectives when it takes up permanent residence in your bank account. Use it wisely, yes, but use it to bless others as well.

*Dear God, Your plan can be trusted. Help me be trustworthy by partnering with You. May You be glorified in a life that wants to count for something. Amen.*

# DAY 351

## THE WISE, THE FOOLISH, THE TRUSTED

*Wisdom is enshrined in an understanding heart;*
*wisdom is not found among fools.*
PROVERBS 14:33 NLT

### MORNING

Proverbs is a great collection of wise sayings. Many powerful truths are found in its short thoughts. In this book of wisdom, we learn that fools can't be trusted. We also learn that God's wisdom and understanding *are* worthy of trust.

Even though God declares He is the source of trust, fools won't believe it and will refuse to trust Him. They tend to do the opposite of everything wise. They trust in the ideas of other foolish humans. They try to convince the wise that they're the foolish ones. Those who are foolish highly regard deception but fail to recognize true wisdom as a priceless treasure. . .

### EVENING

If wisdom is water, then foolishness is oil that separates when in contact with water. Foolishness is repelled by wisdom, and while the wise are willing to teach, the foolish don't want to learn.

The foolish make up their own rules, so there's no reason to trust them. The source of true wisdom is God, so it's foolishness to fail to trust Him. God's wisdom can be trusted, and those who accept His wisdom are worthy of trust.

*Lord, thank You for making it clear that the foolish can't be trusted because their beliefs constantly change. Help me pursue Your wisdom. Help me trust You, the God who never changes. Amen.*

# DAY 352

## BECOME TRUSTWORTHY

*Concentrate on doing your best for God, work you won't be ashamed of, laying out the truth plain and simple.*
2 TIMOTHY 2:15 MSG

### MORNING

Trust God and you can become more trustworthy. While no one is entirely trustworthy, when God is the one you follow, you'll be inclined to become more than a promise maker.

God wants you to reflect His character in your actions, responses, and words. You can inspire others to catch a glimpse of what trust is and then point them to the ultimate source of trust.

Do work you won't be ashamed of. Help others to trust God's simple truth. That's today's message, and it gives you a goal God can help you achieve.

### EVENING

God is trustworthy because He always does what He says He will do. You become trustworthy when you obey what He asks. You can learn what He requires by reading God's Word and doing what it says. The Bible isn't an advice column, a book of suggestions, or one of many inspirational texts to consider. The Bible is God's guide to the best life. God and His words can be trusted.

*Dear God, I would love to be considered worthy of Your trust, and to do that, I must obey what You've asked me to do. Your Word tells me that when You can trust me with small things, You'll entrust bigger things to my care. Help me become more trustworthy. Amen.*

# DAY 353

## ONE MEDIATOR

*For there is one God, and one mediator also between God and mankind, the man Christ Jesus, who gave Himself as a ransom for all, the testimony given at the proper time.*

1 TIMOTHY 2:5–6 NASB

### MORNING

Today's scripture states that there is one God. There are not multiple options of who you want to serve or who has control of your fate. That being said, the passage goes on to tell us that there is only one mediator between God and humans. Christ is your only way to the Father. You need a "middleman." Otherwise, you could not stand before the perfect holiness of God. Christ became a man in order to mediate for the rest of humankind.

### EVENING

Christ was the ransom that set humanity free. Sin was holding you and all of humanity hostage. It would not let you out of your bondage until a ransom was paid. This payment required a sacrificial death. Christ stepped in so that you could be returned to your Father. If not for the mediation of Christ, your sin would put you directly in the line of God's wrath. Instead, He died, and you walk freely. What an incredible mediator you have!

*Lord, thank You for becoming the ransom when I was the one who deserved the wrath of God. You set me free from my bondage to sin. Because of You, I can come before the Father as a blameless child. Amen.*

# DAY 354

## THE GREAT FORGIVER

*Be kind to each other, tenderhearted, forgiving one another, just as God through Christ has forgiven you.*

EPHESIANS 4:32 NLT

### MORNING

In Matthew 18:21 (NLT), Peter interrupted Jesus' discourse on how to settle a disagreement with a fellow believer to ask, "How often should I forgive someone who sins against me? Seven times?" Peter thought he was being generous by using the all-inclusive number seven. Jesus surprised Peter by saying, "Seventy times seven," thus giving a sense of the infinite need to forgive. This is impossible without the prior example of Jesus.

### EVENING

We think how incredible it is that the first Christian martyr, Stephen, forgave his murderers as they were stoning him. People can forgive only because they know the great forgiveness of Jesus, who was killed by His own creation and yet still won the victory over death to bring them salvation. On the cross, Jesus asked the Father to forgive His wayward sheep: "Father, forgive them" (Luke 23:34). They did not know what they were doing, and neither do most people today who reject the peace of forgiveness through Jesus. However, those who lift their hurt and anger to God will find that Jesus sets them free from bondage.

*Lord, set me free to forgive. Provide me with the great love of Jesus. Amen.*

# DAY 355

# BREAKING THE BARRIERS

*There is neither Jew nor Gentile, neither slave nor free, nor is there male and female, for you are all one in Christ Jesus.*
GALATIANS 3:28 NIV

## MORNING

Unfortunately, the widespread stereotype of an American Christian is a smiling person who says, "Have a nice day," but underneath is hypocritical and judgmental. That description also fits the Pharisees, the most religious of the Jews. The Pharisees accused Jesus of being a drunkard and a glutton because He was known for hanging out with people who had bad reputations. Yet, for all the Pharisees' anger, those people loved having Jesus around. He treated them with dignity and shared the truth with them, telling them to sin no more. He reserved His harshest words for the Pharisees and their hypocrisy!

## EVENING

Christ tears down the structures that the world puts up among people—structures of economic inequality, racism, sexism, and other forms of oppression. Through His sacrifice, He unifies believers so that they can be one family, made equal by God's grace. However, the early church struggled with being "respecters of persons" (see James 2), and believers still battle with prejudice today. Whether it's conscious or not, we recoil from certain groups of people, believing stereotypes and passing judgment because of the color of their skin or the lives they've led. Who are they? Ask the Spirit to reveal to you the people toward whom you should better reflect God's love.

*Lord Jesus, "Search me. . .and know my heart; test me and know my anxious thoughts. See if there is any offensive way in me, and lead me in the way everlasting" (Psalm 139:23–24 NIV). Amen.*

# DAY 356

## OVERCOMER

*"I have told you all this so that you may have peace in me.*
*Here on earth you will have many trials and sorrows.*
*But take heart, because I have overcome the world."*
JOHN 16:33 NLT

### MORNING

One in eight people do not have enough to eat. Every ten seconds a child dies of starvation. Across the world, believers are persecuted; many are terrified for their lives. There are wars, sickness, and disease. When we think of all that is happening in our world, when we focus on all its trials and tribulations, our natural response is to become anxious. It is easy to lose hope. . .

### EVENING

As He was about to return to heaven, Jesus prepared His disciples for the worst. Despite the sorrows and trials promised, Jesus offered blessed news: "I have overcome the world." No longer do we have to be anxious and afraid, because Jesus has already overcome. How can you live in such a way that reflects this victorious mindset?

*Jesus, You weren't kidding when You said we would have many trials and sorrows. When I focus on my problems, my heart becomes heavy and weary. Lighten my load. Help me to find my heart and the hope that You have overcome the world. Amen.*

# DAY 357

## A SABBATH CUSTOM

*When he came to the village of Nazareth, his boyhood home, he went as usual to the synagogue on the Sabbath and stood up to read the Scriptures.*

LUKE 4:16 NLT

### MORNING

What is your "Sabbath" custom?

Jesus made a habit of being in worship. Numerous times in the Gospels, there is reference to the fact that Jesus was in the synagogue—sometimes teaching and sometimes healing, but present. Though He was God in the flesh, He followed the principles given to Moses long ago and kept the Sabbath day holy.

The fourth commandment, like the others, is still in effect. We are to reserve one day a week for rest and worship. Because Jesus rose from the grave on the first day of the week, Sunday, the New Testament Christians began gathering on that day instead of Saturday. This has been the Christian tradition ever since.

### EVENING

In recent years, Sabbath-keeping has fallen out of vogue. The "blue laws" of yesteryear are no more. Retailers score big business on Sunday, and arenas are packed for sporting events and concerts. To many people, Sunday is just another workday.

The example of Jesus reminds us to be careful of "the Lord's Day." He had a custom of being in the "Father's house" on the Sabbath. If that was His custom, it should be ours as well.

*Dear Lord, show me how to honor the day we keep as the Sabbath. Guide me as I make choices about how to follow Your example of rest and worship. In Jesus' name, amen.*

# DAY 358

## PRAY FROM YOUR HEART

*"Here's what I want you to do: Find a quiet, secluded place so you won't be tempted to role-play before God. Just be there as simply and honestly as you can manage. The focus will shift from you to God, and you will begin to sense his grace."*

MATTHEW 6:6 MSG

### MORNING

There are two kinds of prayer: rote versus real.

Rote prayer is what you rattle off before meals or bedtime. You know exactly what to pray because you've prayed the same thing so many times. Although you are purposeful about your prayer, it's easy to slip into reciting it without much thought.

Then there is prayer from your heart. Prayer from your heart is honest. It's real. It doesn't have a script or a reason behind every word. It's you talking to your heavenly Father as though He were right next to you. You're explaining your praise, prayers, worship, fears, love, frustration, and joys. You're laying your heart before God with no pretension about what you "should" pray or "shouldn't" say.

### EVENING

Because you do regularly repeat certain prayers, rote prayer will always have its place and can be heartfelt in nature. On the other hand, it's important to purposefully engage in real, honest prayer, which is rarer, because it generates a heartfelt connection with God that can be created no other way.

*Lord, help me to pray like Jesus did: real prayers from the heart. It's in those prayers that my focus can shift to You and Your grace. Amen.*

# DAY 359

## COMPLETE JOY

*"I have told you this so that my joy may be in you and that your joy may be complete."*
JOHN 15:11 NIV

### MORNING

Christ didn't have an easy life. As the son of a carpenter, He undoubtedly grew up knowing what it meant to work hard. As the son of parents who weren't married when they discovered His existence, He surely had to deal with hurtful gossip and rumors. When He finally left the carpentry business for full-time ministry, certain important people hated Him so much that they wanted Him dead.

Yet Jesus was joyful. Despite it all, He carried gladness in His heart because He found delight in doing His Father's work. How could that be? How can we infuse that kind of joy into our own lives? . . .

### EVENING

We must understand the meaning of joy. It's not the same thing as happiness. We may not be happy about our circumstances, the way others treat us, or the current state of our relationships. Happiness has to do with our current circumstances. . .but joy has to do with our future.

No matter where we are in life and no matter what's happening to us, we have a glorious future! Those of us who claim membership in God's family can know without a doubt that we will come out on top. That is certainly reason to rejoice.

*Dear Father, I know You want me to be joyful. Teach me to recognize joy and to live in that joy every day. Amen.*

# DAY 360

## CHOOSE GOD

*God planned to save us from the punishment of sin through our Lord Jesus Christ. He did not plan for us to suffer from His anger.*

1 THESSALONIANS 5:9 NLV

### MORNING

Do you picture God as an angry judge? Do you think He's eager to knock people down and trample them in His wrath? That's not who He is.

The God of the Bible is the image of love. First John 4:8 (NLV) says, "Those who do not love do not know God because God is love." Do you really get that? Not only is God loving, He *is* love. He won't do something that is ultimately unloving, because it would go against His very nature. Love is who He is.

### EVENING

The most incredibly loving act in the history of the world was God sending His Son, Jesus, to die for us so we could live. Do you realize that if you were the only person who needed a Savior, God would have allowed Jesus to pay the price for you? He'd do anything so He could welcome you into His arms for all eternity.

Being the perfect image of love doesn't mean God never gets angry, but His anger is against evil and not against us. We may not understand everything, but we know that the devil rebelled against God, and since then he has done his best to tempt everyone to turn against the Lord. It surely breaks God's heart when people believe Satan's lies and won't receive the love God offers.

*Thank You, heavenly Father, for the salvation we have through Jesus Christ. Thank You for showing us that all we must do is open our hearts to receive Your goodness. Amen.*

# DAY 361

# SAY NO TO BLABBERMOUTHS

*Gossips can't keep secrets, so never confide in blabbermouths.*
PROVERBS 20:19 MSG

## MORNING

If you're like most people, every day you're surrounded with the temptation to gossip. Whether it's at school, in a circle of close friends, or simply out in the community, the rumor mill is always turning.

The wisdom in Proverbs spells plainly its warning: Gossips can't be trusted to keep their mouths shut, so don't share secrets with them!

As Christians, we need to take this attitude a step further and stand up against gossip.

## EVENING

Don't be afraid to voice your displeasure—in love, of course—when your friends talk about others. Introduce encouragement and uplifting words into your conversations, and resist the temptation to fall into old habits.

Words are powerful. If you've ever been the victim of having your secrets blabbed behind your back, you know the pain they cause. Commit yourself to cutting gossip from your life, and your relationships will be strengthened.

*Father, please forgive me for talking about others behind their backs. I don't want to be known as a blabbermouth. Help my words to always be encouraging to others. Amen.*

# DAY 362

## BY OBEDIENCE BLESSED

*Behold, for so shall a man who fears the Lord be blessed.*
Psalm 128:4 NASB

### MORNING

Do you ever wonder if serving God is worth it? After all, acclaim tends to follow those who adopt the world's beliefs. Movie stars who drink and do drugs make millions of dollars per film. Politicians who trade favors for votes inherit power and prestige. And people and companies who cheat on their taxes rack up even more wealth. Sometimes it seems as if nonbelievers prosper and those who serve the Lord suffer.

But God doesn't sit idly by while people flaunt their sinfulness and mock His righteousness. He sees everything—even those acts that the wicked prefer to keep secret.

### EVENING

As the Psalms state over and over, God delights in His faithful children. He sees their suffering, notices their obedience, and revels in their steadfastness. He will never leave the righteous.

Eventually, because He is a God of justice, love, and compassion, He will honor and reward His children. Either on earth or in heaven, the scales will be balanced. He will turn every bit of evil they've experienced into good. And because He made us for Himself, His presence will be His sons' and daughters' greatest gift.

*God, I praise You for being a God of justice and mercy. Help me to keep my eyes on You and not on the world. In Jesus' name, amen.*

# DAY 363

## ETERNAL TREASURE

*"Wherever your treasure is, there the desires of your heart will also be."*
MATTHEW 6:21 NLT

### MORNING

For Melissa's parents, love meant providing for their children's physical needs. They had a comfortable home, drove late-model cars, and never had to worry about whether their children could have a college education.

Unfortunately, this also meant both parents had to work long hours. Throughout their childhoods, Melissa and her sister wanted nothing more than to take a walk in the evening or go on a picnic on the weekends as a family, having their parents' undivided attention. Sadly, Melissa's father died suddenly when he was in his early fifties, and Melissa never did receive the attention from him that she craved. . .

### EVENING

Fast cars, luxurious homes, travel, high-paying jobs, working hard to get ahead. . .these are the values that drive many people today. Most of us know logically that these things aren't the key to happiness, but it's easy to get caught up in worldly trappings of success.

It's not that owning comfortable homes or driving nice cars is wrong, but as Christians, we are called to live our lives differently. Jesus challenges us to place our value in things that have eternal significance and to make choices that have an impact on our spiritual lives—not just on our physical lives. What investments are you making today that will have eternal significance?

*Father, thank You for the promise that there is more to life than material success. Help me to invest my life in things that have eternal significance. Amen.*

# DAY 364

# SKEPTICS AND CYNICS

*For ever since the world was created, people have seen the earth and sky. Through everything God made, they can clearly see his invisible qualities—his eternal power and divine nature. So they have no excuse for not knowing God.*

ROMANS 1:20 NLT

## MORNING

You can see the love of Jesus in the eyes of a newborn baby. You can see the paintbrush of God in the colors of a sunset. It is awe-inspiring to look at the handiwork of God and attempt to grasp His majesty and incredible creativity. For a Christian, it's impossible to see His creation and deny His existence.

There are skeptics and cynics though. They love to question the possibility of a divine Creator. They have seemingly sound arguments based in logic and science. We can share testimonials, blessings, and miracles from our personal lives and from scripture. But these are often met with disbelief and tales of a big bang and evolution. . .

## EVENING

In order for a skeptic to be changed to a seeker, Jesus must grab their attention, often using His children to do that. Take time to really consider the miraculous works of God that prove His existence. Pray for wisdom and compelling words to lead cynics to the throne.

*Father, help me to be a good witness of You and Your miraculous wonders. Give me the words to convince even the most hardened skeptic. Guide me to people, according to Your will, so that I can make a difference. Amen.*

# DAY 365

## WHAT'S THE NEXT STEP?

*What you ought to say is, "If the Lord wants us to, we will live and do this or that."*
JAMES 4:15 NLT

### MORNING

"What does James mean in this verse?" Kirsten asked. "Sounds as if he's saying we should never make plans. If I did that, my life would be a mess!"

Her Bible-study leader explained that God wasn't frowning on our making plans. But He doesn't want us to get so caught up in our plans that we never look to Him for guidance. Planning done without God leads down a dead-end street.

### EVENING

At the end of a year, you're looking forward to 365 new days filled with personal opportunities. Maybe lots of options vie for your attention. Should you try out for a new team, take an advanced course, or start dating someone new?

Though you see the exciting changes ahead, you don't have a God's-eye view of your life. He sees the big picture and wants to help you make the right choices.

So why not ask Him what the next step is?

*The new year needs to be filled, Lord. Let it overflow with Your will for me. In Jesus' name, amen.*

# SCRIPTURE INDEX

# OLD TESTAMENT

## Proverbs



## Ecclesiastes

# NEW TESTAMENT

## Luke



## John



## Acts



## Romans

## 1 Corinthians



## 2 Corinthians



## Galatians



## Ephesians



## Philippians



## Colossians